HUMANI⸗

NGO Information
and Its Impact
on US Foreign Policy

HUMANITARIAN ALERT

NGO Information
and Its Impact
on US Foreign Policy

Abby Stoddard

Kumarian
Press, Inc.

Humanitarian Alert: NGO Information and Its Impact on US Foreign Policy
Published in 2006 in the United States of America by Kumarian Press, Inc.
1294 Blue Hills Avenue, Bloomfield, CT 06002 USA

The text of this book is set in 10/12.5 Sabon

Proofread by Beth Richards
Index by Robert Swanson
Copyedited by Bob Land

Production and design by Victoria Hughes Waters,
Hughes Publishing Services, Worcester, MA

Printed in the United States of America by Thomson-Shore, Inc.
Text printed with vegetable oil-based ink.

♾ The paper used in this publication meets the minimum requirements of
the American National Standard for Information Sciences-Permanence of
Paper for printed Library Materials, ANSI Z39.48-1984

Library of Congress Cataloging-in-Publication Data

Stoddard, Abby, 1966-
  Humanitarian alert : NGO information and its impact on US foreign poli-
cy / by Abby Stoddard.
     p. cm.
  Includes bibliographical references and index.
  ISBN-13: 978-1-56549-227-1 (pbk. : alk. paper)
  ISBN-10: 1-56549-227-7 (pbk. : alk. paper)
  ISBN-13: 978-1-56549-228-8 (cloth : alk. paper)
  ISBN-10: 1-56549-228-5 (cloth : alk. paper)
  1. Non-governmental organizations. 2. Non-governmental organizations--
Political aspects. 3. United States--Foreign relations--1989- 4. Non-govern-
mental organizations--International cooperation. 5. International relief. I.
Title.
JZ4841.S755 2006
327.73--dc22

                              2006019522

CONTENTS

To Nitin Madhav, whose courage
and commitment exemplifies the best
of the humanitarian endeavor.

FIGURES

TABLES

ACKNOWLEDGMENTS

I would like to thank my mentors and friends Michael Barnett, Shepard Forman, Michael Gilligan, Barnett R. Rubin, and Dirk Salomons for their invaluable input and guidance. I am also greatly indebted to my colleagues John Fawcett and Sue Lautze for sharing a wealth of primary source material as well as insights. I am most grateful to the many members of the NGO community, the United Nations, and the US government who gave their time to be interviewed, and to the Aspen Institute, which enabled a large portion of the research through a grant from the Nonprofit Sector Research Fund. Finally, to my family: my love and thanks go to Vanya, Sonia, and Miles for their patience and support, and to Mom, Dad, Vica, and Bernie, without whose enormous help I never could have undertaken, let alone completed, this project.

INTRODUCTION

Background and Overview

No sooner had the waters receded from the devastating South Asian tsunami than the international aid organizations began mounting an unprecedented response. The largest among them were already operating in the affected countries and so were able to use their logistical infrastructure and human resources to move quickly. They also possessed the fundraising mechanisms that local indigenous organizations and governments (the first responders) lacked. The Atlanta-based organization CARE raised $5 million online in just ten days. Save the Children, Oxfam, Médecins sans Frontières, and others experienced similar influxes. In the days and weeks to come, millions more would be transferred to these organizations via grants from donor governments, who, as in past emergencies, would call on these entities to implement a large portion of the international relief and reconstruction effort.

Over the past three decades, an informal international network of humanitarian nongovernmental organizations, or NGOs, has evolved from a modest grouping of charitable ventures operating on the sidelines of emergencies into a crucial pillar of the international humanitarian architecture. Governments rely on NGOs to deliver their foreign relief assistance directly to the people who need it. The two largest governmental donor agencies, the US Agency for International Development (USAID) and the Humanitarian Aid department of the European Commission (ECHO), each channel roughly 60 to 70 percent of their official humanitarian assistance funding "bilaterally" through NGOs (as opposed to the affected governments or to multilateral funds). Although the largest single government grants go to the major UN aid agencies such as UNICEF,

UNHCR, and the World Food Programme, these agencies in turn subgrant much of it to NGOs to do most of the actual implementation of services or delivery of goods at the community level.[1] Overall it is estimated that 77 percent of government humanitarian funding is now bilateral.[2] Contributions from the twenty-two (primarily Western) governments that make up the OECD Development Assistance Committee (DAC)—the main source of global humanitarian aid funding—reached a total of $6.9 billion in 2003. Recent efforts to capture the total picture of humanitarian aid flows, including not only the official reported government flows but also private contributions raised by humanitarian organizations and funding from "non-DAC"[3] governments, have placed the total annual humanitarian assistance figure at approximately $10 billion.[4] Of this total, NGOs are estimated to manage somewhere between $2.5 and $3 billion[5]—a significant share.

The NGOs' percentage becomes more striking when one considers that fewer than a dozen organizations account for over 90 percent of that revenue.[6] The five largest international NGOs (with annual revenues ranging from $250 million to just over $1 billion) can be counted on to launch a response to every major emergency—their in-country budgets and staffs at times dwarfing those of UN agencies—and have often served as lead agencies in their niche sector during coordinated international efforts. These organizations' increasingly visible and intrepid operations in humanitarian crises have been highlighted in the international media, making the term "NGO" almost a household word. Their profile as independent players in political arenas has been raised to the point that a few have warned of their inordinate influence over government policies. In recent years, in fact, some conservative groups in the United States have issued warnings about powerful and "unaccountable" NGOs (humanitarian and others) that pursue leftist agendas and work "to constrain US freedom of action in international affairs and influence the behavior of corporations abroad."[7]

Yet at the same time, despite their status as private, nongovernmental entities, many of the largest and most active humanitarian NGOs receive the bulk of their funding from their respective national governments. The NGOs' growing share in public funds (particularly the US-based NGOs, which tend to have much larger public-to-private funding ratios than their European counterparts) can pose ethical problems for organizations that define their humanitarian mandate in terms of their independence from states and national political agendas. Moreover, donors as a general trend have become more directly involved in all aspects of the needs identification, design, and management of NGO projects.[8] Finally, notwithstanding the size, global reach, or proven expertise of some of these organizations, the US government and other donors still commonly refer to NGOs as "implementing partners," implying an agency relationship where the NGOs execute aid projects at the donor's behest, and in service of donor objectives. From the other end of the political spectrum, therefore, theorists have explained the NGO movement as a new means of power extension by wealthy states into the developing world.

These two opposing images of humanitarian NGOs challenge efforts to understand their role and measure their influence in international relations. Do they function primarily as autonomous—and increasingly influential—nonstate actors in pursuit of their own value-driven agendas? Or do they ultimately serve merely as the paid agents of national governments, providing a service delivery function in line with those nations' foreign policy goals? This book proposes a third view: the humanitarian NGOs, even those dependent on their home government for most of their funding, can and do influence state policy formation, but not in the manner of interest-based advocacy groups—that is, by lobbying, pressure tactics, and (de)legitimization of government policies. Although humanitarian NGOs do engage in these forms of public advocacy activities to varying degrees, their most significant source of policy influence derives from their on-the-ground presence as crucial public goods providers in conflicts and crises, and their behind-the-scenes functions vis-à-vis governments and intergovernmental organizations. The chapters ahead focus specifically on the NGOs' informal and largely unrecognized role in policy making as field-level information sources and technical advisors of governments, and how NGO information and recommendations have influenced policy decisions. Using case illustrations of US policy regarding the conflicts in Somalia, Bosnia, and Kosovo, this books shows how NGO information and organizational interests helped shape the international, and particularly the US, policy response, though not always with the humanitarians' preferred outcome.

The phenomenon of globalization has set off a renewed interest in the study of nonstate actors and their roles in international relations. Consequently, the NGO movement has been examined in numerous works of scholarship and in the media. Yet while there may be growing recognition that NGOs have increasing visibility and influence as international actors, no consensus exists on the extent of their influence, or even how to define and categorize these entities. The literature on "global civil society," as the vast landscape of nongovernmental associations has been dubbed, focuses mainly on transnational social policy movements and advocacy networks around shared causes, such as women's rights and the environment.[9] International humanitarian organizations, although they are often included in the term "global civil society," constitute a unique subset of NGOs, with a physical presence and more active role in crisis settings than their issue-based cousin organizations.

The operational nature of the humanitarian NGOs, I argue, sets them apart. These organizations are engaged in functional activities on the ground and are embedded within the local situation as actors in their own right alongside governmental and intergovernmental bodies, military forces, and various other nonstate entities. In long-term missions, where NGOs have established a solid presence and assistance infrastructure, they often enjoy the recognition and trust of the local community, a measure of political clout, and a not insignificant role in the local economy as an employer, contractor, and consumer.

The NGOs' "operationality" becomes particularly important in conflict-related emergencies. When political conditions become increasingly unstable and insecure, and diplomatic and other government personnel are subject to heavy restrictions on their movements, the NGOs more than ever become the international community's eyes and ears on the ground. Frequently, they provide for the international political actors the principal or sole source of information on local conditions and events. Governments and international organizations readily attest to the importance they place on NGO-generated information in what are usually highly fluid and confusing situations, where, as a UN humanitarian officer recently lamented, the challenge is to sort out what is true from different versions and interpretations of events: "Truth is hopelessly elusive in humanitarian operations. . . . And in the midst of protracted conflict 'truths' shift unpredictably over time."[10]

This book attempts to show how NGOs' information and definitions of a situation—their version of the truth—has provided the basis for decision making in the formation of the US government's response, and filtered up from the humanitarian offices to the higher political reaches of government. As the case studies demonstrate, the role of NGOs as information providers exists in a different realm than their role as humanitarian issue advocates. Unlike the international advocacy movements that attempt to affect the interests and preferences of decision makers (i.e., to "change what actors *want*"[11]), the operational humanitarian NGOs have had their greatest impact on policy by providing the situational information that shapes the understanding upon which the decisions are made— in effect by changing what actors know, and how the policy problem is framed. The process begins with a conflict-based humanitarian emergency in which humanitarian NGOs, as the primary international presence on the ground, provide the lion's share, if not the sum total, of the information received by the international community and policymakers in powerful states. (The study looks specifically at the US government.) Much of this information is transmitted through NGOs' regular communications with the donor agency, which feeds upward to higher levels of government. This information tends to describe the situation through a humanitarian-operational lens, with the most compelling and urgent narratives forming around issues of access and security for humanitarian assistance—for instance, the blocking of aid deliveries by belligerents. This narrative, constructed through NGO-donor communications and often combined with the explicit or implied threat of NGO withdrawal and aid suspension, has proven to be a decisive factor in policy response. In a process that unfolds moment to moment in certain crises, and in ways often not strategic or even fully intentional, the operational imperatives of humanitarian aid have effectively driven or drawn in the larger political/military responses. These responses do not always lead to the best outcomes from the humanitarian standpoint, however, and may even deepen the crisis. Moreover, once states have decided to focus their military and/or political resources on a decisive response, the humanitarian information once seen as invaluable is no longer sought after, and in fact is often ignored by political and military actors.

The cases examined in this book each involve a conflict situation in which the Northern/Western governments intervened diplomatically or militarily, and illuminate the NGO role leading up to and during that engagement. I attempt to trace the NGO contribution in setting the agenda, framing the issues, and promoting particular governmental actions. Although I address NGO interaction with European donors and the United Nations (particularly NGO–Security Council informational sessions), the main focus is on the US government, as the most powerful national actor in international relations and the leading nation in the international interventions in complex emergencies over the past two decades. The case studies examine US government decisions in response to the conflict situations in developing countries to determine the extent of influence exerted by NGOs through their informational role. The word "alert" in the title was originally "advisory," chosen to describe the basic information relayed to governments by the field-level humanitarian actors, as well as to imply a form of prescriptive counsel from experts, and finally, to connote the sense of a warning or urgent alert that is often implicit in their message and can act as a trigger for further policy action.

A few of the so-called forgotten or neglected emergencies share certain characteristics that have so far not allowed the humanitarian advisory dynamic to unfold. One, of course, is the slow disintegration into a state of "chronic emergency" that fails to generate the urgency and problem-solving thinking that a sudden onset crisis or natural disaster provokes in the policy community. What I argue may be more significant, however, is the much sparser aid presence (relative to the size of the affected area) and correspondingly diffuse NGO information emanating from the field. The scant access and coverage of the humanitarian NGOs in the cases of Angola, DR Congo, and Sudan have not facilitated the humanitarian entry point that policy makers used in cases like Bosnia, Kosovo, and Somalia.

Methodology

The research for this book involved the following methods and sources:

Official documentation review. Through the Freedom of Information Act, I obtained copies of the official US Embassy telegrams (cables) sent from the field to Washington, DC. The cables contain situation reports, assessment findings, and other information relayed to USAID headquarters as well as policy makers in the Departments of State and Defense. Other primary US government documents include memoranda; internal reports; commissioned reviews and evaluations; funding overviews; public information; conference reports from USAID and the State Department; transcripts of press conferences, congressional testimony, and briefings; relevant foreign operations budgets; and supplemental funding information. I also reviewed a large amount of NGO and UN agency documentation, including field reports, evaluations, advocacy and publicity materials, internal reviews and policy memoranda, and audited financial statements.

Interviews. The analysis draws on information gleaned from interviews that I conducted specifically for this study, and from those I conducted for other research projects on related topics. Interviewees who gave their permission to be cited in this study include US government officials, UN and Red Cross representatives, and NGO leadership and staff. In some instances I have referenced the interview subject by name, and in others I have made more general attribution, such as "NGO representative," depending on the sensitivity of the topic and the subjects' wishes.

Participant observation. Much of the study is informed by my professional experience working for humanitarian NGOs from 1990 to 2000. This background includes direct or peripheral involvement with the humanitarian response to all three of the main case studies. In addition, though no longer a humanitarian practitioner, I have maintained contact with the field through personal contacts and by attending conferences, seminars, and various information-sharing meetings with UN, NGO, and government representatives on a regular basis.

Secondary literature review. Secondary literature reviewed includes case studies, evaluations, reports, briefing papers, and scholarly articles and books.

Definition of Terms

In the chapters ahead I employ the following definitions for the units of analysis and their attached activities and functions. Many are common usages or terms of art in the humanitarian field, while others have a particular contextual meaning.

NGOs. I use the shorthand "NGO" to refer to the Northern-based, internationally operating nongovernmental private organizations that deliver assistance to crisis-affected populations. Locally operating, indigenous NGOs are distinguished by use of the qualifier.

NGO community. In this book, this term refers to the approximately 260 NGOs currently operational in humanitarian assistance—that is, maintaining relief or rehabilitation programs in at least one country, with the mandate and capacity for additional responses.

Implementers. Organizations providing beneficiary-level delivery of humanitarian services. This term can refer to NGOs, local organizations, UN agencies, or international organizations such as the Red Cross.

Donors. State governments contributing official assistance resources— that is, "foreign aid." "Donor agency" refers to the bureau or office within the government that is mandated with channeling monetary assistance to the implementers through grants or contracts.

International humanitarian community. The network of key implementers, donors, and international organizations involved in humanitarian assistance. This includes several UN agencies such as the High Commissioner for Refugees (UNHCR), UNICEF, the World Food Programme, and the disaster division of UN Development Programme (UNDP); the twelve major donors belonging to the OECD, of which the largest are the European Commission, the United States, Britain, and the Netherlands; and the NGOs, sometimes represented by the three major NGO consortia: InterAction, the Steering Committee for Humanitarian Response (SCHR), and International Committee for Voluntary Assistance (ICVA).

Complex emergency. I use this shorthand to refer to conflict-related crises entailing significant humanitarian need, but which are nonetheless political in origin, unlike humanitarian emergencies caused by natural disaster.

Advocacy. Formal attempts to influence policy through lobbying, public statements, demonstrations, or behind-the-scenes consultations; the "official" means for promoting the NGO's value-based agenda.

Information. As described in chapter 2, NGO information can be classified into two main types: quantitative, which can include such data as mortality rates, malnutrition rates, and other socioeconomic indicators; refugee movements, IDP estimates, and other demographic data; and needs assessments (for example, quantities of food, potable water, relief items required for a given population); and qualitative, such as anecdotal evidence of growing need or imminent crisis, eyewitness accounts of key events or victimization of civilians, and interpretations of political developments.

Policy impact. NGO impact on government policy regarding response to complex emergencies refers not merely to advising on logistical decisions regarding how and where humanitarian assistance should be delivered in emergency situations (NGO input into these decisions can be safely assumed), but whether political and security conditions are established so that it can be carried out. As such, this book examines the extent of government involvement, beyond providing grants, in the diplomatic or military engagement intended to affect the course of a conflict, and how important humanitarian aims are in the government's overall view of the situation.

Structure

Chapter 1 provides some historical background and suggests a conceptual framework for understanding the way NGOs relate to each other and to governments. It begins by profiling the major humanitarian players within the NGO community and elaborating on their market share and operational niche. The chapter goes on to examine how the NGOs belonging to different historical traditions hold different operational and ethical priorities, as well as different financing structures, which lead them to adopt an oppositional/advocacy role in their communications with governments or a cooperative/informational and advisory role.

Chapter 2 begins with an analysis of the two broad ways in which non-state actors can influence the policy decisions of governments. It posits that advocacy action attempts to influence what a government perceives as its interests, while information and technical advice affect the policy-makers' basic understanding of the question at hand. This chapter then describes the various sources of field-level information available to policy-makers dealing with a complex emergency in a developing country, and illuminates their origins, for the most part, in humanitarian NGOs. Also explored in this chapter are the challenges NGOs face in attempting to strengthen their advocacy efforts, which to date have yielded limited tangible results.

Chapters 3, 4, and 5 detail the case studies of Somalia, Bosnia, and Kosovo, respectively, and present the evidence that NGO information and their "humanitarianization" of the situation on the ground flowed up the policymaking hierarchy in the US government via the USAID/OFDA situation reports. The humanitarian framing and the urgency of the message—with the repeated themes of belligerents' obstruction of relief efforts and the threatened departure of the NGOs if security did not improve—is shown to have spurred US action in initiating and driving the international response. In the cases of Somalia and Kosovo the ultimate policy responses were not appropriate to the actual needs on the ground (and in the case of Kosovo arguably precipitated a major humanitarian emergency where there was previously a minor one). In Bosnia, the field-level information provided by NGOs sparked the beginning of active US engagement, and the humanitarian response created momentum within the US policy community for the United States to eventually assume diplomatic and military leadership to force an end to the conflict. However, the humanitarians' introverted focus on the constraints and achievements of the convoy operation may have inadvertently led to delays in the political response.

The three cases also reveal how the level of NGO influence in national government can also change abruptly once political engagement is intensified. Once a military action is under way, for instance, the nongovernmental actors are effectively shunted aside, whereas in the pre-crisis days they served as sought-after sources of information. (As H. Roy Williams, former NGO leader and head of the Office of U.S. Foreign Disaster Assistance, is quoted in this volume, the government tends to listen to NGOs by turns "too much or not at all.")

Chapter 6 addresses the issue of so-called neglected emergencies, where despite long-term conflict, instability, and humanitarian suffering, the international community has yet to devote robust and sustained efforts toward resolving the crisis. After a review of the Rwanda genocide and the (lack of) international response, the chapter goes on to examine the cases of Angola, Democratic Republic of Congo (DRC), and Sudan. The contrasts between these cases and the other three are examined with specific regard to the vastly different levels of humanitarian NGO presence and informational role.

The conclusion synthesizes the lessons of the previous chapters' findings for potential future action by the humanitarian NGO community. An effective joint effort to advance the humanitarian agenda in politico-military situations would require that the NGOs address both the flaws in their information function and the impotence of their advocacy role. Improvements in field-level information gathering and analysis, increased political awareness, and the development of data-driven, strategic advocacy approaches could potentially merge the realms of what some political scientists have called "expert authority" and "moral authority,"[12] allowing humanitarian actors both to provide policymakers with an accurate understanding of the crisis, and to steer them toward principled policy responses.

Caveats

Focus on US policy. Because the case studies focus on the information dynamic between the USAID Office of Foreign Disaster Assistance and its NGO operational partners, the majority of which are US-based, the study could potentially be accused of reducing the whole of the humanitarian enterprise to a small, US-centric subset. It was not possible within this book's scope to closely examine the information dynamic between all other donor governments and their NGO grantees. The US government was chosen due to its leading role in the policy responses that ensued.

Focus on international NGOs. Additionally, with the exception of the Kosovo case study, I am conscious of the relatively little discussion of indigenous NGOs and local Red Cross/Red Crescent societies, and the critical part they play in humanitarian response and information-gathering efforts. Local entities very often work side by side with international NGOs or provide the outreach and coverage necessary for the international NGOs to fulfill their programming objectives. The absence of detail on this score should not be construed as a dismissal of their role, but merely reflects the international relations context of the analysis, examining international NGOs as nonstate actors functioning in the international arena, and their direct connection with the Western governments.

Unique time period—anomalous cases? The decade after the collapse of the Soviet Union represented a relatively small window of time, now termed "post–Cold War," that some have concluded ended abruptly with the events of September 11, 2001, and the emergence of the new US doctrine of "preemptive security." All three of the cases studied occurred within this "heyday" of humanitarian intervention, and so it could be argued that their lessons would not pertain to the post-9/11 global environment. I am inclined to believe that the terrorist threat has not replaced the Soviet threat in the same all-encompassing way that rendered much of the developing world as pawns on a geo-strategic chessboard. Rather, many of the developing countries facing conflict and state failure remain outside the direct security interests of the sole remaining superpower.

Skewed perspective? Another potential pitfall in this research is that having served much of my professional life working for international

NGOs, I may be inclined to overstate their importance and centrality in complex emergency settings. David Rieff and other observers of the humanitarian community have taken NGOs to task for their hubris in attempting to assume political roles in the absence of will and active engagement of political actors. With that admonishment in mind, I endeavored not to fall into the trap of contending that NGOs are increasing their influence on the global stage relative to state actors. Rather, I argue that their influence in shaping areas of state behavior and decision making has been underrecognized and underestimated.

In this regard as well, a final caution concerns the heavily introspective nature of the study of humanitarian assistance. As Hugo Slim accurately observed, "By far the most deafening part of humanitarian discourse is still that part of the conversation voiced by the international (and largely [W]estern) humanitarian system in discussion with itself. Comparatively little in-depth discourse by, about or between people who actually endure war permeates the barrage of this dominant institutional conversation."[13]

Notes

1. For example, in 2000 UNHCR programmed $311 million out of its $706 million total income through NGOs (Development Initiatives, *Global Humanitarian Assistance 2003*, report prepared by Judith Randel and Tony German, London: Development Initiatives, 2003, 53).

2. Development Initiatives, *Global Humanitarian Assistance Update 2004–2005*, report prepared by Judith Randel and Tony German (London: Development Initiatives, 2005), 10.

3. Development Assistance Committee, Organization for Economic Cooperation and Development.

4. Development Initiatives, *Global Humanitarian Assistance 2003*.

5. Ibid.

6. Annual reports; Development Initiatives, *Global Humanitarian Assistance 2003*.

7. Jim Lobe, "NGOs in the US Firing Line," Inter Press Service, June 26, 2003. The article reports on the efforts of two conservative think tanks, the American Enterprise Institute (AEI) and the Federalist Society for Law and Public Policy Studies, from which "no fewer than 42 senior administration foreign-policy and justice officials have been recruited" and which have jointly launched a Web site, "NGO Watch," dedicated to monitoring and cautioning about what they see as "The Growing Power of an Unelected Few," www.NGOWatch.org.

8. Joanna Macrae et al., "Uncertain Power: The Changing Role of Official Donors in Humanitarian Action," *HPG Report* 12 (London: ODI, December 2002).

9. The premier example being Margaret E. Keck and Kathryn Sikkink's book, *Activists beyond Borders: Advocacy Networks in International Politics* (Ithaca, NY: Cornell University Press, 1998).

10. Kathleen Cravero, former UN coordinator in Burundi, "On Being a Humanitarian Coordinator: A Personal Reflection" (unpublished draft, 2003).

11. Richard Price, "Reversing the Gun Sights: Transnational Civil Society Targets Landmines," *International Organization* 52 (Summer 1998): 613–44. Emphasis added.

12. Michael Barnett and Martha Finnemore, *Rules for the World: International Organizations in Global Politics* (Ithaca, NY: Cornell University Press, 2004).

13. Hugo Slim, "International Humanitarianism's Engagement with Civil War in the 1990s: A Glance at Evolving Practice and Theory," *Journal of Humanitarian Assistance* (March 1998), http://www.jha.ac/articles/a033.htm.

ABBREVIATIONS

ACCORD	African Centre for the Constructive Resolution of Disputes
ACF	Action Contre la Faim
CAP	Consolidated Appeal Process
CARE	Cooperative for Assistance and Relief Everywhere
CDC	Centers for Disease Control and Prevention
CERF	Central Emergency Revolving Fund
CHAP	Common Humanitarian Action Plan
CRS	Catholic Relief Services
DART	Disaster Assistance Response Team (OFDA)
DDR	Disarmament, Demobilization and Reintegration
DFID	Department for International Development (UK)
DHA	UN Department of Humanitarian Affairs
DoD	US Department of Defense
DOW	Doctors of the World (Médecins du Monde—USA)
DPA	UN Department of Political Affairs

DPKO	UN Department of Peacekeeping Operations
DPRK	Democratic People's Republic of Korea
DRC	Democratic Republic of Congo
ECHO	European Community (EU) Humanitarian Office
FAO	Food and Agriculture Organization
FRY	Former Yugoslav Republic of Macedonia
HICs	Humanitarian Information Centers
IASC	Interagency Standing Committee for Humanitarian Affairs
ICRC	International Committee of the Red Cross
ICVA	International Council of Voluntary Agencies
IDPs	Internally Displaced Persons
IFOR	Implementation Force (NATO)
IFRC	International Federation of the Red Cross
IMC	International Medical Corps
IOM	International Organization for Migration
IRC	International Rescue Committee
MDM	Médecins du Monde
MONUC	United Nations Mission in the Democratic Republic of Congo
MSF	Médecins sans Frontières
MTS	Mother Teresa Society
NGO	Nongovernmental organization
NSA	Nonstate actor
NSC	US National Security Council
OCHA	UN Office for the Coordination of Humanitarian Affairs
OECD	Organisation for Economic Co-operation and Development

OFDA	Office of US Foreign Disaster Assistance
OLS	Operation Lifeline Sudan
OP	Occupying Power
OSCE	Organization for Security and Cooperation in Europe
PRM	US Department of State Bureau of Population, Refugees and Migration
RBA	Rights-Based Approach
RIACSO	Regional Interagency Coordination Support Office
RPF	Rwandan Patriotic Front
SACB	Somalia Aid Coordination Body
SC	UN Security Council
SCF	Save the Children Fund
SCHR	Steering Committee for Humanitarian Response
SG	Secretary-General
SPLM/A	Sudan People's Liberation Movement/ Army
SRSG	Special Representative of the Secretary General
UN	United Nations
UNDP	United Nations Development Programme
UNHCR	United Nations High Commissioner for Refugees
UNICEF	United Nations Children's Fund
UNSECOORD	United Nations Security Coordinator
USAID	United States Agency for International Development
WFP	World Food Programme
WHO	World Health Organization

CHAPTER ONE

AGENTS, ADVISORS, ANTAGONISTS

Understanding the NGO Community and Its Ambivalent Orientation toward Governments[1]

The NGO Landscape

On the subject of nongovernmental organizations, discussion tends to focus on their dramatic proliferation during the last three decades, as the burgeoning "third sector" of society. A frequently quoted UN estimate from 1995 reports the existence of 29,000 international NGOs, with millions more operating domestically.[2] When this broad conglomeration is disaggregated, the number of NGOs working in international charitable assistance (i.e., emergency relief, antipoverty efforts in foreign countries) appears closer to 3,000–4,000.[3] However, a more useful number may be found in the United Nations' roster of agencies that are currently operational and engaged in international humanitarian assistance activities, which does not include development-only organizations or the numerous "briefcase NGOs" that are established for a onetime relief program in a specific emergency. The UN Office for the Coordination of Humanitarian Aid (OCHA) by 2003 had registered a total of 260 NGOs and NGO consortia from across Europe, North America, Australia, and Japan.[4] Of the 260, 87 were US-based, the largest number from any single country, but European organizations collectively make up the largest share of NGOs.

Even the smaller number derived from the OCHA roster of agencies fails to provide a clear and accurate picture of the humanitarian field, for

Figure 1.1: Operational Humanitarian NGOs Based in Industrialized States

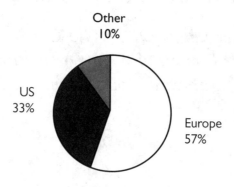

Source: UN OCHA

within those 260 organizations, a handful of giants indisputably dominate the field. These super-NGOs—large and long-standing organizations founded in the United States and Europe—manage the lion's share of relief aid resources in many emergency situations, and increasingly set the terms of debate for the rest of the community. Another dozen or so mid-level organizations round out the core of the operational humanitarian NGO community. Despite the differences in organizational culture and programmatic approach that complicate their relationship, this core group of organizations has proven adept at maintaining its market dominance and raising the bar for new entrants.

This chapter sets out to describe the current constellation of international humanitarian NGOs, and how their cultures and traditions dictate the ways in which they interrelate with political actors, specifically the Northern/Western governments that, for many of them, provide most of their funding. In so doing the chapter focuses special attention on the largest and most influential: CARE, Catholic Relief Services (CRS), Médecins sans Frontières (MSF), Oxfam, Save the Children Federation, and World Vision. This group, in a way a microcosm of the overall NGO population, comprises US, British, and French founding entities, both religious and secular. Other European countries are represented as national affiliates within those large federations, such as the Dutch NOVIB, which existed independently for many years before joining the Oxfam family. Numerous other large organizations have built up solid reputations and wide operational presence, such as the International Rescue Committee (IRC) in particular, as well as Action Contre la Faim (ACF), Danish Refugee Council, Lutheran World Relief, Mercy Corps International, and Norwegian Peoples Aid (NPA), to name just a few, but they remain small in comparison to the six above.

The Maturing of a Movement

The NGO population stayed quite small throughout the first half of the twentieth century (CARE, IRC, Oxfam, and Save the Children are among the few that can trace their roots back to World War II and earlier), and virtually exploded in the second. By the late 1980s, organizations and governments, confronted with mounting urgent needs, disappointed in the development enterprise, and emboldened by new openings in states that were inaccessible during the Cold War, seized the idea of humanitarian action as a way to effect positive change in people's lives in the developing world. Global humanitarian funding increased rapidly, and many hundreds of new NGOs were created—and would continue to spring up around each successive emergency.

Particularly since 1989, when they first ventured into the province of the Red Cross and began programming amidst an active civil war in Sudan, humanitarian NGOs have inserted and asserted themselves as actors in conflicts and emergency settings.[5] The massive humanitarian emergencies caused by conflicts and state failures in the 1990s thrust the humanitarian NGOs into ever more prominent roles on the ground, where they not only served as the primary representatives of the "international community," but also increasingly began to function as public goods providers in the absence of functional states. At times, the humanitarian NGOs have created complete stopgap public sectors for failed or paralyzed governments (e.g., Somalia, Haiti), or taken extreme risks to deliver vital services to civilians in militarily insecure areas (Chechnya, Great Lakes region, Sierra Leone).

Profiles: The Major Players

The largest NGOs actually contain multiple national affiliate organizations that share the brand under various forms of confederation. These NGO federations or "families," of CARE International, Oxfam International, Save the Children Federation, and World Vision International have grown up around founding members that are powerhouses in their own right. World Vision USA's revenues increased by nearly $200 million during 1997–2001 and thus edged out CARE USA as the largest international assistance NGO, with a budget in excess of $600 million. Three years later World Vision USA's budget had grown by another $200 million, and now tops $800 million annually.[6] The budgets of Oxfam Great Britain (Oxfam GB), Save the Children US, and Save the Children UK each fall between $200 million and $300 million.[7]

The four federations range in membership from ten to sixty-five national affiliates, some of which exist only as fundraising and recruitment vehicles while others operate independent programs. The two largest aid NGOs, CARE and World Vision, are heavily weighted toward one large (founding) member. CARE USA, for example, accounts for nearly 80 percent of the total combined revenues of the ten CARE International members. At a distant second is CARE Canada, at 15 percent. Similarly, World Vision US provides 54 percent of total revenues, dwarfing the other sixty-four members. Oxfam International is somewhat bipolar, with Oxfam GB providing 39 percent and the Netherlands 36 percent of revenues, with the other nine members contributing much smaller amounts. Likewise, Save the Children UK and Save the Children US are twin giants in their federation, each accounting for slightly more than 30 percent of federation revenues.

Although budgets fluctuate from year to year, the overall market shares have not changed significantly in several years: World Vision and CARE

Table 1.1: NGO Federation Profiles

Organization	National Affiliates	Countries of Operation	Founding Member	Date Founded	Total Cash Revenues ($USD mil)
CARE	10	70	US	1945	670
MSF	18	80	France	1971	423
OXFAM	12	100	UK	1942	400
Save the Children	27	111	UK	1919	771
World Vision	65	99	US	1950	1,500

Source: Annual reports (figures for 2004)

occupy the number-one and number-two positions, respectively, while Oxfam, MSF, and Save the Children move within the second tier. One explanation for this stability is the comparative advantage positioning of these NGOs over the years. Although all these NGOs conduct programs across sectors (and in fact their staff complain they must "do it all" to sustain their growth in the competitive arena of government funding[8]), most have come to be associated with a specific operational niche in emergency humanitarian assistance that is reinforced by the major donors. CARE established a reputation in large-scale food delivery and logistics, MSF provides medical and primary health care, Oxfam has become the chief NGO expert in water and sanitation, and Save focuses on the needs of children. In emergencies these NGOs often share their niche with other, smaller NGOs, at times serving as the coordinator or lead agency for that sector. World Vision is less strongly identified with any particular niche, though it finds its strengths in food aid and agriculture (World Vision USA is now the largest implementer of WFP food assistance), child rights, and managing the relief-to-development transition.

With the exception of MSF, the youngest and most relief-oriented of the group, each of the super NGOs spent the decades following World War II building up their program portfolios from initial emergency aid deliveries to long-term, antipoverty activities throughout the developing world. Though their raison d'être shifted to development, their operational infrastructures in crisis-prone countries facilitated a rapid response, with a minimum of start-up costs, when crises struck. The major donors came to rely on these already-on-site NGOs to program their relief aid contributions, which provided a significant budget boost to the organizations in each new emergency. These boosts became more important as the development paradigm began to lose its luster and donors' eyes turned increasingly to the massive humanitarian emergencies showcased on CNN and other media outlets. For many of the multi-mandated assistance agencies, UN and NGOs alike, funding for emergency humanitarian relief has grown as a share of their budget. Though many NGOs do not differentiate emergency and development figures in their budget,[9] CARE began in 1998 to make these distinctions within its detailed financial statements. By way of example of the trend, a look back over those five years shows that humanitarian activities (counting both emergency and rehabilitation) grew from an average of 22 percent of CARE's programming budget during 1998–2002[10] to 40 percent in 2004.[11]

Although we tend to speak of the humanitarian community and humanitarian NGOs, very few of the assistance NGOs engage solely in humanitarian relief operations.[12] The vast majority, MSF included, implements both relief and development-oriented programming, and maintains long-term missions in nonemergency settings. In addition to growing awareness of the necessary overlap between relief and development activities, the lines have blurred in basic operational definitions, especially with the phenomenon of the so-called chronic emergency, such as Sudan, where NGOs have been on the ground doing "emergency relief" work for well over a decade.

Depending on their organizational cultures, the NGO federations started out on the opposite ends of the spectrum, either with a strong corporate model of governance (CARE and World Vision) or loose coordinating umbrella bodies (MSF and Oxfam). By the 1990s, however, there was a distinct convergence to the center, with models approaching a confederated style of governance. This common trend reflects at once the perceived need for tighter policy coherence among national members, and the desire to increase Southern participation at all levels of the organization.[13] Of all the organizations, World Vision International rates as the most fully "indigenized" or transnational, and has made indigenization a strategic goal throughout "the Partnership" as it calls itself. Approximately forty World Vision country offices are now fully indigenous, from their boards on down, and the others are making plans to follow suit. Organizations like CARE and Oxfam have also begun down this path, focusing on cultivating partnerships with indigenous NGOs, and project spin-offs that build indigenous capacity.

Despite numerical evidence of NGOs "going global," by internationalizing their organizations,[14] in point of fact they are not yet close to becoming truly transnational entities. On the contrary, despite the newly globalized governance structures of some of these federations, they maintain an identity that is closely associated with their country of origin, and sometimes display a striking tendency to mirror the policies and preferences of their domestic government (one example being the 1999 dispute in Kosovo between the US, French, and Greek affiliates of Médecins du Monde, described in chapter 5).

Traditions and Typologies:
Getting a Handle on the NGO Community

Over the years, various observers of the humanitarian NGOs have made efforts to typologize them by their mission, philosophy, or political stance. Because of its diversity, the international NGO community can be divided up in any number of ways. However, a fundamental division underlying many of the differences and debates between these organizations lies in the nature of their relationship to the great power governments, which is to say the major humanitarian donors and their home governments. In his book *A Bed for the Night*, David Rieff drew attention to the contrasts and conflicts between the European and the US-based NGOs, particularly regarding their orientation to governments.[15] Building on Rieff's distinctions and two previous typologies suggested by humanitarian scholars Thomas Weiss and Steve O'Malley/Dennis Dijkzeul, I begin with a survey of the three main historical strands or traditions in the evolution of modern humanitarian action, and then propose a schematic for classifying the humanitarian NGOs in terms of how they relate to each other and to governments. Understanding the orientations of the major NGOs is crucial to understanding their operational relationships and modes of communications with Western political actors, and their differing emphases on information versus advocacy, as will be explored in subsequent chapters.

Wilsonians

Rieff observed the tendency of many of the large US-based NGOs to cooperate with their government in a "Wilsonian" vision of foreign aid.[16] Whereas the British and French humanitarian groups grew from more political and intellectual roots, the primarily US-based Wilsonian NGOs, to codify Rieff's distinction, emerged from a place of solidarity with the home government. Named for President Woodrow Wilson, who dreamed of projecting US values and influence as a force for good in the world, the Wilsonian tradition sees a basic compatibility of humanitarian aims with US foreign policy objectives. Additionally, European NGO founders came out of leftist movements, while in the United States the leftists engaged in the human rights movement, resulting in a historical and conceptual divide between human rights and humanitarian aid that US practitioners are now trying to bridge, and which essentially does not exist in Europe.[17]

CARE, the large and quintessentially American NGO, came into being during the Marshall Plan after World War II, beginning with the delivery of the original "CARE packages" sent to war-affected populations in Europe. Wilsonian NGOs like CARE exhibit a practical and pragmatic operational perspective, and a number of their senior personnel have crossed back and forth from NGOs to government positions. In one sense the Dutch NGOs might also be included in the Wilsonian realm, as the government of the Netherlands gives generously to humanitarian causes and is politically liberal such that its recipients have few qualms in accepting large government donations.[18] Although the Dutch NGOs have more leftist political leanings and have been vociferous critics of the way the US NGOs have followed their flag, the Dutch and many of the US NGOs both seem to operate with the perception that their home governments represent, essentially, the "good guys," and while they may have differences and conflicts with them at times, accepting government money doesn't automatically compromise the organization's integrity. The Scandinavian NGOs (in particular, the religious ones such as Norwegian Church Aid and Danish Church Aid) are an interesting mix of political activist aid agencies within a Wilsonian mold. Like most US and Dutch NGOs they also receive the bulk of their funding from their respective governments, and at times appear almost quasi-governmental in their programming, but in their own governments' tradition of social democratic ideology[19]: "an ideology," as Norwegian People's Aid puts it in their mission statement, "that among other things has fostered the evolution of the Nordic welfare states."[20]

Dunantists

If Wilson's name can be used to classify the operational bent of the major US humanitarian NGOs, by the same token the European, or classical, branch of humanitarianism that operates distinctly apart from governments might be called the "Dunantist" tradition. The label derives from Red Cross founder Henry Dunant, whose reaction to the aftermath of the battle of Solferino in 1859 launched a humanitarian movement based on the rights of noncombatants, including war wounded, to be protected from the actions of governments at war. Though not technically an NGO, owing to its unique legal status embodied in the Geneva Conventions, the International Committee of the Red Cross (ICRC) was the originating humanitarian organization in this tradition and the codifier of the core humanitarian principles: humanity, impartiality, neutrality, independence, voluntary action, unity, and universality.

The oldest of the modern-day super-NGOs, Save the Children UK was created in the Dunantist image at the end of World War I. Founded expressly to aid war orphans, the organization also held the broader goal of promoting children's rights and international humanitarian safeguards for children during war and peacetime. Save UK and its sister organization of roughly equal size and stature, Save USA, have evolved into mainstream NGOs, but maintain the focus on children (and are frequently at odds over political stance).

Oxfam began as a university movement to send food relief to Nazi-occupied Greece in direct opposition to a British law that prevented aid to countries under occupation. After the war the Oxford Committee for Famine Relief decided to continue and expand its objectives to relieve "the suffering arising as a result of wars or other causes in any part of the world."[21]

Médecins sans Frontières appeared much later, in 1971, after a schism within ICRC's ranks, yet it too remains firmly rooted in this tradition.

These organizations, descendants of ICRC in the Dunantist tradition, were essentially born of war and deliberately distanced from state power. As MSF's Jean-Hervé Bradol has written, this view of humanitarianism defines itself as inherently and necessarily subversive, as it amounts to a "refusal to collaborate" with the decisions of authority figures over who shall live or die.[22] Bradol and other Dunantists argue that humanitarian action "is primarily addressed to those whose right to exist clashes with the indifference or overt hostility of others . . . Consequently, if humanitarian action is to be consistent, it will inevitably clash with the established order."[23]

What separates the original Dunantist organization, ICRC, from its rebellious younger cousins like MSF and MDM, therefore, is the question of consent. The ICRC takes war "as a given" and operates within a framework of rules of war that relies on the warring parties' consent for a neutral humanitarian presence to aid prisoners of war and civilian noncombatants caught up in the conflict. Within this framework ICRC is not a cooperative partner of governments but rather an oppositional force that attempts to hold belligerents to their responsibilities in exchange for not taking sides. If ICRC takes war as a given, NGOs like MSF, MDM, and Oxfam take war as a violation, a crime perpetrated by governments and armed groups against individuals. Consent is not sought by these organizations; rather it is rejected on principle.

Religious NGOs

Finally, the religious or "faith-based" humanitarian tradition is, of course, the oldest of the three, and finds its mandate in the basic tenets of compassion and charitable service common to all the faiths. Religious humanitarianism has evolved out of, and largely away from, the overseas missionary work of previous centuries, with its uncomfortable association with colonialism and coerced religious conversion. On the whole, religious and secular NGOs have for decades worked together constructively in humanitarian emergencies. In policy and practice there is generally no disharmony between the two, except for the rare occasions when a religious NGO is accused of using relief aid as a vehicle for proselytizing to victims. Apart from some evangelical organizations, however, most religious humanitarian agencies do not engage in proselytizing in any direct way.

The Catholics represent some of the largest and most visible aid organizations (e.g., Catholic Relief Services, CAFOD, and the Caritas network). Catholic organizations have a religious purpose in espousing the "teachings of the Gospel of Jesus Christ," but also pursue social justice goals.

Some representatives have described their humanitarian programs as straddling the church and the secular world. Proselytizing is not part of their program, as it would interfere in the delivery of aid, which should be conducted in the spirit of service and free giving. Vatican II also spoke of the potential for aid as a vehicle for ecumenical rapprochement between the Catholic Church and other faiths.

The evangelical NGOs seem to be gaining in prominence in the United States. The Association of Evangelical Relief and Development Organizations (AERDO) now comprises forty-one member organizations, and certain of these organizations are frequently cited by members of the Bush administration, which has many senior officials professing to that faith.[24] In a move that surprised many in the relief community, in 2005 the director of programs for the evangelical NGO Samaritan's Purse (founded by Rev. Franklin Graham, the son of Billy Graham) was appointed director of USAID's Office of U.S. Foreign Disaster Assistance (OFDA).[25] The proselytizing mission of the evangelical movement has created tensions among the humanitarian community, which holds as a bedrock principle that humanitarian aid be given without regard to religious, political, or any consideration other than need. Although the larger evangelical humanitarian NGOs like Samaritan's Purse deny charges of tying their relief aid to religious conversion, accusations have cropped up periodically, and they readily admit they cannot easily divorce their religious mission from their humanitarian work. "We are first a Christian organization and second an aid organization," a representative of Samaritan's Purse was quoted as saying in 2001. "We can't really separate the two."[26]

World Vision International represents a different stripe of religious NGO, one that has a distinctly Christian message but is not governed by any established church. A self-defined "trans-denominational" Christian organization with Protestant leanings, World Vision's field offices partner with local secular and religious organizations of all faiths, and integrate faith into their activities in varying degrees from country to country. (In an example given by a World Vision interviewee, World Vision in Afghanistan consists of a mostly Muslim staff, and their programs are indistinguishable from secular agencies.)

Although their faith may play a role in where some of them decide to initiate programming,[27] the Jewish humanitarian organizations (the most prominent of which include the American Jewish Joint Distribution Committee and American Jewish World Service) do not have to grapple with the issue of proselytizing. As a rabbi speaking at a humanitarian conference explained, God's covenant with the Jews does not preclude universal values. All humans are seen as subject to the laws of God, and this "universal covenant" means that Jews are not driven to recruit for their religion.[28]

This inbuilt tolerance approach is also claimed by the larger independent Islamic humanitarian organizations, such as the Aga Khan Foundation, Islamic Relief, and Muslim Hands in the UK, as the Koran also allows for the possibility of civilized disagreement within a wider framework of universal human values. However, as is the case with some of the major Jewish NGOs, the Islamic NGOs exhibit a preference for programming within the faith, and channel their aid to mainly Islamic countries or populations. Their organizational missions and fund-raising mechanisms also make heavy use of articles of faith such as the Muslim charitable traditions of *zakat* (akin to Christian tithing) and *waqf* (the donation of formerly private property for the public good).[29]

Overall, although these organizations' faith-based mission and orientation may represent a crucial distinction for the religious humanitarian practitioner, the existence or type of religious affiliation has little bearing on how the NGOs relate to governments. Religious NGOs can fall within the Wilsonian or Dunantist camp on that score; organizations like Catholic Relief Services and Mercy Corps International have more in common with Wilsonian organizations like CARE than with, say, Danish Church Aid, with its emphasis on political advocacy on behalf of the poor and oppressed.

The Activist-Pragmatist Split

Growing out of the core difference between the US and the European NGOs regarding how they relate to states are various disparities in operational stance and approach. Leaving aside for the moment the many distinctions among the European NGOs, as a group they stand in sharp contrast to the US organizations by having a higher degree of independence from governments, placing their actions in a longer time range, and being less dependent on governments for their operational budget.

Operationally, these philosophical differences have manifested themselves as an activist-pragmatist split, which can be seen in many aspects of NGO activity. Dunantist organizations such as MSF and Oxfam at times see their advocacy function as of more lasting importance than the actual aid operations. MSF's considerable technical expertise developed over its organizational life, but the organization began as a dramatic humanitarian statement, and continues to stress an advocacy agenda, its "*témoignage*," as its driving force. Oxfam is known also for technical proficiency in the field, but sees its mission as advocating for the poor and victimized, and counts advocacy as one of its three core activities.[30] Generally speaking, the European approach to humanitarian advocacy tends toward the confrontational as opposed to cooperative, and is more inclined to attempt policy suasion through naming and shaming in public forums.

In contrast, the US NGOs' advocacy is largely focused through the umbrella group InterAction, which concentrates on opening and maintaining lines of communication with the US government and inside tracks with key policymakers. In general a US NGO prefers to positions itself as a "friend at court," believing it can be more effective through nudging and behind-the-scenes policy advice. When US NGOs do take policy positions in opposition to the government, which is not uncommon, they more often seek dialogue in private fora to express their views. Their public protests and advocacy statements generally use broad-based, generic means such as joint letters to the White House from a large group of organizations, or signing on to global petitions. NGOs like Oxfam, on the other hand, tend to be more vocal and critical—for example, publishing a list of manufacturers and exposing their ties to a repressive government.

The Wilsonian NGOs are fundamentally pragmatists, focused on the technical and logistical tasks of aid—"what are the practical things we can accomplish, and how effective we can be in the specific context of the current crisis."[31] The Europeans, on the other hand, tend to look further down the road and place their actions within a context of long-range costs and benefits. Much time could be spent arguing back and forth about the relative merits of each other's approach. The Dunantist critique holds that the US organizations offer only Band-Aid solutions to humanitarian needs, having little lasting impact at best, and at worst reinforcing oppressive systems. In complex emergencies involving rights abuses, some of these organizations will question how vital or effective international humanitarian assistance is to the victims and whether they might not do more good by shining a light on the situation by withdrawing or speaking out. For their part, US NGOs have disapproved of some Dunantist organizations' willingness to take on governments, even at the cost of their programming, and accuse them of have reified the concept of humanitarian space to the point where it serves the agencies' ethos more than the actual people in need of assistance.

In reality, such a stark choice is rarely thrust upon an aid agency today. MSF does almost no illicit, cross-border operations at present, and the last time it was forced to shut down its program by a host government was over a dispute on malaria treatment protocols.[32] Those NGOs that witness rights abuses could conceivably pass along the information to human rights bodies or the media without necessarily endangering their mission. Rather, the agency must only choose whether it will speak publicly itself, and many, through commonsense concerns for their mission or the safety of their staff on the ground, may choose not to do so. More common, and increasingly so of late, are NGO decisions to voluntarily withdraw. In the summer of 2004 MSF permanently withdrew its staff from both Afghanistan and Iraq. The withdrawals were painful decisions taken to safeguard its staff, as well as pointed political messages to the United States and its coalition allies that the humanitarian endeavor had been compromised and imperiled by its association with the military occupation in those countries.[33]

Cross-Cutting Alliances

Most political/philosophical typologies of the humanitarian NGOs have centered on the core humanitarian principles and the relative weight the organizations place upon them when they are in contradiction. Yet this has tended to exaggerate the more esoteric philosophical differences while downplaying basic practical similarities, and it obscures the fact that even within one organization different principles are stressed at different times. For example, because MSF was born of an angry split of French doctors from the ICRC—over what they felt was ICRC placing its concern for neutrality over the suffering of Biafran victims of Ethiopia's war campaign—observers have at times classified them, mis-

Figure 1.2: Weiss's "Political Spectrum of Humanitarians and Their Attitudes toward Traditional Operating Principles"

	Classicists ⟷ Minimalists ⟷ Maximalists ⟷ Solidarists	
Engagement with political authorities	eschew public confrontations	advocate controversial public policy
Neutrality	avoid taking sides	take the side of selected victims
Impartiality	deliver aid using proportionality and nondiscrimination	skew the balance of resource allocation
Consent	pursue as sine qua non	override sovereignty as necessary

Source: Thomas Weiss, "Principles, Politics, and Humanitarian Action," *Ethics and International Affairs,* vol. 13, December 1999.

leadingly, as polar opposites. In Thomas Weiss's schematic of humanitarian organizations' political orientations (see Figure 2), ICRC is placed in the "classicist" group, MSF is at the opposite end toward the "solidarist" extreme, and those NGOs advocating a "do no harm" approach fall in between the two under "minimalists."[34] On the issue of consent, Weiss's continuum captures the crucial difference between ICRC and MSF, but the logic of the schematic would make the two organizations appear as polar opposites, when in reality, despite their different approaches to speaking out, they are firmly rooted in the same tradition of humanitarian action independent of states. Weiss's classification system also doesn't capture the arguably more fundamental division (for the purposes of this study at any rate) between what David Rieff called the "disobedient humanitarianism" of an MSF versus Wilsonian or "state humanitarianism" of most US NGOs.

There may in fact be no satisfactory way of pigeonholing all the NGOs according to philosophy. On the ground and in debate, the line

Figure 1.3: O'Malley and Dijkzeul's "Mental Map of Large International NGOs" (2002)

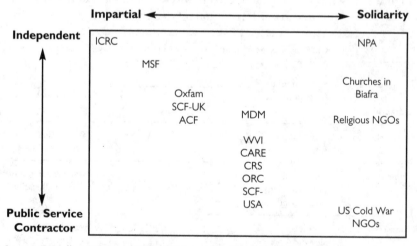

Source: O'Malley, Steve, and Dennis Dijkzeul, "A Typology of International Humanitarian Organizations." Paper presented at International Expert Conference on "Security and Humanitarian Action: Who Is Winning? A US-Europe Dialogue in the Wake of September 11." Columbia University, Arden House, May 24–25, 2002.

Figure 1.4: Lines of Demarcation within the Secular NGO Traditions

	Wilsonian	**Dunantist**
Favoring rule-based coordination	CARE Save the Children US IRC	(Anglophone) Oxfam Save the Children UK Concern Worldwide
Independent/rule averse	Americares Other in-kind dona- tional organizations	(Francophone) MSF Action contre la Faim Médecins du Monde

More dependent on and cooperative with governments	**More independent of and oppositional toward governments**
Short time horizon	**Longer time horizon**
Service delivery emphasis	**Advocacy emphasis**

is typically drawn between US and European NGOS, but pronounced divisions also exist on matters of coordination between Francophone agencies on the one hand and Anglophone agencies on the other, and still another between the majority of agencies that adhere to varying degrees of neutrality versus the unapologetic solidarity of the Nordic agencies.

Seeking more clarity on what differentiates the NGOs from each other, a recent paper by Steve O'Malley and Dennis Dijkzeul reconfigured Weiss's categories and offered an alternative typology, which plots organizations on two axes (see Figure 3): from "Independent" to (the perhaps inadvertently pejorative) "Public Service Contractor" on one, and from "Impartial" to "Solidarity" on the other.[35] Their mental map thus has ICRC as impartial and independent, with MSF as a close second.

O'Malley and Dijkzeul's model is instructive for our purposes in that it addresses the differentiation between NGOs in their way of relating to governments. This schematic captures both the extent of their independence from donors and their means of exercising influence—that is, the relative weight of advocacy versus operations. It does not, however, address another basic split between the organizations: their willingness, or not, to create rule-based codes and self-policing mechanisms within their community.

To add a further dimension to this analysis, therefore, one could also take into account the divisions among NGOs on the question of what sort of community they would like to institute among themselves: one based on shared codes and rules and in time a formal accountability structure, or a more atomistic collection of independent and diverse entities. The matrix in Figure 4 attempts a new typology using the Wilsonian and Dunantist categories superimposed by the rule-based regime question. In doing so it evinces two cross-cutting divides: between Wilsonians and Dunantists, and between the Anglo- and Francophone NGOs.

In regard to the second divide, the Anglophone Dunantists have consistently expressed the need for a tighter, more rule-based community to be constructed from the crowd of NGOs. They wish to see codes and standards with real teeth, to hold NGOs to their agreed-upon responsibilities, and to make sure they are accountable for their programs. The Wilsonian group has been ambivalent to this movement, the centerpiece of which is the Humanitarian Accountability Project, which seeks to establish an ombudsman or watchdog office in the field. However, the largest stumbling block has been the resistance of the Francophone Dunantists, led by MSF. Another case in point was the French rebellion over the inter-NGO collaboration known as the Sphere Project. The Sphere Project began in 1997 as a joint effort between humanitarian NGOs and the Red Cross. Emerging from the scathing reviews of humanitarian effectiveness in the post-genocide Rwandan refugee crisis, the project produced "Humanitarian Charter and Minimum Standards in Disaster Response," a handbook containing a code of ethics as well as operational guidelines and technical standards for humanitarian organizations operating in emergency settings.[36] MSF, despite being one of its initiators, ultimately withdrew from Sphere because it grew concerned that it would become a set of rigid, lowest-common-denominator standards that would inhibit innovation and independence. The French NGOs—MSF, MDM, and ACF—have all expressed the sentiment that Sphere smacks too much of corporate collaboration, that it could too easily be manipulated by donor governments in pursuing their own agendas, and that its main result would be to solidify the dominance of the core group of major NGOs. MSF was also critical of the code of conduct that emerged in response to the West Africa sex scandal,[37] an effort led by UNHCR and Save the Children. MSF maintains that in general, codes of conduct are knee-jerk, media-friendly reactions that don't get to the root of the problem, which in this instance is the whole system of refugee camp structure and management.

In response, some other NGOs complain that MSF has a knee-jerk reaction to rules and codes other than the ones it sets forth itself. In the words of one US NGO representative, "You could fill a library with all the books and manuals MSF has written on the right way to do things, but they don't like it when it's a group effort."

Figure 1.5: Annual Budgets and Public-to-Private Funding Split of Six Major NGOs (in millions of US dollars)

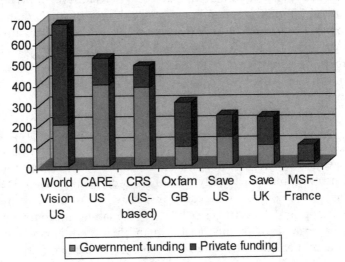

Source: Annual Reports and financial statements (figures for FY ending 2003)

The Financing Split

The way the NGOs are financed both reflects and reinforces their divergent perspectives. The simple truth is that the major (secular) US NGOs could not operate at their current level without public funding. To be in a position where they could regularly refuse donor government dollars on principle they would have to radically reformulate (downsize) their organizations. Their dependence on the US government was arguably expressed also in their movement away from New York City where a number of NGOs like CARE and CRS were once based to cities further down the eastern seaboard closer to the nation's capital. The two US NGO consortia, PACT and InterAction, had already left New York for Washington by the late 1980s. Symbolically the move represented a shift away from the United Nations and the international community (the reason for so many being in New York to begin with) and toward their main source of resources.

CARE, CRS, and Save the Children US regularly receive over 50 percent of their funding from the US government. The Dutch and Scandinavian NGOs also receive about three-quarters of their annual funding in government grants (see Figure 5).

In contrast, Oxfam US is 75 percent privately funded, and Oxfam GB takes only about a quarter of its funding from the British government. MSF has been able to maintain a 70–80 percent level of private funding, with an internally set minimum of 50 percent of funds that must come from private sources. As a matter of policy MSF refuses funding from governments who are "belligerents" in a conflict or whose neutrality is otherwise compromised. For instance, MSF would not accept US government money for Afghanistan or French government money for Rwanda.

The economics of the US NGOs are fundamentally different from the Europeans. In the United States even private donors want to see their grants leveraged with public funds. The private funding raised by Save the Children US, for example, would not be sufficient to support significant programming by any one of its individual country Field Offices (with maybe one or two exceptions) if its US government funding were to disappear.[38] Government's bilateral humanitarian contributions have, in general, grown much faster than their multilateral contributions (from 50 percent in the late 1980s to over 60 percent in the 1990s, topping 70 percent today, during which time humanitarian assistance more than doubled[39]); more government aid funding is now flowing through NGOs, or more precisely through the handful of largest NGOs, for the donors do not distribute equally among the community but rather fund according to track record and absorption capacity. As one illustration, in 2000 a total of $2.5 billion in USAID relief and development assistance was programmed in grants and contracts to over four hundred NGOs. A quarter of that went to just four NGOs: CARE, CRS, Save the Children, and World Vision. Those same four received slightly more than a quarter, 27 percent, of USAID's total aid funding in 2002, and if one excludes the USAID grants to organizations that do not engage in humanitarian assistance, the share of the four largest NGOs rises to a full 50 percent.[40]

MSF and other European NGOs have built up formidable direct-mail bases, which they have leveraged into automatic, repeating credit card donations, providing a more reliable source than earlier direct appeals. The UK's Disasters Emergency Committee (DEC) consortium[41] raises funds jointly around emergencies with special appeals. Oxfam, Red Cross, and Save UK are the biggest recipients of DEC-raised funds, and as a result can respond rapidly to an emergency with a private war chest of $5 or $6 million in advance funding. As a result of their greater financial independence from government donors, the Dunantist organizations are able, in principle, to exercise greater operational independence, or at least have the leeway of launching humanitarian responses without being seen as colluding with one of the parties to the conflict.

The US public is less easily tapped, as it is very domestically focused with its giving. Only 1–2 percent of charitable giving goes to international causes, and much of that is religiously oriented, which is one way World Vision can sustain its lower public percentages. Eighty percent of World Vision's funding is raised from private sources. Of this, a further 80 percent comes from individual donors, largely through child sponsorship and other direct appeals. The remaining 20 percent is from corporate or large gift donors.

Recent Developments and Perennial Debates

The key policy challenges and debates revolve around NGO-donor relations and issues of independence and neutrality; NGO's relationship to the military and security issues; the rights-based programming approach central to the "new humanitarianism" paradigm, and its counterargument in the back-to-basics movement. Humanitarian practitioners have been grappling with these issues for many years, though in the post-9/11 environment and in the context of emergencies in Western-occupied countries, the debates have taken on a new urgency. All of these issues are but variations on the major theme that divides the Dunantists from the Wilsonians: whether to cohere with a Western political agenda or stand steadfastly apart from it.

As governments programmed increasingly larger shares of their official aid through NGOs they have sought closer ties to NGO programming, and applied greater pressure for accountability to donor-defined performance measures.[42] The deepening donor involvement with the design and management of aid projects has once again raised the specter of the "government contractor," and NGOs who go along will have a harder time demonstrating their neutrality on the ground.

NGOs and the Military

The fraught relationship of humanitarianism with the military has been pushed to the forefront of the NGO debate at present, capping a trend that was building since the early 1990s. In the previous decade, when governments were using NGOs as the primary expression of international involvement in complex emergencies, and NGOs began seeing greater numbers of casualties among their own personnel, some of them called for the first time for the use of military force. CARE USA lobbied intensely for an intervention in Somalia, while Oxfam publicly appealed for it in both Rwanda and Eastern Zaire (DRC).

Most NGOs at one time or another have coordinated with military forces in the execution of aid activities. This relationship is handled with varying degrees of caution and reluctance, with the US organizations typically being the most amenable. However, virtually all the NGOs note a big difference between coordinating with the military as a temporary marriage of convenience, and being coordinated *by* them.[43] During the Kosovo campaign, MSF USA was so concerned about the blurring of the lines between the military and humanitarian spheres, and the seeming acquiescence of its counterparts, that it was moved to quit the Disaster Response Committee of InterAction in protest. Finally, even the most amenable Wilsonian NGOs recoil at the notion of playing an instrumental role in the US military effort as, in the words of Graham Allison, "a genuine second front"[44] or, as Colin Powell put it, a "force multiplier" for the US military.[45]

Of the military's three possible roles in humanitarian assistance—providing an umbrella of security for humanitarians to operate, supporting agencies' work with logistical and protection services, or providing direct assistance to populations themselves, in parallel with humanitarian groups[46]—common sense would seem to dictate that the military should pursue its comparative advantage that lies in the first instance: creating a secure environment for humanitarians to do their work. However, the military has increasingly been opting to focus on the third role of direct provider, with Afghanistan being the most obvious example. From the early days of the postconflict response, NGOs called for the expansion of the International Security Assistance Forces beyond Kabul to allow them to travel and do their work safely. Rather than expanding

ISAF's geographic mandate and force requirements, however, the military adopted and expanded the use of the Provincial Reconstruction Teams (PRTs), small groups of military and civilian personnel that seek to provide the stability of an armed international presence, while at the same time undertaking small-scale reconstruction projects in a "hearts and minds" endeavor. The overwhelming consensus of NGOs in Afghanistan held that the PRTs were an inadequate solution to the security problem, and in fact may have heightened the risk for humanitarian workers by blurring the lines between the military and humanitarian presence.

The Rise of the Rights-Based Approach and the Back-to-Basics Backlash

Over the past decade a number of major humanitarian NGOs arrived at a philosophical consensus on the importance of a rights-based approach (RBA), as opposed to needs-based or welfarist approach to humanitarian action. "International humanitarian law imposes limits on permissible behavior during war; human rights law sets the minimum standards to which individuals are entitled by virtue of their membership in humanity; and humanitarian action seeks to restore some of those rights when individuals are deprived of them by circumstance."[47] The adoption of rights-based approaches by more and more NGOs signifies concurrence that the motives and way of thinking about humanitarian aid—not as voluntary acts of charity but in recognition and protection of people's fundamental rights—matters a great deal to its success.

Even the proto-Wilsonian NGO CARE, under the leadership of Peter Bell (president from 1995 to 2005) adopted a rights-based approach and stepped up its policy and advocacy activities. CARE's adoption of the RBA principle surprised many in the field who considered CARE a solid, technically proficient but decidedly nonflashy workhorse of relief and development work, with a well-established niche in food aid and logistics. Attempting to make it otherwise, some thought, was ill advised and counter to CARE's comparative advantage.

The rights-based approach grew out of a trend in the humanitarian movement in the late 1990s that some labeled the "new humanitarianism."[48] The ceaseless refrain heard earlier in the decade was that humanitarians were allowing their aid resources to be manipulated by belligerents, thus fueling economies of war and perpetuating violence. The "Do No Harm"[49] concept fashioned in response begat a more activist agenda, which reasoned that if aid could be used for harm it could conceivably also be used for good, and might in fact be instrumental to peace-building, as some NGOs and international organizations began to attempt.[50]

The back-to-basics response to this trend—which is shared, for somewhat different reasons, by humanitarian practitioners such as MSF's Nicholas de Torrente and Fiona Terry, and observers such as Mark Duffield and David Rieff—has warned that the humanitarian endeavor is imperiled by such forays into politics. The MSF position holds that humanitarians must adhere strictly to the fundamentals of neutrality and impartiality or risk being assimilated into one political agenda or another, to the detriment of their mission to save lives and ease suffering. In a very true sense, of course, this is a incontrovertibly political stance in itself, but one that claims loyalty only to the humanitarian imperative, rather than a particular side or outcome. Taking a somewhat different tack toward the same conclusion, David Rieff has proclaimed the human rights focus an exercise in NGO "hubris" and overstretch, leading perhaps to the end of independent humanitarianism. Rieff believes that rights-based humanitarianism is impossible, because human rights are law-based and absolutist, while humanitarian aid requires flexibility, constant compromise of principles, and the occasional deal with the devil. In "coming to view its commitments as going beyond providing relief, in allying itself with the human rights movement, and in committing itself to an interpretation of international law in which aid must be allowed . . . [humanitarian aid] . . . may never recover."[51] But such warnings of humanitarianism's demise are surely premature, since for the time being this remains more of a problem for the thinkers in headquarters than for operational staff. The rights-based approach in the field is naturally subject to the practical concerns of the day-to-day, as delimited by the organization's mission perception and risk threshold, and the individual staff member's own values.

Of more immediate concern is the future of UN-NGO cooperation in humanitarian action under the "integrated mission" framework. Around the same time that the new humanitarianism began to develop, "coherence" and "integration" became watchwords within the UN humanitarian circles. Frustrated at the lack of strategic coordination between its political and humanitarian arms, the UN evolved the concept of "integrated missions," which seek to place all of UN activity in a crisis country under the coordination of a single UN authority, frequently the secretary-general's specially appointed special representative (SRSG). Many humanitarian NGOs, accustomed to working with UN agencies under a humanitarian coordinator (HC), have protested (to little avail) that this arrangement subordinates humanitarian assistance to political objectives. Its critics have observed that the basic problem with the "coherence" agenda was that the UN was insisting that all the agencies band together to apply political conditionality to aid services, a concept in direct opposition to humanitarian principles.[52]

What Sort of Community?

Humanitarian NGO personnel face peculiar tensions in their work. Whereas a devoted employee of a business venture has the relatively clear-cut goal of generating profits, growth, and market share of his or her enterprise, the typical NGO worker must juggle competing loyalties: the needs and interests of the beneficiary, the desires of the donor, the shared goals of the humanitarian NGO community, and the interest of one's organization to survive and grow. These various sets of interests conflict with each other at least as often as they overlap.

By necessity, NGOs inhabit relationships of mutual dependence. The scale of modern humanitarian emergencies and the comparatively limited capacities of NGOs demand that they coordinate their activities with each other and with multilateral agencies in order to meet needs effectively. In most emergencies not even the largest NGO is capable of launching an effective response individually; it can function only in tandem with other agencies, international organizations, and host and donor governments. The humanitarian organizations must function in symbiotic, if not always harmonious, relationships with each other, with donor agencies, and with the media on whom they depend to get their messages out to the private donor public.

The humanitarian NGOs operate around a shared set of core values. Most NGOs recognize, formally in their mission statements or informally in their practice, the "fundamental principles" of the Red Cross movement as a large component of their guiding ideology. In particular, the first three of the seven principles—humanity (the "humanitarian imperative"), impartiality, and neutrality—are widely seen as the core of humanitarianism and the basis for international humanitarian action. However, NGO representatives frequently point out that humanitarian principles are often contradictory, and there can be many cases where an organization is faced with a choice to favor one principle over another. In Goma, for instance, MSF France withdrew from the refugee camps when it became clear that they were abetting the *genocidaires* among the refugee Hutu population of the camps, and violating the principle of neutrality. In deciding to stay, other NGOs could cite the humanitarian imperative principle, claiming the withdrawal of services would cause more suffering to the innocent individuals in the camps.

Some observers dismiss the term "humanitarian community" as a naïve fiction, much as some deride the notion of "international community." Yet despite the fact that NGOs have different mandates, organizational cultures, and interests, the operational and collegial links among staff members of the major NGOs are quite strong. Over the past ten years the NGOs have greatly increased their coordination, in practice and in principle, covering just about every aspect of their work. Previously existing umbrella groups and consortia of NGOs such as the Steering Committee for Humanitarian Response (SCHR) and the International Council of Voluntary Agencies (ICVA), both based in Geneva, InterAction in Washington, and Voluntary Organizations in Cooperation in Emergencies (VOICE) in Brussels have served the NGOs as fora for dialogue and information sharing, and as vehicles for joint advocacy efforts. A plethora of new mechanisms and initiatives took shape in the second half of the 1990s, spurred on by perceived failures of the humanitarian community in the Goma crisis, and a rising tide of criticism about foreign aid in general. The organizations sought to enhance performance and effectiveness, to strengthen NGO accountability (to their beneficiaries as well as to their donors), and to restore public trust in the humanitarian enterprise. Examples of these efforts include declamatory statements of principle such as the Red Cross Code of Conduct and the Sphere Project's Humanitarian Charter; operational guidelines and best practices such as the NGO Field Cooperation Protocol, the People in Aid Code of Best Practice in the Management and Support of Personnel, and Sphere's Minimum Standards in Disaster Response; and the most recent addition, a code of conduct being developed by a sub-Working Group of the IASC in response to the West Africa sex scandal uncovered by UNHCR and Save the Children UK. (These various measures have gone forward despite objections from MSF and other Francophone agencies.)[53]

Conclusion: A Community Divided

The NGOs today have a wide range of options on how they want to work together, and how to approach the donor governments. They can choose to do so as a group, singly, behind the scenes, or in a public confrontation. The EU's forum, VOICE, and USAID's ACVA serve as centers for NGO-donor dialogue and policy cooperation. The major NGO consortia ICVA, SCHR, and InterAction are all represented on the UN's Inter-Agency Standing Committee, and NGOs typically belong to more than one, using them as they see fit. However, despite their advances in collaborative efforts and field-level coordination, despite the vast increase in inter-NGO communication at all organizational levels, and despite the expressed desire of nearly all the major NGOs to work together more effectively to advance a humanitarian agenda, they find themselves continually falling short of this goal. Reaching agreement on appropriate standards, performance measures, and field protocols is one thing (and even this has not gone smoothly owing to the rule-averse nature of the Francophone NGOs), but the NGO community remains constitutionally unable to present a clear and authoritative humanitarian voice in its interface with the great power governments. As this chapter has explored, the largest fissure that runs through the core of the community between the US NGOs, most of which are Wilsonian in character, and the European NGOs of the Dunantist tradition, regards how they relate to and work with governments—chiefly, the great power governments, their donors. The NGO-government interface and the forms it has taken to date are the subject of the next chapter.

Notes

1. Some portions of this chapter first appeared in my article, "Humanitarian NGOs: Challenges and Trends," in *Humanitarian Action and the Global War on Terror: A Review of Trends and Issues*, ed. Joanna Macrae and Adele Harmer (London: Overseas Development Institute, July 2003).

2. "Sins of the Secular Missionaries," *The Economist*, January 29, 2000.

3. Shepard Forman and Abby Stoddard, "International Assistance," in *The State of Nonprofit America*, ed. Lester M. Salamon (Washington, DC: Brookings Institution Press, 2002), 244. Lindenberg and Bryant estimate twenty-five hundred relief and development NGOs in 1990, nearly double the amount of ten years prior (Marc Lindenberg and Coralie Bryant, *Going Global: Transforming Relief and Development NGOs* [Bloomfield, CT: Kumarian, 2001], 3).

4. Northern NGOs and NGO consortia culled from UN OCHA, ReliefWeb Directory of Humanitarian Organizations, http://www.reliefweb.int.

5. Fiona Terry, among others, has noted the 1989 "negotiated access" agreement with the Sudanese government and rebels that created Operation Lifeline Sudan as a watershed moment in humanitarian NGO operations (Fiona Terry, *Condemned to Repeat? The Paradox of Humanitarian Action*. Ithaca, NY: Cornell University Press, 2002).

6. "2005 Consolidated Financial Statements: World Vision Inc., September 30, 2004 and 2005."

7. Annual reports: figures for FY 2004.

8. Conference remarks and interviews, NGO representatives.

9. Instead they show amounts by program sector, such as water/sanitation, or by geographical region, which can pertain to either relief or development scenarios.

10. CARE USA audited financial statements, 1998–2002.

11. CARE USA Annual Report 2004.

12. Notable exceptions are those NGOs specializing in single bulk deliveries of commodities, such as Americares, Feed the Children, and Gifts in Kind International.

13. Forman and Stoddard, "International Assistance Organizations."

14. Lindenberg and Bryant, *Going Global.*

15. David Rieff, *A Bed for the Night: Humanitarianism in Crisis* (New York: Simon & Schuster, 2002).

16. Ibid., 13.

17. Ibid.

18. Steve O'Malley and Dennis Dijkzeul, "A Typology of International Humanitarian Organizations," paper presented at International Expert Conference on Security and Humanitarian Action: Who Is Winning? A US-Europe Dialogue in the Wake of September 11. Columbia University, Arden House, May 24–25, 2002. See also Lindenberg and Bryant, *Going Global.*

19. Sebastien Chartrand, "Politics of Swedish Humanitarian Organizations: Exporting the Welfare State?" Paper P02-301, Wissenschaftszentrum Berlin for Sozial Forschung, January 2002.

20. NPA Web site, http://ips.idium.no/folkehjelp.no.

21. www.oxfam.org.uk/atwork/history/oxhist1.htm.

22. Jean-Hervé Bradol, "Introduction: The Sacrificial International Order and Humanitarian Action," in *In the Shadow of Just Wars: Violence, Politics, and Humanitarian Action,* ed. Fabrice Weissman (Ithaca, NY: Cornell University Press), 9.

23. Ibid., 6.

24. The much publicized "faith-based initiative" of the Bush administration supports and encourages the charitable works of religious NGOs within a wider promotion of voluntarism. President Bush signed an executive order in 2002 that established a center for faith-based initiatives

within USAID as a part of the overall effort to make "it easier for faith-based organizations to work with the federal government." In one noticeable development, World Vision, which until 1994 was listed as two separate entities for USAID registration purposes—World Vision USA and World Vision Inc. (USAID funds)—is now registered as a single entity. The dual registration had been done in past years to separate out the religious activities, which were not supported by regulations. The structure of World Vision, according to senior staff, has not changed.

25. In perhaps another sign of the US government's blessing on Samaritan's Purse, the organization, though still on the small end of the NGO spectrum, has exhibited a remarkable growth rate in US public funding in recent years. In 2002 the US government gave $4.7 million in grants and other support to Samaritan's Purse, up from $370,940 in 1999.

26. David Gonzalez, "U.S. Aids Conversion-Minded Quake Relief in El Salvador," *New York Times*, March 5, 2001. The article quotes Salvadoran aid recipients as saying Samaritan's Purse workers asked them to "accept Jesus Christ as their savior"—that is, convert to evangelical Protestantism.

27. For instance, although American Jewish Joint Distribution Committee programs in many countries throughout the world, its principal mission is to "serve the needs of Jews throughout the world, particularly where their lives as Jews are threatened or made more difficult" (www.jdc.org/who_mission.html). American Jewish World Service, however, makes clear that it represents "a Jewish response to the needs of communities throughout the globe, regardless of race, religion or nationality" ("Mission Statement," http://www.ajws.org).

28. Remarks by Rabbi H. J. Wechsler at "Traditions, Values, and Humanitarian Action," a symposium held by the Center for International Health and Cooperation and the Institute of International Humanitarian Affairs at Fordham University, New York, November 20, 2002.

29. Jonathan Benthall, "Humanitarianism and Islam after 11 September," in *Humanitarian Action and the "Global War on Terror"*: *A Review of Trends and Issues*, ed. Joanna Macrae and Adele Harmer (London: Overseas Development Institute, 2003).

30. "Oxfam's global programme includes three types of intervention—humanitarian response, development work, and campaigning. All our work comes from a rights-based approach. To overcome poverty and suffering we work to ensure that the rights of women and men are

fulfilled and protected" (*Oxfam Annual Report and Accounts 2003/2004*).

31. Rudolph von Bernuth, vice president for Children in Emergencies, Save the Children US, interview with author. September 26, 2002.

32. The dispute was with the government of Burundi in 2002, where MSF was illegally using a treatment known as Artemisinin Combination Therapy, the approach favored by experts for the treatment of drug-resistant malaria. The government eventually yielded to pressure and revised their protocols the following year.

33. MSF representatives' remarks and press statements.

34. Thomas Weiss, "Principles, Politics, and Humanitarian Action," *Ethics and International Affairs*, vol. 13, Winter (1999): 1–22.

35. O'Malley and Dijkzeul, "Typology of International Humanitarian Organizations."

36. Though Sphere does not comprise a formal membership or list of signatories, being a purely voluntary endeavor, it is "used" widely across the humanitarian sector (www.sphereproject.org).

37. In 2001 a review of UNHCR operations in West African refugee camps revealed that refugees and displaced people (girls and women) living in the camps were being subject to sexual abuse and exploitation, including at the hands of humanitarian workers. An IASC task force of UN agencies and NGOs was created March 2002 and established the code of conduct (Inter-Agency Standing Committee Report of the Task Force on Protection from Sexual Exploitation and Abuse in Humanitarian Crises).

38. Von Bernuth interview.

39. Development Initiatives, *The Reality of Aid 2000*, ed. Judith Randel, Tony German, and Deborah Ewing (London: Earthscan Publications, 2000).

40. USAID, *Voluntary Foreign Aid Programs: Report of Voluntary Agencies Engaged in Overseas Relief and Development (The VOLAG Report)*. Reports from 2002 and 2004.

41. The DEC consists of fourteen British-based NGOs: Actionaid, British Red Cross, CAFOD, CARE International, Children's Aid Direct, Christian Aid, Christian Children's Fund GB, Concern, Help the Aged, Merlin, OXFAM, Save the Children UK, Tearfund, and World Vision UK. Its activities consist mainly of joint fund-raising appeals for specific emergencies, but it also serves as an interagency forum for consultation, evaluation, and dialogue.

42. Abby Stoddard, "The US and the 'Bilateralisation' of Humanitarian Response," HPG Background Paper (London: Overseas Development Institute, December 2002).

43. Hugo Slim, "Military Intervention to Protect Human Rights: The Humanitarian Agency Perspective," Background paper for the International Council on Human Rights' Meeting on Humanitarian Intervention: Responses and Dilemmas for Human Rights Organisations, Geneva, March 31–April 1, 2001.

44. Quoted in Larry Minear, "Humanitarian Action in the Age of Terrorism," Background paper presented at International Expert Conference on Security and Humanitarian Action: Who Is Winning? A US-Europe Dialogue in the Wake of September 11. Columbia University, Arden House, May 24–25, 2002.

45. US UN Press, Remarks by Secretary of State Colin Powell to the National Foreign Policy Conference for Leaders of NGOs in Washington, DC, October 26, 2001.

46. Steve Hansch, "NGOs and the Military: A Practitioner's Perspective," Paper presented at International Expert Conference on Security and Humanitarian Action: Who Is Winning? A US-Europe Dialogue in the Wake of September 11. Columbia University, Arden House, May 24–25, 2002.

47. Terry, *Condemned to Repeat?* 17.

48. Joanna Macrae, *The New Humanitarianisms: A Review of Trends in Global Humanitarian Action* (London: Overseas Development Institute, April 2002).

49. From Mary Anderson, *Do No Harm: Supporting Local Capacities for Peace through Aid* (Cambridge, MA: Collaborative for Development Action, 1996); and *Do No Harm: How Aid Can Support Peace—Or War* (Boulder, CO: Lynne Rienner, 1999).

50. Macrae, *New Humanitarianisms.*

51. Rieff, *Bed for the Night*, 302.

52. Terry, *Condemned to Repeat?* Joanna Macrae and Nicholas Leader, *Shifting Sands: The Search for Coherence between Political and Humanitarian Action* (London: Overseas Development Institute, 2000).

53. The MSF leadership freely admits that it resists regulation by anyone else, and its members occasionally lament the fact that its reputation as a nay-sayer has led other NGOs in the community to dismiss what it is saying out of hand (Fiona Terry, interview with author). It worries also that the professionalization movement of NGOs is a form of "busi-

ness ethics" that serves to further marketize the humanitarian community. MSF's strongest objections to the unification efforts stem from its belief that whatever the technical competence problems with the small NGOs, they are far outweighed by the accountability and political/ethical problems with the big ones.

CHAPTER TWO

ANTS IN THE GROUND, GNATS IN THE EAR

The Separate but Intersecting Realms of Humanitarian Information and Advocacy

Unraveling the Policy Equation

Having reviewed how the historical traditions of the major humanitarian NGOs condition the manner in which they relate to great power governments, this chapter tackles the question of whether the humanitarian NGOs matter, in any appreciable sense, to the conduct of political actors, and if they can lay claim to any impact on the policies of those governments in regard to complex emergencies in developing countries. My contention is that the traditional advocacy efforts (pressuring, lobbying, public statements) when employed by humanitarian NGOs have had, at most, a very modest effect on policy decisions. However, a larger and generally unrecognized source of NGO influence has shaped international perceptions and behavior around these crises, which stems from their informational function and their emerging role as a group of expert witnesses and advisors. By virtue of being the singular originating source of information on humanitarian conditions in many areas, however spotty or soft the information, NGOs in fact play a significant role in shaping the ultimate policy decisions of donor governments and intergovernmental bodies dealing with a crisis. Specifically, this chapter examines the way NGO information from the field shapes the understanding of the situation and the resulting policy decisions of the US government and the UN Security Council as an intergovernmental unit in cases of conflict-rated crises.

The question inevitably raises methodological difficulties, foremost of which is the problem of how to identify causation in policy formation. Political scientists do not agree on a single formula or set of factors that produces a nation's foreign policy. Undoubtedly such policies are forged from a complex mix of numerous sets of interests held by the individual policymakers and their constituencies. Depending on the unit of analysis—the state, the individual leader, interest group—one can find multiple explanations for why a policy decision was taken and which interests it serves. Authors Eugene Wittkopf and James McCormick have described US foreign policy in particular as a type of jigsaw puzzle, constructed from numerous, fragmented sources of authority.[1] In the broadest sense, not only do the US executive and legislative branches exert different influences, but certain periods have also seen heightened involvement of various government departments thought of as domestic (Agriculture, Justice) behaving as stakeholders in foreign policy. From these various layers of inputs it is difficult, to say the least, to determine the extent to which one group or individual steered the policy outcome.

Policy formation can be viewed though a number of different prisms; domestic pressures, organizational process, bureaucratic politics, and other models of decision making can all provide insight into why governments choose certain actions.[2] International relations theorists generally find it most useful to treat states as unitary, rational (interest-maximizing) actors for the purposes of studying their behavior in the international arena, taking for granted that foreign policy preferences are the result of compromise between the interests of policymakers, constituents, lobby groups, and so forth. Game theory and other formal modeling approaches to political science also begin with this assumption in modeling states' international behavior. These approaches view policymaking in a strategic framework, describing the elements of political decisions as follows:

1. A set of acts, A, one of which will be chosen as the decision.
2. A set of states of the world, S . . . The "world" defined to encompass all matters relevant to the problem beyond the control of the decider . . .
3. A set of consequences or outcomes, C, with one consequence for each pair of acts and states.
4. A preference ordering that's complete, transitive, and fixed.
5. Behavioral axiom: Actors choose the act that maximizes the possibility of achieving their most preferred outcome.[3]

In other words, before taking a policy decision, the actor weighs both the preferences for certain outcomes and the likelihood of those outcomes occurring given the actor's understanding of the "state of the world." From these elements one can calculate an expected utility function for the actor who is deciding on what course to take based on the probability of several possible alternative states. The Von-Neumann-Morgenstern utility function measures the appeal of actions to the decision maker against the probability of preferred outcomes expressed as follows:

$$EU(A) = \sum p(S)u[C(S,A)]$$

The decision maker will choose a course of action A such that EU(A) is maximized—that is, the action with the highest expected utility given the likelihood of consequences it could produce (The decider's order of preferences is considered fixed; however, the probability calculus is subjective—a judgment call by the decider on the likelihood of the true "S" based on his best available information. [4] Simplifying then, policy decisions (D) can be seen as deriving from the decision maker's outcome preferences (interests or I), conditioned by their understanding of a particular context (information or i): D=I(i).[5]

Much of international relations theory, it has been argued, fails to take into account the transformative effect of information on actors' interests—that is, "that the diffusion of new ideas and information can lead to new patterns of behavior and prove an important determinant of international policy coordination."[6] When viewed in the way presented above, information (and by extension the information provider) has an independent determining influence on policy decisions. When the information is drawn from multiple different sources, as is usually the case, the influence of each provider will be small. When the information sources are concentrated in a small number of providers, their influence, naturally, will be greater.

In the majority of the literature on the influence of NGOs and other nonstate actors on state policy, their impact has mostly been assumed to be on the interests side of the equation. That is to say, by lobbying or publicly appealing for a certain policy they add their voice to the other constituencies being weighed by the decision makers, attempting to affect their preference ordering—to persuade the decision makers that it is in their interest to decide on a certain course of action for reasons of humanitarian principles, or for fear of public shaming if they do not. In doing so, NGOs attempt to steer the policy compromise toward their goals, and in the process, as "constructivist" theory argues, can in fact create new norms and preferences.[7] As Richard Price wrote in his article about the successful NGO campaign for a treaty to ban landmines, such issue-based advocacy is a value-driven exercise that attempts in effect to "change what actors want."[8]

The above describes the traditional humanitarian advocacy that many NGOs engage in, the "speaking out," which is more strongly associated with members of the Dunantist tradition. Humanitarian NGOs in general, frustrated by the limited success in this area, have committed to strengthening their advocacy capacity and devoting more resources to campaigns and lobbying efforts, both individually and in joint efforts with other organizations. Though many in the NGO community believe strongly in the importance of the advocacy endeavor, and believe equally strongly in the potential of NGO advocacy for positive change, they can point to little direct evidence—in the humanitarian sphere at least—that these efforts have made an impact.[9] Few seem to have considered that NGOs may actually weigh in much more heavily on the information side of the equation, by influencing decision makers' perceptions and their understanding of a situation as policy is being formed.

National Interests and International Behavior: The Scope for Nonstate Influences

The question posed in this chapter also necessarily raises the staple debate in international relations theory: whether it makes sense to view nonstate actors as capable of exerting a significant modifying influence over state behavior in the global state system, or in any way mitigating what Kenneth Waltz referred to as "the enduring anarchic character of international politics."[10] The foundation of realist and neorealist theory rests on a rejection of this premise, and the state-centered paradigm continues to hold sway in mainstream international relations theory today.

However, an alternative hypothesis keeps presenting itself in one form or another. Beginning in the 1960s, the schools of functionalism and later institutionalism emerged to challenge the state-centered view. Emphasizing the postwar growth of transnational linkages, international organizations and movements, and other forms of international cooperation that seemed to defy realist interpretation, theorists such as Ernst Haas, David Mitrany, Robert Keohane, Joseph Nye, and John Ruggie argued that neorealist theory was insufficient to describe or explain the workings of the international system, and more attention needs be paid to the phenomena of international regimes, interdependence at multiple levels of government and civil society, the modifying effects of institutions, and changes in the functional capabilities of governments. In particular, most variations of this alternative conceptual framework highlighted the emerging roles of nonstate actors and how they function to influence, take up, or circumvent national actors in pursuit of independent agendas.

The late-twentieth-century phenomenon of globalization gave a new spin to the alternative hypothesis. Globalization's revolution in cross-border flows of people, capital, and information has revived theoretical interest in nonstate actors and their influence in international relations, with the focus shifting from multinational corporations, regimes, and intergovernmental institutions to what some observers have heralded as the birth of a "global civil society" of transnational interest groups proliferating in numbers and growing in power and leverage over policy setting in the international realm. These like-minded individuals and groups have organized across borders, forming advocacy networks to campaign for social change. Authors Margaret Keck and Kathryn Sikkink examined three such "transnational advocacy networks" of (nonhumanitarian) NGOs—in human rights, the environment, and violence against women— and found them to be influential on state behavior through raising issues, setting new norms, and promoting their implementation "by pressuring target actors to adopt new policies, and monitoring compliance with international standards."[11]

The global civil society school of thought centers on the notion that value-based coalitions can use advocacy tactics to create new constituencies and promote their interests. Many of the international advocacy campaigns that have received attention, such as the landmines ban and the movement to forgive developing country debt, were formed through linkages between NGOs and later themselves institutionalized as NGOs.[12]

The United States and "Global Civil Society" in the Post–Cold War Era

The decade following the demise of the Soviet Union and up until September 11, 2001, terrorist attacks seemed to hold greater possibilities than ever before for the influence of nonstate actors and nonstrategic agendas in the conduct of foreign policy. The deadlock of veto powers that had stymied the UN Security Council gave way to new activism, as powerful states came to define conflicts in the developing world not as stakes in the superpower rivalry, but rather as humanitarian emergencies—the product of failed states.

In the US government, writes James Lindsay, the former foreign policy consensus behind countering Soviet power dissolved, lessening for a time the dominance of the office of the president in foreign affairs, and opening the field to other influences and actors such as Congress and other executive departments. The author notes previous examples of waxing influence in foreign policy by other parts of government to past instances of "declining perception of external threat" such as in the 1970s after the US withdrawal from Vietnam and détente seemed to prove that communist revolutions in the developing countries did not directly threaten US security.[13]

Within the State Department, government officials attempted structural reform of the foreign affairs apparatus to better reflect the new realities of globalization. During his term as deputy secretary of state, Strobe Talbott oversaw what he called "a strategy of working 'multi-multilaterally'"[14] by forming new partnerships, coalitions, and operational linkages between State and "other American agencies, other countries, and numerous governmental and intergovernmental institutions." By way of example he notes, "In Bosnia, nine agencies and departments of the U.S. government are cooperating with more than a dozen other governments, seven international organizations, and 13 major NGOs—from the Red Cross to the International Crisis Group to the American Bar Association—to implement the Dayton Peace Accords."[15]

In his 1999 article entitled "Redefining the National Interest,"[16] Joseph Nye observed that after the Cold War's end removed the Soviet threat to US national survival, low-level, indirect threats to US interests, such as the conflicts in Bosnia, Kosovo, Rwanda, and Haiti, had "come to dominate today's foreign policy agenda." Nye maintained that a country's national interest is broader than its strategic (military or economic) interests. It also encompasses expression of public values, such as those set on human rights: "A democratic definition of the national interest does not accept the distinction between a morality-based and an interest-based foreign policy. Moral values are simply intangible interests." Other analysts writing during the period interpreted the "humanitarian intervention" phenomenon as signaling that in the post–Cold War era humanitarian values came to play a greater, and at times central, role in U.S. foreign policy,[17] or, alternatively, that the liberal democratic governments in the Security Council were able to push their humanitarian-centered agenda while the United States had relaxed its position. Still others maintained during this period there was simply no domestic agreement on what should constitute the US foreign agenda or the means to pursue it.[18]

If we are to draw one lesson from the post–Cold War humanitarian interventionism it may be that when foreign policy preferences are fuzzy, the door opens for new influences on policy, such as humanitarian advocacy. When preferences are clear and compelling, on the other hand, policies take on a more predetermined character. Since September 11, 2001, a new A-list threat to the survival of the United States has emerged, in the form of a global radical Islamist movement that uses terrorist tactics. While politicians may debate the appropriate strategy to take to counter this threat, the compelling interest to the United States is no longer in question. Suddenly the stakes appear much clearer than they did during the ten years of the post–Cold War era when it was adrift due to what Samuel Huntington referred to as the "loss of 'the other.'"[19] If "the other" has now reappeared in the form of al-Qaeda or similar transnational terrorist threat (a recent US government contingency planning report for terrorism used the ominous-sounding term "Universal Adversary"), the door for other influences and agendas could conceivably swing shut once again.

The Unique Potential for Influence of Humanitarian NGOs as a Community of Principled Experts

Where do humanitarian NGOs fit within the vast sea of nonstate, non-commercial actors known as "global civil society"? Like the human rights, women's rights, and other international movements the humanitarian NGOs are value-based and altruistic in their mission, but they differ from other philanthropic and advocacy organizations in important ways. The key difference lies in the humanitarian NGOs' "operationality." More than witnesses and advocates, these organizations maintain a field presence in crisis situations, employ nationals of the country in question (indeed at times serve as the largest local employers), negotiate with governmental and local authorities or rebel groups, and work in parallel with UN agencies, military forces, and various other actors. Increasingly in developing country crises the major international NGOs have emerged as key actors in their own right, complete with casualty rates often exceeding those of the international armed forces involved. Their operationality thus puts them in a different category than groups campaigning for policy change, or even than field human rights workers who play an important role in witnessing and documenting abuses. Governments and UN agencies rely upon NGOs to physically deliver the aid to affected populations, and in turn to communicate the conditions and needs of the populations back up to the policymakers.

As demonstrated in the previous chapters, a small group of the largest and oldest NGOs have built up solid track records, reputations of know-how, personal networks, and long-standing working relationships with the major donors. Donor and host governments, UN agencies, and other political actors to varying degrees have come to view these organizations as experts in their field rather than mere contracted service providers or charities. The professionalization and standardization movement of the 1990s has increased the general perception that in humanitarian response there is a right way to do things, and a cadre of people with the NGO community who possess the experience and training to do it.

In their book *Rules for the World*, Michael Barnett and Martha Finnemore argue that international organizations (IOs) such as the United Nations and the IMF have "social construction power," meaning the ability through their knowledge and authority "not only to regulate but also to constitute and construct the social world."[20] As such, they put forward, the IOs are essentially creating the reality, not just interpreting it. Humanitarian NGOs lack the regulatory authority, but as the cases in the following chapters show, by virtue of being the only international actors providing ground-level information in some crises, and by dint of their working relationship with the government donor agency, they too have the power to shape political actors' understanding of the world. Yet as the cases also show, this information is a crude instrument that is wielded clumsily, when it is consciously wielded at all.

Barnett and Finnemore also draw attention to moral and expert authority, which may be related to the spheres of advocacy and information, respectively. Some international groups have successfully combined both, such as Amnesty International or Human Rights Watch on international legal issues pertaining to human rights. The expert authority of the humanitarian NGOs, and the weight afforded to their information by policymakers, derives from their practical experience in humanitarian emergencies, and is one important route to more effective policy influence. Once again it is their functional, operational nature, their ability not only to prescribe solutions to problems but to effect them on the ground, that separates the humanitarian NGOs from the organizations studied by Barnett and Finnemore and Keck and Sikkink. For this reason it is useful to look back to earlier, functionalist schools of thought, and in particular the idea of the "epistemic community."

Peter M. Haas first drew attention to the power of "epistemic communities" in his article about how a community of international environmental experts influenced international coordination around pollution control in the Mediterranean.[21] An epistemic community, in his definition, consists of a "network of professionals with recognized expertise and competence in a particular domain and an authoritative claim to policy-relevant knowledge within that domain or issue area."[22] Their power vis-à-vis state actors comes from their possession of information on the given state of affairs and their expert opinion on the appropriate policy response. These individuals were legitimated by states as experts to prescribe policy solutions and thus affect the states' future behavior. NGOs through their practically based expertise have begun to take on an epistemic function vis-à-vis states, not only in practical matters of how to feed and shelter crisis victims, but also in interpretations of political events and their humanitarian consequences.

The previous chapter showed how long-standing differences among the humanitarian NGOs can manifest themselves in deep philosophical disagreements. Yet it also demonstrated that despite the internal diversity, despite the variety of missions, mandates, and priorities stemming from their separate traditions, this conglomeration is nevertheless unarguably a community. This fact is borne out in the field, where operational coordination happens perforce (sometimes smoothly, sometimes not) and at the global level through consortia groups, countless conferences and seminars, collaborative training programs, and joint advocacy. Moreover, this community, although associated with voluntarism, charity, and altruism, has significantly professionalized itself, especially over the past fifteen years, to an extent where it fits fairly closely Haas's description of an epistemic community. In his words, epistemic communities are groupings of professionals possessed of:

"(1) a shared set of normative and principled beliefs, which provide a value-based rationale for the social action of community members" . . .

Humanitarian NGOs share common norms of humanitarianism, embodied in the fundamental principles of the Red Cross movement: humanity, impartiality, neutrality. Although it is not uncommon in emergency cases for one principle to contradict another, and for NGOs from different traditions to favor different principles, it is nonetheless striking how universally the NGOs maintain these common norms.

"(2) shared causal beliefs, which are derived from their analysis of practices leading or contributing to a central set of problems in their domain" . . .

On causation the humanitarian NGOs generally find themselves in agreement about which policies or practices by political actors have caused suffering and death to civilian populations, whether conflict, corruption, participation in illicit economies, or international sanctions that place the greatest burden on civilian populations.

(3) shared notions of validity—that is, intersubjective, internally defined criteria for weighing and validating knowledge in the domain of their expertise" . . .

This is more and more the case in humanitarian assistance. As well as the standard-setting and best practices initiatives such as People in Aid and the Sphere Project, the community has created and widely shared evaluation and assessment models, formed applied-learning networks such as ALNAP, and established an increasing number of internationally accredited training certificates, diplomas, and master's degree programs in humanitarian assistance. And of course there is a large and growing body of practitioner-driven research and literature on all aspects of international humanitarian assistance.

"(4) a common policy enterprise—that is a set of common practices associated with a set of problems to which their professional competence is directed, presumably out of the conviction that human welfare will be enhanced as a consequence."[23]

This would be the area in which most humanitarian practitioners would agree their community has fallen short of the ideal epistemic community. Although now general agreement reigns on the technical matters of how best to provide aid, major sections of the community are frequently at odds about what policies they should advocate to political actors. Although NGOs have established consortia for the purpose of common advocacy, and frequently lobby in unison with joint statements, and so forth, the common policy prescriptions often provoke dissension in various corners of the community. This is where the Dunantist-Wilsonian split is sharpest, as witnessed in recent debates over the appropriate humanitarian response to political policies in Iraq and Afghanistan.

Although Haas's environmental scientists remain the archetype of the epistemic community, the theory holds that such community can be "individuals from any discipline or profession who have sufficiently strong claim to a body of knowledge that is valued by society." So, with their shared principles and causal beliefs, and with aspirations toward a common policy enterprise the core group of major humanitarian NGOs conform in large part to the epistemic community label.[24] Humanitarians not only have the expertise on humanitarian needs and the ways to meet them, but moreover have the unique advantage of being the primary source of information on ground conditions in the areas of concern.

Epistemic communities serve as one important source of information that serves policymakers' demands in order to make decisions that will advance their interests. They provide neither guesses nor straight empirical data, but rather knowledgeable interpretations of conditions and events. The more their expertise is solicited, the higher their profile as actors and the more influential their information. And unlike Haas's environmental scientists, who were limited to scientific analysis, the policymakers in the humanitarian context rely on NGOs not only to explain problems and prescribe solutions, but also to implement those prescriptions, and the actions of political policymakers have major implications on their own work as well as their physical safety.

"Epistemic communities" says Haas, "can help define the self interests of a state or factions within it. The process of elucidating the cause-and-effect relationships of problems can in fact lead to the redefinition of preconceived interests or to the identification of new interests."[25] This is where NGO advocacy sometimes runs afoul of their ultimate objectives. Though in many ways the two spheres of field-based information and policy advocacy are complementary, and the epistemic role can certainly add weight and legitimacy to NGO advocacy positions, certain types of oppositional advocacy can complicate and hinder the humanitarian agenda (no matter how principled and "correct" the message).

Influence or Instrument?

Before proceeding further, however, it is necessary to address the counterargument, which holds that any form of policy influence exercised by NGOs on states, either as epistemic communities or as advocacy movements, is so small as to be negligible, and perhaps no more than wishful thinking on the part of anti-realpolitikers. Some of those rebutting the global civil society concept contend that the NGOs and other globalized institutions represent no more than a creative new way for dominant states to extend their power across the international system. In this view globalization has brought about a redefinition of governance based on privatization, and the operational humanitarian NGOs in particular play a crucial instrumental role in this new form of governance. British scholar and humanitarian aid expert Mark Duffield has argued that, contrary to the notion that new nonstate actors have weakened the state with their growing influence and overlapping jurisdictions, the "metropolitan" state in fact uses these entities as tools to maintain its position and advance its interests in the peripheral states of the developing world, or in the case of failed or conflict ridden states, the far-flung "borderlands" of the international system. Duffield thus places international aid in a systemic, dependency theory–based framework with the aid providers as tools of the center to oppress the peripheral states.

> Indeed, if globalisation has any meaning in relation to the borderlands, it is the thickening of international aid networks as opposed to the augmentation of financial, production and technological networks within and between metropolitan regions (Castells 1996). Without the growing social and political role of

private and non-state actors—together with the new forms of public-private partnership and systems of public management originating in private calculation that they imply—the internationalisation of public policy could not have taken place. . . . Indeed, it is possible to argue that the networks of international aid are part of an emerging system of global governance. Since the aim of most of the strategic actors involved is to establish functioning market economies and plural polities in the borderlands (World Bank 1997), one could say that such complexes are the representatives of global liberal governance (Dillon and Reid 2000). . . . A radical reworking of international authority is taking place. . . .[26]

Duffield believes the dominant Western powers have effectively linked relief and development aid to security. Since the balance of power and arms superiority proved useless against guerilla warfare in the borderlands, metropolitan states needed to find new forms of control, aimed this time at the conduct of populations, hence aid.

Within this public-private framework, security is achieved by activities designed to reduce poverty, satisfy basic needs, strengthen economic sustainability, create representative civil institutions, protect the vulnerable, promote human rights, and so on. . . . In realising the borderlands as a potentially dangerous social body, metropolitan public-private networks bring together donor governments, UN agencies, NGOs, private companies, and so on.[27]

But because these problems seemed so distant and unthreatening to metropolitan populations, Duffield explains, they have been recast as rights issues. Similar views have been expressed by developing-world scholars and policymakers. Professor B. S. Chimni of Jawaharlal Nehru University told a conference of NGO representatives in Geneva that NGOs serve primarily, albeit unconsciously, to maintain the global status quo:

"Humanitarian NGOs are assigned by Northern states the role of ensuring globalization doesn't cause a crisis. . . . The structural role of NGOs is to legitimize a dominant world order that holds no promise for most people. The fact that they are so effective means that they can be used as instruments by Northern states."[28] Using the humanitarian NGOs, the dominant states are able to ameliorate the worst consequences of globalization, he explained, and later help "stitch together a post-conflict democracy."[29]

No one could dispute that powerful states use foreign aid to advance their interests, whether these lie in stabilizing chaotic states in the developing world or to create markets for their products. Yet Duffield's positing of dispersed and decentralized networks of control comprising NGOs and the various other mechanisms of international humanitarian systems embodying a power relationship between wealthy capitalist nations and poor ones has arguably stretched to the point of tautology the notions of power and control. To paraphrase, it is in the interest of powerful and wealthy nations that networks of public and private actors engage in assistance the way they do, and these networks do so because it is in the interest of the wealthy and powerful nations. The theory does not point to a specific process of control, or what he calls "governing at a distance." Surely it is in the interest of all parties that conflicts are managed, humanitarian needs met, and peace and stability fostered, most of all for those populations that Duffield concludes are the objects of control.

Global civil society theorists as well as practitioners within the NGO community have rebutted that the governing-at-a-distance view reflects naiveté about the influence of nonstate actors and the complex way that international policy is articulated. Paul O'Brien, former advocacy director of CARE Afghanistan, contends that "the frugality of Duffield's analysis sells the new humanitarianism short," by its failing to take into account the many levels at which NGOs, by adopting rights-based approaches to their work, are countering the politicization of aid by powerful and weak states and NSAs alike.[30] The question boils down to the independence of the NGO actors, the motives and agendas of those who make up their staff, and whether they serve as mere tools of liberal governance, or if they are able to inject their own agendas into the process and influence the outcome.

The view that NGOs are the unwitting tools of metropolitan governments' political and economic domination becomes particularly puzzling when contrasted with growing fears expressed from conservative groups in these states that NGOs are a growing danger to democratic governance, are exerting undue influence on governments' foreign interests (and business interests), and are potentially subverting the national agenda to their own liberal agendas. In a development noted in press reports that made furious rounds of emails among NGOs on both sides of the Atlantic, a new Web site, NGO Watch, was launched by the conservative think tanks American Enterprise Institute (AEI) and the Federalist Society for Law and Public Policy Studies. The Web site project, kicked off by a conference entitled "NGOs: The Growing Power of an Unelected Few," promotes the position that the largely left-wing NGO sector wields undue influence and constraining power over US foreign policy and corporate interests. From the Web site:

NGO officials and their activities are widely cited in the media and relied upon in congressional testimony; corporations regularly consult with NGOs prior to major investments. Many groups have strayed beyond their original mandates and have assumed quasi-governmental roles. Increasingly, non-governmental organizations are not just accredited observers at international organizations, they are full-fledged decision-makers.

The favored charge of conservatives behind NGO Watch and similar fora holds that NGOs lack accountability and that they claim to speak for people who had no part in electing them to their positions.[31] Similar rumblings in Australia came to a head when Prime Minister John Howard commissioned a conservative think tank, the Institute of Public Affairs, to investigate NGO influence on some government agencies. IPA's director Mike Nahan was quoted as explaining, "NGOs are becoming very influential today—they sit on various committees and are seen to influence governments and big business."[32]

US NGOs were particularly alarmed at these pronouncements, noting that a few dozen senior administration officials have come up through those two particular think tanks. USAID administrator Andrew Natsios seemed to be responding to the frustrations of government at the independence of NGOs when, in a speech to NGOs at a conference in May 2003, he reprimanded them for not clearly identifying their aid activities in Afghanistan as US government–funded.[33] He stressed that it was important in the fight against global terrorism to show that the US government, not CARE or Save the Children, was providing this aid. As he put it, "The work we do is now perceived to affect the national survival of the U.S."[34]

The tone of Natsios's statements seemed to indicate USAID is itself under siege, after a decade of cutbacks and mission closings, losing its independent agency status and being brought more directly under State Department authority, and given a subordinate role to the military in the reconstruction of Afghanistan and Iraq. It is therefore appealing to as much as remonstrating with its NGO partners to fall into line with its effort to show it can get results on the ground and remain relevant in the foreign policy dialogue.

If NGOs are the means of power extension by strong states, it seems they are unwieldy tools indeed. The most conservative observers clearly believe them to be a powerful independent force that threatens and subverts rather than advances state interests. Yet despite harsher rhetoric from the right wing and certain government officials, none of this has yet affected in any measurable way the numbers or types of partnerships the US government maintains with NGOs. Private independent organizations remain the primary implementers of US aid contributions[35] for the simple reason that they have been doing it for over fifty years, are already present in the region or countries of crisis, and have a proven track record of accomplishment and a reputation for competence and expertise in the field. They may exasperate US government officials, but, as one recently declared, "These organizations are our indispensable partners in post-conflict humanitarian assistance and reconstruction."[36]

The Important Role and Multiple Consumers of NGO Information

It is not merely the US government and other Western governments that rely so extensively on NGOs. The UN humanitarian agencies such as the World Food Programme, the High Commissioner for Refugees, and UNICEF lack the service delivery capacity and reach to implement most projects at the ground level in their large number of countries of operation. Therefore they too rely on an extensive network of local and international NGOs to implement their projects and subcontract government contributions. Apart from this "indispensable partnership" in implementation, NGOs also provide the crucial information and expert advice on which decisions are taken on how to proceed. As this chapter shows, their provision of field-level data—however little or soft they may be—frames the situation for political actors and provides the backdrop for their policy decisions. In addition, their reputation as authoritative sources to interpret this information and prescribe actions further guides the policy decision process. We will see how they perform this role not only for states, through donor agency and foreign service representatives restricted to capital, but also the UN agencies. The crucial point to be emphasized is that, in conflict or crisis situations in the developing world, most of the ground-level information on which policymakers proceed originates not from the local government, the press, the UN, or government intelligence or foreign service professionals, but from NGOs. As the chief information manager for the UN coordinating body in the southern Africa region explained, no government or intergovernmental body possesses the reach or the roots in local settings that NGOs do. "NGOs" he says, "are like ants in the ground,"[37] and therefore critical to provide the foundation for building the knowledge base for aid programming.

Types of NGO Information and Its Place in Post–Cold War Policymaking

Prior to September 11, 2001, there was a widespread, mistaken assumption of an omnipresent US intelligence-gathering capacity. This myth "derived from the expectation that U.S. interests must be matched by US capabilities . . . [and] . . . the intelligence community is loath to admit that it is not true."[38] Before al-Qaeda's stunning blow against the United States underscored the critical importance of fielding human operatives, the consensus in the intelligence community was that the days of large covert operations during the Cold War had given way to a greater reliance on technological methods of information gathering such as monitoring communications and aerial photography. The legions of CIA agents with Russian language and expertise (if there ever were legions) were not replaced by Arabic-speaking operatives who could infiltrate the diffuse networks composing the new threat. The defense community and the CIA played diminished roles in the post–Cold War era, and people with their ear to the ground in most of these places were NGOs. If information-gathering resources of the United States and other great powers had fallen short (and continues to fall short) in these areas, it can be assumed these services were even less capable and willing to gather information in areas such as West Africa or the Great Lakes, where no strategic threat is perceived.

Bruce D. Berkowitz has written that policymakers—the consumers of intelligence—tend to view intelligence as a policy support, the end goal being a successful policy, whereas intelligence services see their function as value-neutral and geared to providing predictive accuracy. Therefore, where strong policy preferences are extant, "The consumer helps set the agenda, from intelligence priorities, to collection, to format."[39] In such cases, the intelligence messages that don't support the policy agenda may be downplayed, doubted, or ignored, giving the intelligence producers strong incentive to provide something closer to that which the consumers are seeking to support their policies. It would seem Berkowitz's scenario was clearly and publicly played out in the recent debate over the role of intelligence in the lead-up to the US invasion of Iraq.

If we are to take the corollary of this argument, then where strong policy preferences do *not* color the message, the information, and hence the information producer, will have greater influence over the policy agenda. And unlike government intelligence entities, humanitarian NGOs hold no intrinsic interest in making their messages conform to the policy preferences of the consumer.

The embassies of the United States and other governments have strict security regulations to keep their personnel safe. Travel restrictions are routinely put in place to prevent personnel from venturing outside the capital city when conflict has erupted in the country. If the situation deteriorates further, government personnel might be restricted to embassy compounds. The humanitarian wing of government aid agencies has some more leeway, but very little. The UN agencies have a similarly constrained sphere of activity in situations considered a security risk, with all agencies and secretariat representatives operating under the same security parameters and phased evacuation procedures. Since the August 19, 2003, bombing in Baghdad, security concerns have come to drive every aspect of humanitarian planning and programming, according to OCHA officials. Of course NGOs also have security protocols, but being independent entities, they exhibit a wide variety of procedures and risk thresholds across organizations. In addition, many international NGOs leave local staff and local organizational partners in place and operating when they withdraw their international presence.

NGOs have three levels on which they can communicate to governments and intergovernmental organizations. The first is raw, factual information on the conditions and situation at hand. This can be classified into two main types:

> **Quantitative,** based on spot surveys or ongoing surveillance activities, such as mortality and morbidity rates, malnutrition rates and other socioeconomic data; refugee movements, estimates of population displacements, and other demographic data; needs assessments—for example, quantities of food, potable water, and nonfood relief items required for a given number of affected people.

> **Qualitative,** which can include anecdotal evidence of growing need or imminent crisis; eyewitness accounts of key events or victimization of civilians; and interpretations of political developments and their current and potential impact on humanitarian conditions.

A second level of communication between NGOs and political actors is through providing technical advice (expert opinion). In other words, transmitting information on a particular situation, forecasting humanitarian consequences outcomes, and prescribing possible solutions. In a sense, an NGO project proposal itself can be considered to be emblematic of this level of communication. Often it is in the form of telephone calls or face-to-face meetings with donors at headquarters, or in statements made at joint meetings of NGOs and donors.

The third level on which NGOs communicate to governments, discussed in greater detail in a later section, is through advocacy. Advocacy entails policy promotion and lobbying efforts to advance the organizations' overt arguments for a particular course of policy action. (Advocacy efforts can, of course, be strengthened by the former two levels of communication, as the field data, experience in the region, and technical know-how of the messenger lends credibility to the message.)

When discussing the information-provider role of NGOs, the term "NGO information" is used here to describe the first two levels of communication, raw information and expert advice, as distinct from political advocacy.

The next part of this chapter examines the mechanism for transmitting NGO information to political actors. In the field this occurs through communication from NGOs to their government donor representatives, either a field office or through the embassy, to the UN country team and chief coordinating representative. In the case of a military peacekeeping or "humanitarian intervention" presence, NGOs also play a direct informational role. At the global realm it is through NGO briefings and informal meetings with government representatives, and increasingly in humanitarian briefings to the Security Council.

Principal-Agent Dynamics in the Donor-Implementer Relationship

Perhaps unsurprisingly given that the humanitarian field has formed itself into a small, insular group of donors and agency grantees dependent on each other to administer a humanitarian response, the donor-implementer relationship can be a tense one. The tension is common to principal-agent relationships and stems often from the variable reliability of ground-level information and the interpretation of that information. A study on the practice of needs assessment conducted by ODI's Humanitarian Policy Group found that donors as a whole tend to view NGO assessments with skepticism, and for their part the NGOs doubt that objective needs will have much of an impact on the donors' interests and plans for the response.[40] However, the degree of cynicism expressed by the two sides while talking of generalities does not always reflect the reality of this mutually dependent working relationship.

Although donors may claim to take it with a grain of salt, the fact remains that NGO information is often the best or the only thing they have to go by. In such cases, the information coming from NGOs can't help but contribute to shaping the donor's response, whether it is providing a true picture of needs or self-serving snapshots. Moreover, a donor agency and an implementing organization can develop a relationship of trust that carries forward into future crisis situations. (Or as oftentimes is the case in the United States, the trust relationship forms between individual donor officers and individual NGO representatives.)

Even if government donor agencies possessed the staff resources to field multiple information officers in every area of humanitarian activity, which they assuredly do not, security restrictions would make their work impossible in many cases. Very often when an emergency begins to heat up, travel restrictions are placed on government personnel, who are often already isolated in the capital cities. As one example, on June 29, 2001, in Macedonia as UNHCR and NGOs were staffing up to meet the impending displacement/refugee emergency, the US embassy was calling for the departure of dependents and nonessential personnel. This situation results in the common occurrence of NGO or their local staff and counterparts being the only international presence on the ground in the cases of most extreme need.

The US Government and NGO Information

"NGOs are the eyes and ears on the ground where diplomats may not have access. NGOs are at the forefront of program development. The synergy between our work is crucial," said Undersecretary of State for Global Affairs Paula Dobriansky, speaking at InterAction's Annual Forum in June 2001.[41]

A GAO review of the USAID-NGO partnership found that USAID uses NGOs not only to program its relief resources, but to give them a picture of conditions and needs. USAID then determines priorities for US humanitarian action in the crisis in large part based on what NGOs already on the ground say is needed. In the wake of Hurricane Mitch, the GAO report concludes:

> [T]he USAID mission relied heavily on proposals it received from NGOs to establish a portfolio of assistance activities it could implement quickly; NGOs operating in Nicaragua were considered the most knowledgeable about the hurricane victims' needs, and USAID funded many of the proposals they submitted.[42]

The Office of U.S. Foreign Disaster Assistance (OFDA) serves as the primary programmer of rapid humanitarian assistance of the US foreign aid agency USAID. Together with the office of Food for Peace, OFDA is the main channel through which emergency supplemental funds allocated by Congress go to crises developing overseas. As the major "bilateral" wing of US foreign assistance, it programs over 70 percent of its money, mostly in grants, to NGOs. Of all the government donors,

OFDA may be the most hands-on or operational in the field. OFDA's Disaster Assessment and Response Teams (DARTs), initiated in the 1990s, are trained to assess emergency needs, gather information including performing statistical surveys and public health surveillance, set up logistical infrastructures, and determine material inputs required. Yet even with the expertise and on-the-ground capacity unprecedented by a donor agency, OFDA is admittedly highly dependent on NGOs for information. In its *Field Operations Guide for Disaster Assessment and Response* (known as the FOG) NGOs are listed alongside local governments and community groups as key informants[43] and throughout the FOG in all aspects of assessment and response. The NGOs are typically the first stop on a DART tour, and they tend to make the most of DART's introductions to the local community organizations, and even local authorities. NGO personnel also regularly participate in DART assessment missions, as prescribed in the FOG.

When OFDA establishes a field presence, the team will include an information officer who "collects, analyzes, documents, and distributes information on DART activities; prepares all situation reports and assists with the preparation of cables, briefing papers, the DART operational plan, maps, and final disaster report; tracks DART resources; and coordinates information gathering and reporting activities with UN/PVO/NGO/IOs, other donor countries, and the affected country."[44] Both the field officer and information officer are instructed in their checklist of "immediate actions to make contact with the "UN/PVO/NGO/IOs working in the country" (the acronym PVO meaning "Private Voluntary Organization," the USAID term for NGOs that are registered as implementing partners with USAID).

OFDA operational staff members say they receive the bulk of their information from NGOs and from UN offices (valued for their ability to condense large amounts of information) that also originated from NGO sources.[45] Like government representatives, UN staff members also face strict security limits on their movements in country when security conditions deteriorate, and typically do not have sufficient staff capacity to gather information on every area of interest. Information transmitted back to OFDA Washington from OFDA information officers in the field goes in the form of a "Disaster Cable,"[46] which goes simultaneously to OFDA headquarters in the Bureau as well as to the applicable State Department desk and the State Department's main humanitarian assistance bureau, the Bureau of Population, Refugees and Migration (PRM); to the US embassies in Brussels and Rome; and the US mission to the UN in New York.[47] In addition, the National Security Council is always copied on these cables. The disaster cables and subsequent "sitrep" cables go out under the ambassador's name and form the factual basis for subsequent government planning and policymaking around the crisis country. From the cables, OFDA headquarters personnel compose the official situation reports, which are publicly disseminated. When there is no DART or other OFDA field staff present, the information on potential or brewing humanitarian situations is gathered from the NGOs and IOs and cabled by US embassy staff and is transmitted back to Washington.

In countries where there is little or no access for US government staff, for instance prewar Iraq and Afghanistan, the NGO information becomes critically important. Between 40 and 50 percent of disasters in OFDA's portfolio at any given time have no OFDA field presence.[48] By 2004 in DR Congo OFDA had dispatched two program officers in the field for the express purpose of gathering and ground-truthing, where possible, the NGO information in order to report back on the humanitarian situation. These officers, like other OFDA field officers, are responsible for ensuring the information is as accurate as possible. So in addition to ground-truthing where they are able to get access, they also attempt to triangulate the information with other sources such as the existing USAID mission, if present, other donors, and the United Nations, all of which might have separate, if overlapping, sets of NGO informants. The veracity of reports in highly fluid and often dangerous situations can never be wholly assured, and in reporting the OFDA field information officers try to include any differences and discrepancies they come across. In the end they are going by what the NGO says, with as much confirmation or corroboration as possible under the circumstances.

Although in most cases the channel goes in the other direction, OFDA also occasionally receives information on country conditions from other parts of government, the military, and the CIA, particularly in places where the US military is engaged. This information, say OFDA staffers, does not preempt what it gathers from NGO sources, but is treated as simply another piece in the triangulation process.

Whether or not OFDA will establish a field presence depends upon the amount of money it is programming in the emergency. An allocation of $10 million has become the unofficial benchmark for fielding an OFDA office or officer. OFDA has significantly increased its field presence and in-house technical expertise over the past five years. The increasing technicalization, and the more common ground presence or operationality of OCHA, is testament not to declining dependence on NGOs, but rather the extent to which political actors have come to view humanitarian aid as a technical professional field. In OFDA's view, the NGOs' reputation for expertise and reliability varies from country to country and the staff of NGOs in the field. OFDA also points out that the NGOs perceive them as out of touch with countries where OFDA does not have any field presence.

OFDA staff members tend to agree that the biggest difference in the NGO community over the last ten years is in how the community sees itself and the professional training that they are engaged in, including many academic programs across the United States and Europe that now have humanitarian assistance as a specific field of study. Not only do the NGOs see and conduct themselves in a much more professional manner, but USAID has in fact put a lot of resources into building their capacity, so that the interaction between donors and implementers can be smoother and more trusting.

Although the post–Cold War "humanitarian intervention" may be a thing of the past, with humanitarian action now taking a minor role to security concerns, one holdover may be the seriousness with which the US government has come to hold the strategic importance of the public message of delivering aid. In a new ideological battle between the United States and radical Islamists, humanitarian aid is seen as central to the US hearts-and-minds campaign, and the issue flows straight to the top. As excerpted in *Bush at War*, Bob Woodward's account of the administration's activities in the months following September 11, 2001, the transcripts of National Security Council meetings during the military campaign in Afghanistan show several instances of humanitarian issues being raised with references made to NGOs as important players. A typical example comes from Colin Powell reporting on the humanitarian situation at the morning NSC meeting of October 11, 2001: "Remember that most of the food is distributed by NGOs. That's the distribution network. We need them to get coordinated and coordinated with CENTCOM."[49]

Another NSC meeting the following month provided a brief example of the principals at the highest levels of the US government turning to NGO information where the CIA had none to offer. "'What's the humanitarian situation?' Rice asked. 'We don't know,' Tenet answered. 'Relief organizations must know,' Powell interjected. 'We'll pulse and find out.'"[50] USAID administrator Andrew Natsios attended several of these meetings to report on how aid was getting through and where the main pockets of need were. Natsios came armed with maps and data provided by his staff at OFDA and elsewhere in USAID, which in turn was provided by NGOs on the ground.

Natsios, who previously ran the USAID's Bureau for Humanitarian Response during the administration of the first President Bush, has long observed in his own analyses the extensive NGO connections to US policymakers. In his 1997 book *U.S. Foreign Policy and the Four Horsemen of the Apocalypse* he observes:

> Increasingly, NGO executives have been called to testify before Congress on complex emergencies and give off-the-record briefings to the foreign policy staff of congressional committees. The same executives have been invited to meetings of the National Security Council, USAID, and the State Department to exchange field reports on what occurred in a given emergency, to offer advice on response tactics and strategy, to solicit NGO support for administration policies (or the absence of them), and to identify operational problems. The contacts are more intensive, more regular, and take place at a more senior level than any in the past.[51]

The Military and NGO Information

Over the past decade the US military has also increasingly come to rely on NGOs as a vital information resource. In 2005 a US military publication in its role in the tsunami response reaffirmed the importance of NGOs in constructing the forces' "situational awareness" on the ground,[52] acknowledging that they are able to offer concrete information based on their proximity to local actors and events, and expertise on topics that derives also from this proximity, and is enhanced by their "street cred." As a US army issues paper reviewing the response to the crisis in Haiti in the early 1990s noted:

> Haiti's humanitarian assistance community was well established and had great credibility with the people because of its proven effectiveness. The NGOs knew what logistics issues had to be addressed and proved to be a valuable source of information on main supply routes, facilities, and regional politics. The cooperation and support of these groups were essential. Their ability to influence the Haitian people and to continue their work—whether feeding, educating, building, or healing—was central to achieving the end state of the U.S. military mission: a safe and secure environment in Haiti.[53]

Similar sentiments were expressed in numerous US military papers, briefings, and conferences during the 1990s on the topic of military humanitarian intervention and the importance of coordinating with

NGOs. A Joint Chiefs publication in 1996 reported as follows:

> NGOs and PVOs are frequently on scene before US forces and are willing to operate in high-risk areas. . . . The connectivity between NGOs . . . and the Department of Defense is currently ad hoc, with no specific statutory linkage. But while their focus remains grassroots and their connections informal, NGOs and PVOs are major players at the interagency table. . . . The extensive involvement, local contacts, and experience gained in various nations make private organizations valuable sources of information about local and regional governments and civilian attitudes toward the operation. . . . To the extent feasible, joint planning should include all the participants from the outset.[54]

Beginning with Operation Provide Comfort, to aid the Kurds fleeing northern Iraq, the military and humanitarian actors have been thrown together in several complex emergencies. The Wilsonian NGO view of problems with the military traditionally was one of clashing organizational cultures—a management problem that could be mitigated through closer communication, joint training, guidelines, and so forth. During the 1990s the military, under the banner of Operations Other Than War (OOTW), sponsored many such exchanges and training sessions. In the pre–September 11, 2001, emergency cases where US security interests were not seen to be at stake, the civil-military dynamics of the NGO-military relationship were troubled but tolerable, at least as far as the US NGOs were concerned. This group on the whole was slow to pick up on the Dunantist view that cooperation with military actors posed a basic ethical problem that shook the foundations of humanitarian assistance in wartime.

In Afghanistan in late 2001 the US NGOs became far less sanguine. Not only was the US military engaged in what it saw to be a matter of critical national interest, but the crop of military leaders who had been so solicitous of NGOs during the operations of the 1990s had largely retired, and the new commanders were not coming from the same point of understanding that had been reached through years of exchanges. The military was hard-pressed to understand the NGO fear and anger when US forces (dressed as civilians in order to "blend in" with local populations) were dispatched to areas in Afghanistan to perform reconstruction and aid projects. Not only were these teams no better qualified for this task than most NGOs, they argued, but the locals would conflate the occupying force with the supposedly neutral humanitarian aid providers, making the NGOs targets for anticoalition elements.

Despite the friction in Afghanistan between coalition forces and NGOs, and the complaints even from Wilsonian NGOs that they were not being listened to by military commanders, the military still deemed NGOs an important source of information to be tapped. The military would send teams out to areas where there was no international aid presence and would undertake needs assessments, but in all other areas would use the NGO assessment and respect their ongoing activity—that is, the military would "not duplicate an area or an assessment that's already been done."[55]

The military also considers that NGOs need to say one thing publicly, but can be pragmatic about cooperating with the military behind the scenes, as observed by Brigadier General Jack Kern in remarks about Afghanistan:

> When we started this last year, we had NGOs with us in Tampa. We couldn't use the word coordinating or cooperating, so we talked about "parallel planning." We had NGOs and the UN down there that helped us. If it wasn't planned, at least we got a better view of what our partners, or at least compatriots, in all of this were. And we put people in Pakistan to talk to the NGO community there and to talk to the U.N. community there very early on in the game. . . . So there's a lot going on under the surface of the pond.[56]

HICs and Other New Loci of Information

As part of a broader effort to consolidate support services and coordinate policy and advocacy, the UN interagency community, working with NGOs, has established what are known as Humanitarian Information Centers (HICs) in crisis countries or regions. HICs are funded by the major humanitarian donors (principally OFDA, the US State Department, ECHO, and DFID), and were created in large part to meet donor demands for better coordination, harder data, and more consistent information from the community of field actors. In these centers, which exist in both physical and "virtual" space, the NGOs' and UN agencies' reports, surveys, and findings are consolidated and made available to the rest of the humanitarian community. They also serve to inform what each organization is doing or is capable of doing to assist in the coordination of aid activities. Some notable examples are the HIC in prewar Iraq, AIMS (Afghanistan Information Management Service), and SAHIMs, which was established in southern Africa in 2002 as part of the coordinated response to the twin problems of HIV and acute food shortages. Predecessors of the HICs include the Web-based IRIN and ReliefWeb, which cover broader swaths of emergencies and serve as sources of information to donors and policymakers. The consensus among policymakers and practitioners alike holds that these information services are generally only as good as the on-the-ground sources—that is, NGOs—are willing to participate in them and contribute postings. It is precisely the channel into NGO field information that makes the HIC valuable. As remarked at a USAID conference, "Unlike the news media, the HIC has better access to the NGO community, better data management, and the best field information to analyze."[57]

It is generally admitted that while the NGOs can provide the raw information, most have neither the time nor the in-house capacity to analyze or use it to best effect. In this regard, the HICs have not yet attained the added value desired. Though appreciated for their central clearinghouse role, in most areas they remain little more than a compilation of raw data and listings of "who's doing what where" rather than serving as real tools for analysis and planning. Some humanitarian practitioners in the field have complained that the glut of information centralized in the HIC mechanisms can actually hinder effective strategizing and policymaking; indeed "information overload represents a real constraint to informed judgment."[58]

Other humanitarian information systems, however, have performed much more poorly. In 2002, when it became clear that once again a serious famine was looming over six southern African nations, the major donors were gravely disappointed that regionally based information and early warning systems they had helped initiate and had been funding, such as the Famine Early Warning System (FEWS) and the Food and Agriculture Network of the Southern Africa Development Committee (SADC/FANR), had so clearly dropped the ball. So too, nearly, did the United Nations, as reviews of the UN interagency performance during that period show.[59] In fact it was an NGO, Save the Children UK, that first turned up troubling signs of impending famine through its nutritional surveys in Malawi, and raised the alarm to international agencies and donors. A similar scenario unfolded in Niger in 2005. This time MSF signaled the impending crisis and prodded a reluctant or preoccupied aid community to take notice. The resulting emergency interventions were hailed as successfully averting catastrophic famines, and only just. The experience has left donors, particularly the United States, disheartened and skeptical about further investments in regional information systems.

NGO Information in Agenda-Setting

Along with providing policymakers with the factual basis for their planning and decision making, NGOs contribute to the agenda-setting process through "media framing," advising their donors, and actively participating in joint planning. Each of these three mechanisms is discussed below.

Media Framing

NGO information containing their humanitarian perspective and priorities, as filtered through the media, can lead to the framing of an issue for a global audience.[60] Like government representatives, members of the international media reporting on a brewing or ongoing crisis in remote areas will frequently engage with NGOs, not only to provide them with the background to the events, but also to serve as hosts to journalists, providing them with accommodations, letting them ride along in project vehicles as they do their work, and introducing them to their local partners and people they deem of importance in the local goings-on. This relationship serves both the journalist who receives an orientation to the area, and the NGOs that receive visibility in the media, which can boost fund-raising efforts. It arguably can also result in the reporting of political events through the lens of humanitarian crisis.

Despite the much-ballyhooed "CNN effect," by some accounts the media is drawn in more by the Western humanitarian response than by the initial crisis itself. For instance, as Warren Strobel writes:

> While journalists undoubtedly were drawn to the drama of the famine in Somalia, they had a lot of help getting there. Much of this came from international relief agencies that depend on TV images to move governments to respond, and the public to open its wallets. . . . There were very few television reports on Somalia (15 on three networks to be exact) prior to Bush's August 1992 decision to begin an airlift. That decision resulted in a burst of reporting. The pattern was repeated later in the year when Bush ordered 25,000 U.S. troops to safeguard humanitarian aid.[61]

Humanitarian actors help influence the way crises are defined politically, and once a paradigm has been embraced by political actors and the media it is exceedingly difficult to substitute alternative explanations.[62] The use of key terms, implicit moral judgments, interpretations of causality, and—once the paradigm is accepted—the unwitting practice of "gatekeeping," that is, not reporting that which does not fit the paradigm, all contribute.

The actions of UNHCR and ICRC in the early months of the Bosnian war, according to some, amounted to an effort to "equalize" blame and causality in the war, which helped to frame the issue as an explosive ethnic conflict rather than a case of Serbian national aggression, which in turn limited options for response.[63] As is discussed at greater length in chapter 4, the deliberately neutral language they used in public statements, and the reports of Serbian atrocities that they delayed or withheld in the interest of "mission protection" (they did not want to be kicked out by the Serbs and lose access to victims) have been cited as contributing to media framing and the initial political and public understanding of the war. According to this argument, that early understanding consisted of a narrative wherein there were no good guys or bad guys, and hence no clear policy option beyond protecting humanitarian corridors and safe havens in Bosnia, "setting up its people for years of sustained conflict and low-level slaughter."[64]

Advising Donor Counterparts

Communications between NGOs and government representatives, either donor agency or foreign service personnel, ramp up sharply in the pre- and acute crisis period. For the US NGOs, the most likely to be operating with US government funds or anticipating them, this means at times maintaining daily direct (and/or through the NGO headquarters) telephone or email communication with both the representative US embassy and with State Department and USAID officials in Washington. During the beginnings of the 1998 Kosovo crisis, well before the refugees began flooding into neighboring Macedonia, the OFDA regional coordinator was in constant contact with a small group of NGOs in the field who were reporting on population movements and which villages were under attack. In such communications, occurring in real time and often emotionally charged, the necessity of response becomes implicit in the assessment of need. The recipient of the information then relays the perceived severity of the humanitarian situation, with its implied necessary response, to his or her superiors in the donor agency, who in turn relay it upward in the State Department or foreign ministry.

Joint Planning

NGO information provided to OFDA and other USAID entities makes its way up the policy ladder not only through the State Department, but also in direct line to the US military. OFDA's Military Liaison Unit has maintained formal planning and operational coordination with the US military since the crisis in Bosnia Herzegovina, and its representative sits in Central Command. William Garvelink, the head of the Bureau for Democracy, Conflict, and Humanitarian Assistance in USAID, described this relationship vis-à-vis Iraq in his congressional testimony:

> USAID has a Military Liaison Unit that stays in constant contact with U.S. Combatant Commanders around the world. Prior to the conflict in Iraq, the U.S. interagency community worked in an unprecedented fashion to create a plan addressing future Iraqi relief and rehabilitation needs. Staff from USAID; the Departments of State, Treasury, and Commerce; the National Security Council; the Joint Staff, Office of the Secretary of Defense; the U.S. Military's Central Command; and others collaborated in the Joint Interagency Planning Group to ensure that all organizations' activities would complement and support each other. . . .

And, as previously noted, Bob Woodward's account of the Afghanistan military campaign describes how US officials, including Defense Secretary Donald Rumsfeld, perceived the USAID and DoD joint planning as both important and quite successful.[65]

NGOs can use the firsthand information and advice to more directly influence the policy process when the government includes them in joint planning for missions, as began in the 1990s. During the Kosovo crisis, for example, Julia Taft, then head of the Bureau of Population, Refugees, and Migration, the main humanitarian wing of State, chaired regular interagency planning and coordination meetings that included NGOs at the table with State Department and military officials. During the action in Afghanistan the NGO consortium Center for Humanitarian Coordination obtained agreement with the military to place its representative within CENTCOM to represent NGOs and UN humanitarian agencies. During the coalition's activity, operations in this co-location allowed for dialogue on the issues that concerned NGOs, including the airdrops, location of mines and unexploded ordnance, and the use of military personnel in civilian clothing to deliver aid (which the military eventually conceded).

The Advocacy Challenge

When the communication between NGOs and political actors leaves the realm of reporting and advising on practical matters of humanitarian aid, and makes formal appeals for a policy change for the benefit of their beneficiaries, it becomes advocacy. NGOs' efforts in advocacy are directed at governments to effect policy change, and at publics to educate and build constituencies behind certain values and ideas. It can be conducted through a variety of means, including lobbying, public statements, publications, press articles and editorials, mobilization of demonstrations or petition campaigns; and in all manner of international fora, government offices, and corridors. Advocacy can take an oppositional tack—for example, public shaming through media statements, the mode often employed by Dunantist organizations—or a more collegial one adopted by Wilsonian NGOs, such signing on to joint letters,[66] briefing congressional staff, or giving formal testimony. Of course, even Dunantist organizations sometimes engage in more cooperative methods and vice versa. In the past several years, as advocacy issues have risen in importance to NGOs, they have added new internal structures and training activities for the purpose of crafting and disseminating clearer messages on key issues. CARE, for instance, went from zero staff devoted to policy and rights-based advocacy in headquarters in 1996 to a full-fledged department of more than ten people in headquarters and regional offices by 2002.[67] (CARE, along with Save the Children US and other NGOs, has maintained a Washington liaison office encompassing their Office of Public Policy and Government Relations for over twenty years, but this office serves to maintain contact with the donor and follow congressional activity on issues relating to foreign aid, i.e., more the traditional lobbying type of function.)

Public advocacy can be important, even central, to the identity and mandate of some humanitarian organizations, but historically can point to few successes. The numerous public statements released by Oxfam, for example, related to Western governments' handling of specific humanitarian crises have little concrete to show for them. During the Rwanda massacres, Oxfam publicly called for four things: UN troops, an immediate ceasefire, humanitarian access, and an end to the genocidal killings. In *A Bed for the Night* David Rieff points out that these demands in fact contradict each other.[68] In 2001, Oxfam similarly made public statements and issued press releases calling for a pause in the air strikes on Afghanistan in order to allow for humanitarian deliveries. Although Oxfam's appeals came to naught when the coalition refused to consider a bombing pause, the organization's annual report curiously credits their media announcement with resulting in "a much greater determination to get food into the country, resulting in a massive increase in food entering Afghanistan from the end of October."[69] More recently in Sudan, both Oxfam and Save the Children UK mounted a vigorous direct advocacy effort with the Sudanese government to promote the rights of victims and better humanitarian access in Darfur.

Fairly or not, some observers have argued that these organizations' advocacy focus in Khartoum came at the expense of their operational capacity on the ground in Darfur—to the end result that they assisted fewer people, and ultimately faced expulsion of their senior representatives by the government in November 2004.

Intracommunity divisions over operating principles and terms of engagement make it difficult for NGOs to effect policy persuasion even amongst themselves. When MSF France and later IRC decided to withdraw from the Goma camps after it became clear to them that their aid was being manipulated by *interahamwe* forces within the camps, they were the only NGOs to do so (and not even all national affiliates of MSF followed suit). And with scores of other agencies on hand to fill the vacuum, the act of withdrawal in itself made no appreciable difference in what was happening on the ground. Rieff, in his book, referred to it as a gesture "both principled and hollow."[70]

Thus, despite the Dunantists' traditional emphasis on advocacy, and the general community-wide trend toward increased advocacy efforts, this remains the area where many humanitarian NGOs express the most frustration, and the feeling that as a community they have fallen short. Authors Keck and Sikkink describe transnational advocacy groups as "networks of activists, distinguishable largely by the centrality of principled ideas or values in motivating their formation . . . [S]imultaneously principled and strategic actors, they 'frame' issues to make them comprehensible to target audiences. . . . They also promote norm implementation, by pressuring target actors to adopt new policies."[71]

Humanitarian NGOs likewise have a set of core humanitarian principles, at the top of which is to save lives and relieve suffering—what is known as the "humanitarian imperative." Yet the picture Keck and Sikkink paint of principled and strategic advocates skillfully setting and advancing agendas is far beyond what operational humanitarian NGOs could currently hope for. What differentiates the relief and development NGOs from transnational issue networks is the dual and de facto secondary role of advocacy and reporting to the operational function of providing practical assistance. While Keck and Sikkink's subjects comprised issue-centered advocacy networks first and foremost with advocacy as their sine qua non, the advocacy of operational humanitarian NGOs must compete with the daily work of humanitarian response. It also commonly raises dilemmas for the organizations about whether to speak out publicly against government abuses, which may put their program at risk of expulsion or their staff in physical danger.

The "framing" activity Keck and Sikkink describe also differs between transnational advocacy groups and humanitarian NGOs. The former's type of framing, as defined by Doug McAdam, consists of "conscious strategic efforts by groups of people to fashion shared understandings of the world. . . ."[72] Although many humanitarian NGOs may aspire to this goal, most humanitarian framing by the operational NGOs is neither strategic, nor in some cases entirely conscious. It occurs not around issues, but around specific events. As the cases in the following chapters show, NGO framing in crisis situations has been influential, but came about less by design than as a function of their functioning, so to speak. Their own operational lens and immediate programming needs provided the frame.

Domestic Constituencies

Another important component of advocacy work is public information/ education/awareness-raising campaigns to try to build domestic constituencies for the humanitarian agenda. Undertaking these campaigns has proved easier in Europe than in the United States. The major European NGOs, such as Oxfam and MSF, have achieved a level of respect and recognition among their respective publics quite beyond that of the US NGOs. Even such a venerable name as CARE, from which the iconic CARE package was introduced into common parlance, does not have the same cachet among the US public that MSF does in France or Oxfam in Britain. US NGOs in fact believe quite firmly that the public generally does not distinguish one aid organization from another, and therefore their fortunes, from a public giving standpoint, tend to rise and fall together. This belief is both explained and reinforced by the US NGOs who have pledged not to publicly critique one another.

At a meeting of NGO leaders in the wake of the September 11, 2001, attacks in New York and Washington, the organizations expressed the determination to stay true to their missions and to focus their advocacy efforts on urging the United States to not allow its geopolitical interests to determine aid flows. At the same time, some ventured to suggest that perhaps the attacks might be a turning point that would at last engage the inward-looking American public with international issues. Now, maybe, was the time to recast the advocacy message to the US public and introduce the new rights-based paradigm for development and relief. Nonetheless, the NGOs by their own admission remain flummoxed on how to impart such a complex message to the general public in a clear and compelling way. Program staffers at many NGOs tend to cede this responsibility to the public relations and fund-raising departments, all the while cringing at the self-congratulatory or exploitative tone of the materials that result.

It may be that US NGOs have decided that owing to the particular politics of the United States, attempting to galvanize public opinion around humanitarian and antipoverty concerns simply may not be the most effective route to effect policy change. A Brookings Institute study entitled *Misreading the Public* (by Steven Kuel and I. N. Destler, 1999) states:

> The American public does not give priority to international issues when it chooses public officials. The executive branch does not give priority to public opinion when it makes foreign policy. The legislative branch cares a great deal about public opinion, but not opinion on international matters, [knowing that] whatever the Members' position on foreign affairs, they are unlikely to be punished by voters for disagreeing or being disagreeable. . . . And individual policy practitioners, particularly in the executive branch, do not challenge the widely held belief in public neo-isolationism because they fear they will be labeled unrealistic or even naïve, and this will undercut their influence. . . .[73]

One Voice or Many?

The head of office for Oxfam International laments as the community's biggest failing "the poverty and paucity of efforts"[74] at joint advocacy by the NGOs and their UN agency counterparts vis-à-vis political actors, and many others agree. For instance, they decry the lack of focus by the broader NGO community on the small arms issue,[75] or on joint strategizing on how or whether to respond to needs in Iraq under the US occupation. As we saw in the previous chapter, the problem reaching consensus and advocating common positions stems largely from their different traditions, which dictate the NGOs' modern-day funding structure and approach toward governments. The rule-promoting Dunantists such as Oxfam and other British NGOs have taken great pains to bring the NGO community together around certain key points of consensus or common bottom line on operating principles. The more independently minded, rule-averse Dunantists, namely the French organizations such as MSF and ACF, are determined not to answer to anyone else in deciding the parameters and targets of their advocacy. The Wilsonian organizations are by nature and by necessity reluctant to come out too strongly against their major patrons, question the value of public shaming techniques, and have trouble understanding the divisions and depth of feelings about these issues of principles among their European counterparts.

Despite Oxfam and many others underscoring the importance of presenting a united front, joint advocacy has proved a troubled venture in the past, and has grown more so after September 11, 2001. Through their consortia such as ICVA, SCHR, and InterAction, many NGOs have been able to unify their advocacy efforts vis-à-vis governments and international organizations. Depending on its mission and proclivities, an NGO may choose the degree to which it wants to be part of a unified NGO voice. Often the varying levels of commitment and consensus among NGOs around an advocacy issue lead to dilution of the policy message to a generic, lowest-common-denominator product.

Other times this situation has led to serious rifts in the NGO community. MSF, for example, is strongly opposed to being associated with generic statements on poverty or the environment, say, and will only speak out on things that it deems to be within its expertise. Because it doesn't want anyone to speak for it, especially when it doesn't agree with what's being said, MSF first pulled out of InterAction's Disaster Response Committee in InterAction, and later removed itself from the entire consortium after the InterAction president sent a letter on behalf of NGOs calling for US military intervention in Liberia. MSF, which called for military intervention only once, in Rwanda, maintains that only in the case of genocide is an NGO justified in calling for military force.

Speaking only within one's ken is an essential element of what Hugo Slim has called "voice accountability," which requires both truth telling and authoritative knowledge on the part of the NGO. "This sort of 'voice accountability' had to respond to two areas of interrogation: the *veracity* of what they said and the *authority* with which they spoke. Although obviously linked, questions of veracity were essentially empirical (can you prove it?) while questions of authority were essentially political (from where do you derive your power to speak?)."[76] The concept of voice accountability fits within the epistemic model raised earlier. When NGOs are able to bring to bear in dialogue with political actors both veracity (owing to the NGOs' field-derived data and firsthand knowledge of the situation) and authority (owing to their expertise gained from experience) and when they are in consensus on a general position, they play a role similar to the epistemic community modeled by Haas and others. This, I argue, is happening in nascent form in the UN Security Council.

The Intersect: NGOs at the Security Council

A stronger link must evolve between the United Nations, the Security Council and organizations like Oxfam—who are on the ground, doing humanitarian work, who are touching those societies, looking into the eyes of the people in danger, learning who they are and what is going on and who the factions are and what relations people have with their leaders—much of which never gets to the table of the Security Council.

Ambassador Juan Somavía of Chile [77]

In early 1997 the UN Security Council for the first time met with humanitarian NGOs, who briefed them on complex emergencies in Africa.[78] That February meeting was the first of many in which NGOs were invited to give information and advice to the Council on issues of humanitarian concern, and a core group of NGOs had formed close bilateral relationships with Council members as well.

The Big Five NGO families all maintain liaison and policy offices at the United Nations. The UN-based representatives of CARE, MSF, Oxfam, World Vision, and Save the Children (a federation office, but spearheaded by Save UK) enjoy an informal and collegial relationship with each other that has facilitated a high level of strategic policy coordination in their dealings with UN bodies and member states. Their circle is sometimes joined by the human rights organizations Amnesty International and Human Rights Watch. The broader community at the UN, known as the NGO Working Group, consists of forty members and is chaired by the Global Policy Forum, a research NGO focused on Security Council reform. Through this body the NGOs have developed strong relationships with representatives from both permanent and rotating Council members. In 2004 the Irish ambassador made a special point of introducing all newly incoming Council members to the NGO group, saying they were a prime source of information.

Before 1997 there was very little contact between humanitarian NGOs and the Council, and in the past six years it has dramatically increased. According to James Paul, director of the Global Policy Forum, this development began with the drastic increase in the Security Council's workload during the crises of the 1990s. Freed from the fetters of Cold War veto-deadlock on the Permanent Five (P-5) council members, and driven by a general perception of developing-country crises as humanitarian emergencies, Council meetings increased from 55 to 171, consultations from 62 to 253, presidential statements from 8 to 88, and resolutions from 20 to

93.[79] The ten rotating members found it difficult to keep up with the dozens of active crisis spots now covered by the Council's agenda. Unable to gain firsthand, reliable information from their own national intelligence services, their embassies, or the media, these delegations felt the information gleaned from NGOs would assist them in policy formation and counterbalance what they perceived was the information advantage held by P-5 countries due to their superior intelligence technology, as well as assist in policy formulation. Moreover the new framework for thinking about these conflicts—as humanitarian emergencies, systematic human rights violations, and development failures—called for NGO expertise. Though not technically an NGO, ICRC had been granted UN observer status in 1991, which gave it some access to the Council, including meetings with Council presidents, and set a precedent for Council consultations with an operational humanitarian entity.

Under the "Arria Formula" (so named for Ambassador Diego Arria of Venezuela, who devised it in 1992 to allow Council members to hear from a Bosnian priest), any nonpresiding Council member can organize a meeting outside of Council chambers, off the record, and invite as many NGOs as they wish, and all fifteen Council members must attend. Arria meetings have afforded a major opportunity for policy impact to the NGOs, enabling them to reach all fifteen Council member states at once (though not always at the highest level of representation), and providing a unique glimpse into the workings of the Council.

Additionally, the NGO Working Group on the Security Council, organized by the Global Policy Forum in 1995, arranges ninety-minute meetings for the NGOs with each member state on a regular ongoing basis, one ambassador at a time. By NGO accounts this process works very well, allowing delegates the freedom to be more frank. Some have developed really strong relationships with NGOs, and the NGOs perceive a positive momentum and strong outcomes. "From just 15 meetings in 1997, Working Group activity had grown by 2002 to 40 meetings with ambassadors and 5 with UN Under-Secretary-Generals. In 2001–2002, Working Group members also met with foreign ministers of the UK and Ireland."[80]

The Arria briefings allow the NGOs not only to report on humanitarian developments but also to frame certain issues for Council action. Prior to Arria briefings, the NGOs' New York offices typically marshal the efforts of their field and headquarters staffs to compile the most current information and together prepare briefing documents in advance of the meetings. The NGO Working Group cites a few key examples of Security Council resolutions on issues of humanitarian concern that were adopted immediately following NGO Arria briefings on each topic:

- November 1998: Security Council Resolution 1209 on "Illicit Arms Flows in Africa"
- April 2000: Resolution 1296 on "Protection of Civilians in Armed Conflict"
- October 2000: Resolution 1325 on "Women and Peace and Security"

Other resolutions resulting from NGO persuasion included provisions on humanitarian and human rights issues. In a highly effective example of NGO reporting influencing global opinion and prompting action, the organization Global Witness was invited to brief the Security Council upon release of its 1998 report "A Rough Trade," which examined the illicit diamond trade in Angola, exposing how UNITA rebels were helping to finance their war efforts by selling to de Beers and other Western corporations. The report and subsequent briefing resulted in a tightening of the international sanctions regime in Angola to stem the trade of "blood diamonds."

Starting in 2000, the Security Council began to undertake its own field visits to get a firsthand look at crisis areas. In preparation for these missions the NGOs provided the delegations with the latest information and arranged for NGO visits in country to be included on the mission's itinerary.

To be effective interlocutors with the Security Council, NGO representatives need to be senior staffers who demonstrate diplomatic skills as well as consummate expertise in their field. According to James Paul, the current cadre of NGO representatives has established quite good relations with Council members at the highest levels, who take the representatives seriously and listen to them.

In general, the tone of the meetings between NGOs and Council members remains diplomatic, respectful, and decidedly nonconfrontational. Problems with tone, when they have cropped up, surprisingly tend not to be with the Dunantist NGOs, but rather with the Wilsonians. The US NGO representatives have been known not to censor their comments when addressing their fellow Americans in the US delegation, which has caused some friction with the "P-1" in the past. When an NGO representative in this context steps out of the collegial, consultative role into that of oppositional advocate, he or she runs the risk of alienating ambassadors who, of course, are meeting with the NGOs on a voluntary basis. Paul is adamant that successful interactions are not just a matter of giving information and technical advice, but to transmit the tacit message, in the gentlest of diplomatic ways, that "lurking behind those diplomatic faces is the threat of public campaign. You have to be a little insane."

It appears, however, that once that threat becomes overt, the small window of influence for NGOs can be lost. The influence of an epistemic community may function only within a relatively small space between neutral technocrats imparting information and strong spokespersons advocating a principled position. As a case in point, in 1997 Ambassador Juan Somavía of Chile, a former NGO leader and a strong proponent of Council consultations with NGOs, attempted to expand the Arria formula to include NGOs alongside Council members as non-Council delegates, as opposed to invited "expert witnesses." On February 12 the Council members met under this format with MSF, Oxfam, and CARE to discuss the crisis in the Great Lakes region of Africa. With the NGOs thus empowered to take on a more direct advocacy role, they were forceful in their policy critiques; the meeting was contentious, and ultimately a failure. "During the meeting and in a press conference afterwards, the organizations were highly critical of the Council's failure to take action and to find political solutions in the region, an outcome with which P-5 delegations were not pleased. The 'Somavía Formula' never got a second chance."[81]

It is important to note also that some NGO-proposed meetings on certain topics have been blocked by Council members. Kashmir and Sudan, for instance, were deemed too politically sensitive for Arria briefings.

This is not to say that, even playing the middle space to perfection, the NGOs will be successful in influencing the Council in every instance. On issues where P-5 members have strong national interests, such as the Middle East, Iraq, or Chechnya, NGOs are often unable even to broach discussion.

Conclusion: The Limits and Potential of NGO Information and Advocacy

The preceding discussion has indicated some of the strengths and weaknesses of NGO information and advocacy as separate spheres of activity. In sum, NGO public advocacy has suffered from a lack of consensus on its appropriate parameters and targets, causing divisions within the community particularly since September 11, 2001; a track record consisting of empty gestures and statements that have accomplished little or nothing in the way of policy change; and, partly as a result of the former two, a credibility deficit in the eyes of the political actors toward whom the advocacy efforts are directed. On the other hand, while this chapter argues that NGO information has unrecognized influence on policy through a variety of bilateral channels, the information gathering remains too uneven and insufficiently rigorous to adequately inform and guide policy and operations in many cases. The information coming from multiple points in the field is diffuse and fragmented, impossible to integrate into a strong, concerted strategy for policy influence.

This chapter has treated information and advocacy as distinct spheres of NGO activity because that is how the NGOs approach them in practice. Advocacy represents a more conscious attempt at impacting policy, and to the extent that it is backed up with firsthand information on ground conditions and hard data, it becomes more credible and persuasive. But more often it focuses on making public statements and calls for action to prod or shame governments into doing something, which have a poor track record in obtaining the desired results. This approach is favored by the Anglophone Dunantists such as Oxfam, owing to their organizational history and culture as a champion of humanitarian principles in opposition to government.

NGO field-based information and implementer-donor communications, on the other hand, filter up through government channels and shape agendas and policy at a number of levels, but often lack quality and rigor, are not conscious or coordinated, are not strategically delivered, and can result in policies wholly contrary to the NGO humanitarian agenda. A small example was seen in Afghanistan in 2001, when the one nutritional survey that was available from inside Afghanistan (by Save the Children US) showed pockets of need in certain areas. The United States, keen to include a humanitarian component to the military campaign against the Taliban and al-Qaeda in Afghanistan, used that information to plan air drops of humanitarian daily rations, a practice that NGOs are opposed to in virtually every situation on the grounds that it is an ineffective, overly costly, and potentially dangerous method of delivery. If that information had been more strategically applied and delivered, perhaps it would have produced a more favorable policy outcome.

The Francophone Dunantists have in just the past few years significantly widened the interorganizational rift by vehemently critiquing their counterparts' advocacy interventions that they deemed overstepped the line between humanitarian action and politics, and by withdrawing from consortia so as not to be associated with a "generic" advocacy message that they do not ascribe to or feel is outside their scope of expertise. While many of their fellow NGOs have cried hypocrisy (MSF began as an organization dedicated to speaking out against human rights abuses, and a review of their public statements since the late 1980s shows numerous examples of political analyses and statements outside its field experience[82]), the debate has nonetheless highlighted the widespread dissatisfaction with the way NGOs have pursued the humanitarian agenda vis-à-vis governments.

To the extent that these two spheres can merge, as the NGO UN liaison group has managed more or less successfully at the Security Council, an epistemic community function begins to emerge for the NGOs. The final chapter examines this potential in greater depth. The following three chapters tackle specific case studies to demonstrate the critical impact NGO information has made on state policies (specifically on the United States) in conflict-driven emergencies.

In the following three chapters, I attempt to show how field-based humanitarian organizations provided the bulk of the information on ground conditions in humanitarian emergencies, and the ways this information fed into US policy decisions at critical points.

The cases examine how humanitarian concerns regarding civilian populations came to be defined as "threats to global security," engendering a Chapter VII peace operations response from the international community and the engagement of US military in leading roles. These chapters postulate that NGO information coming from the field directly through donor channels, and supported indirectly through the media framing of the issue, set the tone of urgency and drove the policymaking process up to the decision point. Without the presence of the aid community on the ground, thwarted in their efforts to deliver aid and vividly attesting to the dire humanitarian conditions, the interventions would have been later in coming or absent altogether, and policy responses would have taken a different form.

Notes

1. Eugene R. Wittkopf and James M. McCormick, eds., *The Domestic Sources of American Foreign Policy: Insights and Evidence* (Lanham, MD: Rowman & Littlefield, 1999).

2. Graham Allison, *Essence of Decision: Explaining the Cuban Missile Crisis* (New York: Harper Collins, 1971).

3. James D. Morrow, *Game Theory for Political Scientists* (Princeton, NJ: Princeton University Press, 1994), 22.

4. Morrow, *Game Theory*, 23.

5. Restating the Von-Neumann-Morgenstern utility function: The A with the highest expected utility (EU(A)) = preferred action = decision (D) is the product of Sp(S) = sum of probabilities of all possible states = informed guess of what reality is = information (I) and C(S,A) = the preferred outcome = interests (i) or D=I(i).

6. From Peter M. Haas, "Introduction: Epistemic Communities and International Policy Coordination," *International Organization* 46, no. 1 (Winter 1992): 2.

7. See, for example, Michael Barnett and Martha Finnemore, *Rules for the World: International Organizations in Global Politics* (Ithaca, NY: Cornell University Press, 2004); Friedrich Kratochwil, "Constructing a New Orthodoxy? Wendt's 'Social Theory of International Politics' and the Constructivist Challenge," *Millennium: Journal of International Studies* 29, no. 1 (January 2000); John Gerard Ruggie, "What Makes the World Hang Together? Neo-Utilitarianism and the Social Constructivist Challenge," *International Organization* 52, no. 4 (Autumn 1998); and Alexander Wendt, "Constructing International Politics," in *Theories of War and Peace: An International Security Reader,* ed. Michael E. Brown, Owen R. Cote Jr., Sean M. Lynn-Jones, and Steven E. Miller (Cambridge, MA: MIT Press, 1988).

8. Richard Price, "Reversing the Gun Sights: Transnational Civil Society Targets Land Mines," *International Organization* 52 (Summer 1998), 615.

9. Informal survey of NGO representatives.

10. Kenneth Waltz, "Reductionist and Systemic Theories," in *Neorealism and Its Critics*, ed. Robert Keohane (New York: Columbia University Press, 1986).

11. Margaret E. Keck and Kathryn Sikkink, *Activists beyond Borders: Advocacy Networks in International Politics* (Ithaca, NY: Cornell University Press, 1998), 3.

12. Anthony Judge, "NGOs and Civil Society: Some Realities and Distortions. The Challenge of 'Necessary-to-Governance Organizations' (NGOs)," Union of International Associations (http://www.uia.org/), Adaptation of a paper presented to a Seminar on State and Society at the Russian Public Policy Center (Moscow, December 6–8, 1994) under the auspices of the Council of Europe.

13. James M. Lindsay, "End of an Era: Congress and Foreign Policy after the Cold War," in *The Domestic Sources of American Foreign Policy: Insights and Evidence*, ed. Eugene R. Wittkopf and James M. McCormick (Lanham, MD: Rowman & Littlefield, 1999), 178.

14. Strobe Talbott, "Globalization and Diplomacy: The View from Foggy Bottom," in *The Domestic Sources of American Foreign Policy: Insights and Evidence*, ed. Eugene R. Wittkopf and James M. McCormick (Lanham, MD: Rowman & Littlefield, 1999), 191.

15. Ibid.

16. Joseph Nye, "Redefining the National Interest," *Foreign Affairs* 78, No. 4 (July/August 1999): 22–35.

17. Thomas Weiss, "Principles, Politics, and Humanitarian Action," *Ethics and International Affairs* 13 (Winter 1999): 20.

18. Stewart Patrick, "Multilateralism and Its Discontents: The Causes and Consequences of U.S. Ambivalence," in *Multilateralism and US Foreign Policy: Ambivalent Engagement,* Stewart Patrick and Shepard Forman, ed. (Boulder, CO: Lynne Reinner, 2001), 26.

19. Samuel Huntington, "The Erosion of American National Interests," in *The Domestic Sources of American Foreign Policy: Insights and Evidence*, ed. Eugene R. Wittkopf and James M. McCormick (Lanham, MD: Rowman & Littlefield, 1999), 12.

20. Michael Barnett and Martha Finnemore, *Rules for the World: International Organizations in Global Politics* (Ithaca, NY: Cornell University Press, 2004), 7.

21. Peter M. Haas, "Do Regimes Matter? Epistemic Communities and Mediterranean Pollution Control," in *International Organization: A Reader*, ed. Friedrich Kratochwil and Edward Mansfield (New York: Harper Collins, 1994).

22. Haas, "Introduction," 3.

23. Ibid.

24. Epistemic communities may be cross-cutting within a field. In the same series of articles introduced by Peter Haas, Raymond Hopkins writes of an epistemic community existing in the issue area of food aid, comprising aid providers together with development and agricultural economists. Raymond F. Hopkins, "Reform in the International Food Aid Regime: The Role of Consensual Knowledge," *International Organization* 46, no. 1 (Winter 1992): 225–64.

25. Haas, "Introduction, 15".

26. Mark Duffield, "Governing the Borderlands: Decoding the Power of Aid," paper presented at seminar entitled "Politics and Humanitarian Aid: Debates, Dilemmas and Dissension," Commonwealth Institute, London (February 1, 2001).

27. Ibid.

28. Ruth Gidley, "NGO Motives on Refugees Challenged at ICVA Conference," *Alertnet*, February 21, 2003, www.globalpolicy.org/ngos/credib/2003/0221refugee.htm.

29. Ibid.

30. Paul O'Brien, "Serum or Snake Oil? Rights-Based Responses to Aid Politicization in Afghanistan" (unpublished article, 2004).

31. The "democratic deficit" has been an issue of concern in the NGO world for some time. In his book, *NGO Rights and Responsibilities: A New Deal for Global Governance* (London: Foreign Policy Centre, 2000), the Ford Foundation's Mike Edwards proposes a three-point "New Deal" between governments and civil society actors to address concerns of a lack of accountability of NGOs. First, he says, NGOs' right to a voice should be structured, building on strong local foundations and moving up from there to global campaigns. Edwards suggests a set of "compacts" between governments, businesses, and NGO networks that lay out the roles and responsibilities of each set of actors around particular issues and institutions.

32. Janaki Kremmer, "Australia Scrutinizes Influence of Nongovernmental Groups," *Christian Science Monitor*, September 5, 2003.

33. Andrew S. Natsios, "Remarks at the InterAction Forum, Closing Plenary Session," May 21, 2003, http://www.interaction.org/forum2003/panels.html.

34. Ibid.

35. In fact the government has taken pains to rebut accusations that the United States was shifting away from implementing partnerships with independent NGOs, preferring to contract out to more malleable for-profit contractors for more and more humanitarian assistance work. According to statistics disseminated by Natsios at a 2003 conference, NGOs still account for 60 percent of global procurements, as compared to 23 percent to the private sector, 12 percent to international organizations, and 5 percent to US agencies. The large amounts going in reconstruction contracts to corporations in Iraq and Afghanistan, he argued, are for large-scale, infrastructural projects not traditionally performed by NGOs (ibid.).

36. U.S. House of Representatives, Subcommittee on National Security, Emerging Threats, and International Relations, testimony of James Kunder, deputy assistant administrator for Asia and the Near East, *Humanitarian Assistance Following Military Operations: Overcoming Barriers, Part II*, July 18, 2003, http://www.usaid.gov/press/speeches/2003/ty030718.html.

37. Georges Tadonki, Programme Manager, Southern African Humanitarian Information Management System (SAHIMS), UN Office for the Coordination of Humanitarian Assistance, interview with author (April 2000).

38. Bruce D. Berkowitz, "Information Age Intelligence," in *The Domestic Sources of American Foreign Policy: Insights and Evidence*, ed. Eugene R. Wittkopf and James M. McCormick (Lanham, MD: Rowman & Littlefield, 1999), 259.

39. Ibid., 265.

40. James Darcy and Charles-Antoine Hoffman, "According to Need? Needs Assessment and Decision-Making in the Humanitarian Sector," Humanitarian Policy Group Report 15 (London: ODI, September 2003).

41. "New Global Affairs Undersecretary Wishes to Engage with NGOs," *Monday Developments* 19 (June 25, 2001), 5.

42. US House of Representatives, Subcommittee on National Security, Veterans Affairs, and International Relations, Committee on Government Reform, GAO Report to the Chairman, "USAID Relies Heavily on Nongovernmental Organizations, but Better Data Needed to Evaluate Approaches" (2002), 15.

43. USAID/OFDA, *Field Operations Guide*, version 3.0, II–9.

44. Ibid., IV-41.

45. OFDA operational staff, Washington, DC, interview with author, March 22, 2004.

46. "Cables are the official means of communication for the US foreign affairs agencies: USAID and State Department. . . . They are transmitted over secured lines even if the material contained in the cable is not classified." From OFDA online cable course, http://cable.devis.com/.

47. A cable training course OFDA provides to its staff instructs that "At a minimum, the reporting cable should be addressed as follows:

SECSTATE WASHDC
DCHA/OFDA (Regional Bureau)
AMEMBASSY BRUSSELS (INFO) (for USEC)
AMEMBASSY ROME (Rome pass FODAG)
USMISSION GENEVA (for USAID and RMA)
USMISSION USUN (New York)
AMEMBASSY (OFDA Regional Advisor for the region)"

From OFDA Cable Course, http://cable.devis.com/Tutorial/Field_Section/Drafting_Content/#2.

48. OFDA operational staff, interview with author.

49. Bob Woodward, *Bush at War* (New York: Simon & Schuster, 2002), 228.

50. Ibid., 307.

51. Andrew Natsios, *U.S. Foreign Policy and the Four Horsemen of the Apocalypse: Humanitarian Relief in Complex Emergencies* (Washington, DC: Center for Strategic and International Studies, 1997), 59.

52. Rear Admiral David J. Dorsett, "Tsunami: Information Sharing in the Wake of Destruction," *Joint Force Quarterly* 31 (Fourth Quarter 2005): 12–18.

53. Captain Nancy C. Henderson, "Civil Affairs and Logistics in Haiti," http://www.almc.army.mil/ALOG/issues/mayjun/ms922.htm.

54. US Joint Chiefs of Staff Joint Pub 3-08, *Interagency Coordination During Joint Operations* 1, no. 9 (October 1996), http://www.dtic.mil/doctrine/jel/new_pubs/jp3_08v1.pdf.

55. LTC Michael Stout, CHC Civil-Military Cooperation Conference, January 16, 2003 (hosted by United States Institute of Peace), 4.

56. Kern, CHC Civil-Military Cooperation Conference, January 16, 2003 (hosted by United States Institute of Peace), 17.

57. Joe Donahue, VVAF, "Humanitarian Action in an Increasingly Complex World," speaking at a panel on HICs, USAID Conference Proceedings, DCHA/OFDA 21st Biennial NGO Conference, Washington, DC, November 21–22, 2000, 42.

58. Darcy and Hoffman, "According to Need?" 53.

59. Bruce Jones and Abby Stoddard, "External Review of the Inter-Agency Standing Committee," "Annex 4: IASC Support for Southern Africa Crisis Response" (New York: UN Office for the Coordination of Humanitarian Affairs, December 2003).

60. Gregory Kent, "Humanitarian Agencies, Media, and the War against Bosnia: 'Neutrality' and Framing Moral Equalisation in a Genocidal War of Expansion," *Journal of Humanitarian Assistance* http://www.jha.ac/articles/a141.pdf (August 2003).

61. Warren P. Strobel, "The CNN Effect: Myth or Reality?" in *The Domestic Sources of American Foreign Policy: Insights and Evidence*, ed. Eugene R. Wittkopf and James M. McCormick (Lanham, MD: Rowman & Littlefield, 1999), 88–89.

62. Roger W. Cobb and David A. Rochefort, eds., *The Politics of Problem Definition: Shaping the Policy Agenda* (Lawrence: University Press of Kansas, 1994); Kent, *Journal of Humanitarian Assistance*, (August 2003).

63. Kent, *Journal of Humanitarian Assistance* (August 2003).

64. Ibid., 10.

65. Woodward, *Bush at War*, 175, 222.

66. One of many examples is the April 4, 2003, letter to President Bush signed by the heads of CARE, IRC, Mercy Corps, Save the Children US, and World Vision. The letter urges the president to allow

humanitarian distributions in Iraq to be implemented by State and USAID rather than the Pentagon, and for overall humanitarian responsibility to be given to the UN.

67. Karen Thomson, CARE, interview with author (January 2003).

68. David Rieff, *A Bed for the Night: Humanitarianism in Crisis* (New York: Simon & Schuster, 2002), 171.

69. Oxfam Annual Report 2001/2002.

70. Rieff, *Bed for the Night*, 187.

71. Keck and Sikkink, *Activists beyond Borders*, 1–3.

72. Doug McAdam, John D. McCarthy, and Mayer N. Zald, *Comparative Perspectives on Social Movements: Political Opportunities, Mobilizing Structures, and Cultural Framings* (New York: Cambridge University Press, 1966).

73. Quoted in speech by Ambassador William J. vanden Heuvel, "The United Nations and its Enemies," The Arthur Ross Lecture Series, Foreign Policy Association, October 30, 2003.

74. Nicola Reindorp, Oxfam International, interview with author (January 24, 2003).

75. *Talk Back*, the Newsletter of the International Council of Voluntary Agencies (ICVA) vol. 3, issue 3, 28 (June 28, 2001).

76. Hugo Slim, "By What Authority? The Legitimacy and Accountability of Non-governmental Organisations," lecture at the International Council on Human Rights Policy, International Meeting on Global Trends and Human Rights—Before and after September 11, Geneva, January 10–12, 2002.

77. Somavía, "Humanitarian Responsibilities," quoted in James Paul, "NGOs and the United Nations Security Council" (unpublished article, 2004), 9.

78. Larry Minear, *The Humanitarian Enterprise: Dilemmas and Discoveries* (Bloomfield, CT: Kumarian Press, 2002), 88.

79. Data from UN Secretariat; see Global Policy Forum, "Table on Meetings" and "Table on Resolutions," and James Paul, interview with author (January 15, 2004).

80. James Paul, "NGOs and the United Nations Security Council."

81. Ibid., 12.

82. MSF, "Case Studies: Médecins sans Frontières Speaks Out," ed. Laurence Binet (Brussels: MSF, September 2003).

CHAPTER THREE

SOMALIA

US-led coalition forces in Somalia left the "largest military footprint in Africa since World War II."[1] Somalia represents an unprecedented case of U.S. military intervention on purely humanitarian grounds, without attendant geo-strategic, political, or economic interests. It occurred at the height of the short-lived "New World Order," following the USSR's demise, and with the United States fresh from military victory in the Gulf and the subsequent Operation Provide Comfort, the highly praised military-humanitarian collaboration to deliver aid to Kurds trapped on the Turkish border.

President Bush's decision to send troops into Somalia in 1992 has received a fair bit of scholarly scrutiny, and gave birth to the notion of the CNN effect. This chapter argues that humanitarian NGOs, by virtue of their presence in country and the information they provided to the government, set the wheels in motion for a policy decision that was initially looked at very unfavorably in the administration.

Background: Famine as a Weapon of War and the International Humanitarian Response

Major fighting in Somalia began in November 1991, eleven months after the overthrow of President Siad Barre. In the resulting anarchy, armed rival factions, one supporting interim President Ali Mahdi Mohamed and the other behind General Mohamed Farah Aideed, initiated the violence in the capital of Mogadishu, which then spread throughout the countryside. Other armed elements began seizing control of different areas of the country and either aligned themselves with one of the two factions or

77

remained separate. Taking advantage of the disorder and the plentiful supply of arms, numerous groups of bandits joined the fray, and the country
descended into chaos. The disruption of civil war combined with a
drought led to a major famine throughout the country. Armed factions
took over food production and controlled distribution. Donated food
brought in by the international community was plundered from ports,
warehouses, and relief convoys. Stolen food became the chief political and
economic currency of Somalia. By late 1991–early 1992 approximately
three hundred thousand people had died, 1.5 million were in imminent
danger of starvation, 1 million refugees had fled the country, and 4.5 million—half the total population—were threatened by severe malnutrition
and related diseases.

There had been no official US government presence in Somalia for most
of that year, the embassy having evacuated its staff on January 6 in
response to the coup. Foreign service officers from the Somalia embassy
were relocated to Nairobi, with many assigned to other posts. Having
ceased to be a point of strategic interest for the United States, Somalia
merited no focus and little discussion in the State Department or in other
foreign policy circles.[2] In light of the chaotic and dangerous conditions on
the ground, the United Nations followed suit and evacuated all its personnel from Somalia some months later and withdrew its personnel from
Somalia, not to return in any major mission presence for over a year—a
point for which it would ultimately face harsh criticism.[3] However, the
ICRC and approximately ten international NGOs remained in country,
throughout the chaos and the fighting, as the sole international presence
in Somalia.

NGO Activity in Somalia, 1991–1992

Unlike the ICRC, which is mandated by the Geneva Conventions to provide a neutral source of aid to combatants and victims of conflict, NGOs
at this time were still fairly new to operating under conditions of active
combat. What they found in Somalia was a largely engineered famine,
with the incoming international aid resources being flagrantly hijacked by
rival warlords to exert control over populations and enrich their supporters. Small arms were plentiful in Somalia; to protect their personnel and
their aid convoys, NGOs began hiring armed guards known as "technicals"[4] (typically khat-chewing teenagers with machine guns) to ride along
on their vehicles. These arrangements existed on a thin line between security and extortion. Many NGOs dared not fire their guards, for well-
founded fears of violent reprisals. For those NGOs committed to stay
amidst a violent, fluid, and highly complex political crisis, the crux of the

problem, as they conceived it, was singular and clear: people were starving, and food aid was not being allowed to reach them. This was the substance and the message of the stream of information that they alone provided to the absent national and international political actors, beginning in the fall of 1991.

The UN Somalia Missions:
A Late, Weak, and Disorganized Presence

Throughout the entire first year of the crisis the presence of the United Nations in Somalia, even its humanitarian agencies, was "sporadic to non-existent."[5] When the United Nations returned to the country in 1992 they did so with a thin staff, and not without fostering some bitterness among the NGOs, who resented what they saw as the United Nations telling them how to do their jobs after having abandoned them and the Somali people.[6] Accustomed to working with and through local government bodies, the United Nations was struggling to reorient its work to a situation of total and enduring state collapse. The UN mission was further hampered by the early resignation of the SG's special envoy Ambassador Sahnoun in October 1992, after a public dispute with Secretary-General Boutros-Ghali, who had reprimanded Sahnoun for criticizing the United Nations' lackluster response to Somalia.

Not long after Sahnoun's resignation, the UN-appointed humanitarian coordinator, UNICEF's David Bassiouni, was forced to leave the country when General Aideed issued a death threat against him. (He continued in his role as HC, but from Nairobi.) The UN body charged with coordinating the humanitarian efforts of its various agencies—at that time known as the Department of Humanitarian Affairs (DHA)—was understaffed and widely perceived as dysfunctional by the NGOs in Somalia.[7] In the face of the United Nations' troubled operation, DHA chief Jan Eliasson chose to appoint not a UN staffer, but an NGO president (Phillip Johnston of CARE) as the head of the 100 Day Plan, and as such the effective humanitarian coordinator for Somalia. NGO workers were therefore not only the primary implementers of the international community's humanitarian response, but were also in charge of organizing it.

In April 1992 the UN Security Council approved a force of 550 to monitor the ceasefire in Mogadishu and protect humanitarian convoys delivering food.[8] The UN Operation in Somalia (UNOSOM) proved unable to fulfill its protection mandate when faced with violent opposition from Aideed's forces, who attacked the peacekeepers and humanitarian workers, and obstructed and looted aid deliveries intended for starving civilians.

The way UNOSOM was organized, with thirty-five hundred troops from four nations controlling their own zone and reporting to their own governments, it was unable to fulfill its mandate. According to Johnston, "the troops were totally out of proportion to their respective populations" and the level of security risk.[9] They were very slow to deploy in any event. By November 1992 only the five-hundred-man Pakistani contingent was in place. Although tasked with protecting the humanitarian relief supply effort, it could not be simultaneously at the airport and the harbor.

An Unprecedented Intervention

By August 1992 Somalia had become a topic of intense discussion in the US White House and on Capitol Hill. Though the Pentagon and others were still reluctant to consider military action to send troops into a country with no clear strategic or economic significance, the government did initiate a massive airlift of donated food on August 28. The decision to undertake the airlift was recounted by officials as an effort to do something in response to the humanitarian crisis, without engaging US armed forces.

Between August and November, however, something happened to change the minds of the president, senior administration officials, and military leaders to deploy ground troops. At a National Security Council Deputies Committee meeting on November 21, 1992, Admiral David Jeremiah of the Joint Chiefs of Staff made the surprising announcement that, "If you think US forces are needed, we can do the job," and days later the president decided to send over twenty-five thousand US troops to Somalia. Jon Western and others have questioned the motivations and analyzed the dynamics behind the decision that seemed such a stunning departure from typical US foreign policy: "For more than a year, the Bush administration, and General Powell and the Joint Chiefs of Staff in particular, had steadfastly opposed calls for U.S. humanitarian military interventions in Somalia, Liberia, Bosnia, and elsewhere. None of these conflicts was relevant to U.S. vital interests. They were simply humanitarian tragedies."

So why was the decision taken? How did a "simple humanitarian tragedy" become a call for military action? A number of theories have been offered, including the CNN effect; the relative "doability" of the mission as opposed to Bosnia, where the United States was also under pressure to act at this time; the prevailing of a "liberal humanitarianist" strain within the government; a lame duck president's concerns for his legacy; even the recent death of Bush's mother and the sentiments of the Christmas season. In fact, the decision-making process had begun far prior to the arrival of television cameras, when the only information coming from

Somalia was from humanitarian workers on the ground. In fact it was NGO information—the only source of factual information coming out of the country during the year between the fall of Siad Barre and the launch of Operation Restore Hope—that highlighted the need. NGOs framed the issue not just around the humanitarian suffering but around the relief workers and operations themselves—at risk, obstructed by warlords, and in need of a military security umbrella. The humanitarian-centered information played a direct role in the unprecedented Security Council decision, which held that blocking of relief aid constituted an international security risk warranting a Chapter VII intervention.

CNN Effect?

Somalia remains to many the archetypal example of how media coverage can sway government policy. Many analysts have attributed President Bush's decision to send in the troops to Somalia as a direct result of the CNN effect—both his own viewing of the images and the pressure from Congress and the public that had viewed them. Two typical such observations:

> The United States, which had lost interest in Somalia after the end of the Cold War, took a negative attitude on the issue at first. It was the power of mass communication that changed such U.S. policy.[10]

> We went into Somalia because of horrible television images; we will leave Somalia because of horrible television images.[11]

The legend of the CNN effect persists, despite the fact that authors such as Warren Strobel and several others have persuasively debunked it vis-à-vis Somalia and other cases.[12] In his data on televised news broadcasts on Somalia in the months running up to and during the August airlift and the deployment of troops in December, Strobel illustrates how media coverage actually spiked immediately *after* these policy decisions were taken. The famine received significant coverage by the news media only after the August 12 decision to airlift food. This dipped again in September and October, rising again in November and surging in December immediately after Operation Restore Hope was announced at the end of November.[13]

Government officials referred often to the pictures when making statements about Somalia (as in, no one could be unmoved by these images), but is this what actually moved them to a policy decision, or were they using them to support policies already in place? Research suggests the latter. Lawrence Eagleburger, acting secretary of state at the time, recounts that the press coverage was a necessary but not decisive factor in the US decision to send troops, noting that the policy wheels were in motion in the government already, and that CNN and other media began to take interest when they saw the government beginning to take action. Eagleburger's fellow participants at a Brookings Institution conference on the CNN influence made similar statements. "[Before the media focused attention on Somalia] one series of American relief aircraft along with a small contingent of U.S. service personnel were involved in the Somalia operations. Then the news media, including CNN, started to pay attention to that."[14] Several of them noted in particular the efforts of USAID's Andrew Natsios[15] to draw attention to the crisis during the summer of 1992, postulating that it was the lower levels of government using the media to bolster their preferred policy outcomes. "We see that 'the CNN effect' isn't the idea of the media leading in the dance, but rather you have a circumstance of whether some government officials are using the news media to move their agenda items further up the pay scale, to get it to the Secretary's desk."[16]

Natsios himself has argued strongly that media coverage is "tangential or irrelevant" to the US government's decision to provide a humanitarian or military response, though it may influence levels of funding from Congress to maintain the response. Often the response is well under way before the media arrives (as in the southern Africa drought of 1992), following the information making its way through field-based reporting to the embassy to Washington.[17] He observes that coverage generally becomes "more intense and influential" the longer a disaster continues.[18] Natsios insists that USAID, particularly the Office of Foreign Disaster Assistance (OFDA), is able and willing to launch a humanitarian response—without direction or prompting from White House, Congress, or State—from the earliest signs of crisis, which in complex emergencies tend to come not from the media or the affected government, but from NGOs. "Even if bureaucracies do not provide early warning and there is no free press, international NGOs frequently provide U.S. embassies, AID missions, and the media with information on what is happening in the field."[19] Prior to the heavy media coverage, and in advance of the American public's raised awareness of the Somalia situation, the US Congress had also became engaged, with fact-finding missions and resolutions calling for actions passed in the months leading up to the August 1992 airlift, dubbed Operation Provide Relief. According to State Department official and retired army officer Jeff James, who was in the NSC at the time, "In my opinion, the national media followed the action in Congress, and there was plenty of it concerning Somalia."[20]

Other analyses show clear evidence of the US government and military, after the decision was made, using the media to their advantage. Many cite the moment US Marines landed on the beach with a swarm of television crews lighting and filming their nighttime operation. Said members of the Brookings panel, "Somalia was an example of careful planning for involvement of the media. . . . The American forces brought the correspondents along. . . ."[21]

Like the government and the United Nations, CNN and other media outlets did not have a presence on the ground during most of the Somalia emergency:

> CNN has a very specific role but it also has a very small market share. It's extremely powerful but it doesn't address the audience at large. The audience at large in the country still gets the bulk of their international information from the big—declining but still big—television network news. They have decided for purely commercial reasons that having bureaus in Africa with constant staffs, with constant reporting, is not economically feasible.[22]

NGOs have varying relationships with and approaches to the press. MSF and MDM founder Bernard Kouchner, famously posing with a bag of rice on the shores of Mogadishu, believed strongly that the press can be used to prod governments into action.[23] Other Dunantist organizations like Oxfam use press releases and media inputs to shame and pressure governments. Generally speaking, the US organizations aim their media efforts more at the public for fund-raising purposes, raising awareness among domestic audiences with the goal of getting private individuals to open their hearts and wallets to the victims. They are less confrontational with governments, but also hope that the public sympathetic reaction will have a secondary effect of prodding government action. In Somalia there were numerous examples, some of which are described below, of NGOs hosting the media representatives in country ("at one point in August, MSF France had 17 journalists staying at their compound"[24]), assisting in their access to the story, and often becoming the story themselves.

The press may have followed the government's actions, but there is no doubt that the pictures made an impact and may have contributed to the momentum. A closer look at what started the policy ball rolling in the first place shows the process is far more complicated and began half a year before the major coverage.

Do Something: A "Liberal Humanitarianist" Coup?

The "do something syndrome," as observed by Donald M. Snow,[25] is a supposition that governments are compelled to take action in the face of humanitarian suffering as a result of media-led public pressure. If one dispenses with the CNN effect as a significant driver of policy in this case, popular alternative explanations center around the US government's leeriness of the prospect of a difficult Bosnian operation, combined with the apparent relative ease of a Somalia mission, and the rise of a liberal internationalist bent among some in government who sought to use American might, now unfettered by the strategic constraints of the Cold War, for altruistic ends.

In the words of Lawrence Eagleburger, recalling the decision ten years later:

> Here was the Somali case where there was clearly a humanitarian need but there was also a way for the administration to make its point on that subject and at the same time, to be blunt with you, take some of the pressure off not doing anything in Bosnia or what part of Yugoslavia it was at the time we were supposed to be doing something about. . . . I went to the president, and to my great surprise nobody, including the chairman of the Joint Chiefs, nobody raised any objection. On the understanding, and on this Bush was very clear, on the understanding that we went in, fed, and got out. . . . Then Bush sent me up to talk to Boutros Boutros-Ghali to try to get things organized, but I've got to say from the beginning in President Bush's mind and clearly in mine, it was feed and get out.[26]

Although television images just as compelling were coming from Bosnians at the same time, the decision was made to go into Somalia, recalls Eagleburger, because it was easier done.

In a *Foreign Policy* article published in 1999, Jon Western argues that the Somalia mission was in fact far from doable, as DoD and State had been insisting all along, and that in fact the Somalia mission violated the "Powell Doctrine" of overwhelming force and a clear exit plan.[27] Yet Western's analysis seems a conclusion drawn more in hindsight than a stark contradiction perceived at the time. There is every reason to believe the president and his senior advisors considered the mission to be doable, particularly in comparison with Bosnia, and were ultimately reassured of this belief by the military. In fact, by fall 1992 CENTCOM had already considered the eventuality, and despite the relatively short notice of the Somalia mission, felt well prepared with its "on the shelf" plan (published in January 1992 and tested in command post exercise in May) for responding to disaster in central Africa.[28]

Western's article postulates a competition in US foreign policy circles within and outside of government, in which the "selective engagers" in the administration and the military ultimately lost to the "liberal humanitarianists" who populated the NGO community and much of the succeeding administration. The debate was over competing frames, with the selective engagers viewing the conflict as a quagmire of ancient, tribal hatreds, and the liberal humanitarianists posing the alternative view of ruthless political leaders manipulating the conflict, aid, and innocent populations to their power advantage. With the tide turning toward the liberal humanitarianist tendency, the lame-duck administration made the calculation that of Somalia and Bosnia, Somalia was easier. As both crises continued, notes Western, "Liberal humanists started to gain the information advantage."

Western's article discusses the liberal humanitarianists the way the "neocons" in the Bush administration are described today—as an organized group adhering to a set of political tenets and pushing a far-reaching policy agenda. It seems more likely that those in government who were calling to send US troops to Somalia were simply individuals who had become convinced, based on the information coming from the field, that here was a humanitarian emergency that required a military response in order to keep the aid flowing. Western states correctly that those in power inclined to want to respond to a humanitarian crisis (i.e., of a liberal, internationalist bent) were a receptive audience to the information that was coming from the field. The process was not so much one group gaining the "information advantage" to use as ammunition for their cause, but rather one of awareness raising, agenda setting, and momentum building driven by the NGOs in the field, carried forward by their donor agency counterparts. Therefore, though this account does not share Western's image of competing foreign policy schools engaged in an articulated debate over whether Somalia's emergency had bottom-up or top-down causes, it does take his premise that field-level information was crucial to turning the decision. The mechanism was more diffuse, however, than the high-level advocacy campaign Western describes. It derived first and to a greater degree from the field-Washington connection between NGOs and their donors than from lobbying at the most senior levels of government. The ultimate consensus on the mission's "doability" came from the facts provided by the humanitarian NGOs, which made it clear what needed to be done.

A piece by Andrew Natsios refuting the CNN effect notes, "If a systematic analysis of State Department cable traffic preceding complex human-

itarian emergencies were done, this analysis undoubtedly would be confirmed."[29] In the course of my research I have attempted to undertake
such an analysis, which shows not only that policy wheels were in motion
before media became engaged, but also that the NGOs were feeding the
information in the cables that OFDA then took forward to push policy. A
look back to see what was happening on the ground a year before can
shed light on what led up to Operation Restore Hope, and why humanitarian aims were so central to the mission.

The NGO Effect: NGO Information from Somalia, 1991–1992

The NGOs that remained in Somalia after the evacuation of foreign government representatives and the United Nations, and much of the aid
community, were relatively few in number. The first USAID/OFDA situation report on the Somalia crisis, beginning July 17, 1991, lists ACCORD,
CARE, German Emergency Doctors, MSF, SOS, Save the Children UK,
and World Concern—together with the ICRC—as the only aid agencies
present and operational on the ground in Somalia.[30] Other organizations
and donors were providing material support through these implementers,
but foreign governmental and intergovernmental presence did not reap-
pear until after Operation Restore Hope. During the peak points of the
crisis the NGOs on the ground consistently numbered under a dozen. For
two years leading up to that mission, the operational NGOs provided the
main channel for US government (and the international community's)
relief assistance into and information out of the country.

The mass closings of USAID country offices during the 1990s
increased the agency's reliance on NGO reporting in general,[31] a
dependency only partly mitigated by beginning the fielding of OFDA
DARTs (Disaster Assessment and Response Teams), including information officers to do "ground truthing." As noted in the previous chapter,
even when OFDA maintains a direct field presence in the form of
DARTs, information must still be gleaned from the more numerous,
experienced, and well-connected NGO field staff across the crisis region.
Moreover, in emergency conditions OFDA is constrained to a similar
degree as the rest of the US foreign service, and typically cannot get to
the field in the height of the crisis, but must take the reports from NGOs
who have access. Likewise in Somalia (which, for US foreign assistance
purposes, had been officially declared a disaster back in March 1991),
for the two years prior to Operation Restore Hope, USAID and OFDA
were operating from Nairobi along with US diplomatic personnel.
According to interviews and documents, the only US government repre-

sentative during most of that period who entered Somalia for sporadic and short-term visits (one to two days at a time) was OFDA's coordinator for the Somalia emergency, Jan Westcott.[32] Westcott was one of a very small number of US officials ever on the ground in Somalia after the US government staff evacuated, and was waiting on the beach in Mogadishu when the US forces landed. Her position before the evacuation was as coordinator for an umbrella grant to international and Somali NGOs. When the crisis broke and the US mission was evacuated, she was the sole US official who remained in Nairobi to assist with the emergency response, and was placed in charge of providing regular status reports on the emergency to OFDA/Washington. In both these functions she continued to work primarily with and through the NGOs who remained operational in Somalia.

The information pipeline to Washington was therefore quite narrow— essentially a handful of NGOs reporting to Westcott, who relayed the information in embassy cables from Nairobi. Westcott's cables, which formed the basis of the Somalia Situation Reports, and her interactions with members of Congress and the press played an important role in setting the scene and shaping the agenda for US policymakers.[33]

Wagging the Dog: The OFDA-NGO Partnership in Agenda Setting and the Key Role of Field Reporting

USAID's Office of US Foreign Disaster Assistance (OFDA) had used its institutional discretion to begin programming relief aid to Somalia in 1991, and in January 1992, well prior to the military-supported airlift and discussions of Somalia in the NSC, OFDA's efforts, along with the Office of Food for Peace (FFP), already were part of a "large-scale U.S. government response"[34] in terms of humanitarian relief. OFDA can, and typically will, act on its cable traffic and field assessments to launch an aid response in advance of and independent of the State Department and the White House. This was possible in Somalia because a small group of NGOs, through which OFDA could channel relief assistance, had restarted operations quickly after the crisis onset, while the UN agencies and diplomatic community remained outside. ICRC and MSF, the more emergency-oriented organizations, returned to Somalia shortly after the initial phase of the crisis and helped to define the new crisis-oriented operational approach.[35] CARE and World Concern had long-standing development operations in Somalia, as well as ties to the local community and a sense of responsibility to their Somali employees, and so were committed to return and maintain their presence throughout the crisis.

In Westcott's personal account of the initial crisis period in Somalia, she writes that most of her time was taken up with "following security incidents involving NGOs,"[36] trying to run their aid programs while Somalia descended into an anarchy of looting and violence. In January 1991 in Nairobi, Westcott, the last remaining member of the former US mission in Somalia, sat down with representatives of four NGOs (CARE, Africare, World Concern, and AMREF) to discuss the way forward in aiding Somalia. The group formed a coordinating body for Emergency Relief Assistance to Post Civil War Somalia, later known as the Inter-NGO Coordinating Committee for Somalia (INCS), which met weekly and provided an early focal point for NGO, UN, and donor coordination. It also served as a liaison body with representatives from clan factions. INCS's stated purpose, in addition to coordinating resources and operations of humanitarian providers, was to focus international attention on the Somalia situation (which at the time was nearly completely overshadowed by Operation Desert Storm in Iraq) and to "attract maximum donor funding."[37]

The relatively small cast of characters and the enormity of the problem they were facing helped forge an exceptionally tight OFDA-NGO connection in Somalia. A sense of solidarity with the NGOs and disdain for the UN's impotence on the ground is reflected in Westcott's accounts of the crisis[38]—a feeling that was ultimately shared by many of her colleagues in the US government. In August 1992, OFDA director James Kunder spoke at a press conference upon his return from Mogadishu, lauding the work of the NGOs: "The men and women relief workers who have been working in Somalia since this tragedy began are among the most heroic people I have met. The conditions and the situations they have had to endure are beyond comprehension."[39]

Since Westcott was not allowed the security clearance from the State Department to enter Somalia until May, and her early visits were restricted to twenty-four hours, the US government had essentially no direct ground presence in the country for some time.[40] The United Nations was not operational in Somalia during 1991, and its aid agencies like UNICEF were for the most part also limited to quick forays in and out of the country. In addition to Westcott, there was only one other international donor representative (the EC's humanitarian coordinator) who was making trips into Somalia to monitor the situation. The NGOs and ICRC provided Westcott and the rest of the international community with information on what was happening inside Somalia's borders. In early 1992 aid organizations were already reporting severe malnutrition rates among displaced populations, two expatriate aid workers had been killed, and security incidents continued to rise.

Wescott's cables reported on her visits to displaced camps and feeding projects, the desperate conditions of the people, progress reports of the NGOs' programs, as well as their operational challenges and security incidents. They also relayed NGO findings from nutritional surveys and other public health indicators that they were monitoring that demonstrated a worsening crisis. The cables, at least one of which reportedly made it to President Bush's desk,[41] were written in blunt and often emotional language. One from May 13, 1992, concludes: "The tragic situation in Somalia continues to go from bad to worse with prospects of more fighting, displacement, and starvation in the months to come. The general population of the country is so desperate that death from a bullet or from starvation is of no consequence to a displaced Somali with no hope."[42] The cable ends on a note of praise for the work of the NGOs and Red Cross, and the recommendation that "the USG should continue to support them as well as their proposed expansion of activities."

As is standard in USG emergency aid response, OFDA staff in Washington produced a series of situation reports ("sitreps") on Somalia. These were compiled from information in Westcott's embassy cables (without the source citations of the specific NGOs she obtained the information from), and distributed widely among government offices in Washington. The tone of these reports is urgent, and, even when compiled monthly, they have the feel of late-breaking news. The effect of urgency is inadvertently heightened to the reader by the practice of underlining certain passages to distinguish new information from what was included in past reports. The deteriorating humanitarian conditions of the population are presented alongside reports on the risks and challenges to the humanitarian effort.

A few typical examples of the language excerpted from the Somalia sitreps follow (underlining not shown):

May 7, 1992:

Conditions for displaced populations are worsening, and relief workers report that several children die each day in each of the roughly 100 displaced camps that have sprung up on the periphery of the city. . . . The most desperate situation was found among displaced populations around Merca, where in one location an alarming 99% of the children were found to be malnourished (of which 70% were severely malnourished). . . . [Reports of increasing] violence and lawlessness . . . [R]elief workers report a sharp increase in the number of wounded being treated in hospitals. . . . [O]ver the past several months, all of the NGOs operating in the Northwest have had their compounds attacked, warehouses looted, vehicles stolen and personnel threatened.[43]

June 23:

The death rate in Mogadishu is unknown, but NGOs estimate that between 100 and 200 people are dying every day in and around the city. . . . CARE has taken responsibility for distributing all WFP food in Mogadishu and is working closely with local clans and relief communities. . . . Ironically, since the food shipments began arriving in Mogadishu, the number of casualties arriving at city hospitals has gone up significantly, as armed gangs fight civilians and each other for the food.[44]

August 14:

The situation in much of southern and central Somalia remains desperate. . . . The are no reliable figures for deaths in Mogadishu, but it is clear that the indiscriminate violence has left tens of thousands of people dead and has displaced several hundred thousand, and that more people are dying every day.[45]

As viewed from the humanitarian NGO standpoint, and filtered through OFDA, the information in the sitreps naturally places humanitarian needs front and center, and interprets political and military developments through that lens. The sitreps therefore focus on NGO activities, accomplishments, problems, obstacles, and (mostly informal) assessments of needs. Because the sitreps dealt with humanitarian issues, they naturally contained only very little political or military analysis, and this sort of information wasn't forthcoming from any other source. As the months went on, the sitreps began to do more than interpret the problem, they in effect proposed specific policy prescriptions and actions:

August 14:

Relief workers are concerned that unless the international community acts to stop the flow [of displaced people] into Mogadishu by providing relief and rehabilitation assistance in the countryside, these displaced will face deprivation in Mogadishu for a long time.[46]

October 1:

[S]ecurity incidents continue to bedevil the relief effort. . . .
NGOs are reporting increased harassment. . . . The NGO community has urgently asked the UN to take steps to lessen the
danger to relief workers.[47]

The sitreps made a deep impact in Washington for the simple reason
that they were the only source of ground-level information coming from
Somalia. They were not only read by USAID officials, but at State and on
the Hill they became the essential "must-read" documents for anyone participating in discussions on Somalia and wanting to be abreast of the most
current developments. Policy prescriptions forwarded up from NGOs in
sitreps were in fact ultimately acted upon. In the sitrep following the
arrival of the first contingent of US forces in December, the US decision to
send troops is reported matter-of-factly as a response to the humanitarian
community's appeals:

Operation Restore Hope is in response to sentiment
expressed by the United Nations, non-governmental organizations, US Government representatives and others involved
in the relief effort that insecurity in Somalia has rendered
relief methods inadequate to meet the needs of the desperate
population.[48]

Andrew Natsios writes, "Sustained media attention did contribute to
the Bush administration's decision to use U.S. troops to protect the relief
effort, but that contribution postdated USAID's resolution to be a robust
relief presence in the country."[49] So in fact, the troops were ultimately dispatched to protect this robust (albeit remote—through NGOs), ongoing
US relief response. Natsios was also unapologetic in his attempts to draw
media attention to the famine; US relief officials in partnership with
NGOs, he writes, "played a particularly important—perhaps even decisive—role in generating media coverage of the Somalia famine and influencing internal policy debates."[50]

William Garvelink, now head of USAID's Bureau of Democracy, Conflict and Humanitarian Assistance, was Natsios's deputy at the time. He
insists that NGOs and OFDA moved the policy by hammering the information from the field and feeding the sense of urgency up through the
government. When met with stonewalling at the State and Defense departments, he says, they took a second track and got the ear of Congress,
brought the press in, and generally increased the pressure for the decision.

Like many others who were involved in the process at the time, Garvelink doesn't set any store in the CNN effect, whether in Somalia or elsewhere. The press generally follows the relief agencies, he argues, "and sometimes not even then."[51]

However, the NGOs and OFDA who wanted to see a stronger US response to the emergency did seek to get the media involved. Their representatives in Washington would strategize together on ways to use the media to push policy. Warren Strobel points to how

> Natsios would hold weekly meetings with representatives of the NGOs. "They are all in there planning strategy. . . . How do you inform the world?" said [Assistant Secretary of State for Africa Herman] Cohen, who, as an ally, attended one such session. Because Natsios focused on the suffering and the dying, he could depart from the official policy "in a way that couldn't be called on the carpet." . . . If the images had an impact, it was because the U.S. government had pressured itself into acting.[52]

Before USAID lost its autonomous agency status under President Clinton and was incorporated more formally into the State Department, it nevertheless still found its main source of field information—particularly during emergencies when diplomatic staff are constrained or evacuated—in reports originating from NGOs. The humanitarian wing of the State Department, the Bureau of Population, Refugees and Migration (PRM), although it has far fewer direct partnerships with NGOs than does OFDA, also looks to NGOs as crucial sources of information. The sitreps, compiled by OFDA using NGO reports, bear the official signature of the ambassador or senior foreign service officer for the country in question, and State offices are foremost on the recipients' list of the OFDA cables.

According to a PRM official, the bureau "is rather flat, so the assistant secretary sees the information that is gleaned from NGOs, and it is used immediately at the PRM policy level."[53] Additionally, the assistant secretaries of state heading the regional bureaus consult closely and regularly with PRM on information and developments, their impacts on the region, and what US policy should be. Secretary of State Colin Powell, a former leader of an NGO himself, has been particularly attuned to humanitarian issues. According to the same PRM official, on a 2002 trip to the Middle East, the secretary's first order of business, after meeting Sharon and Arafat, was to find out what was being done for the humanitarian situation in Jenin refugee camps. His experience in the NGO world, according to some on his staff, kept humanitarian issues high on his agenda while in office, and his military background meant that the military was usually at the table for those discussions as well.

At the same time there is no "single authoritative humanitarian voice"[54] in the US government, which has split its humanitarian response operations between USAID and State/PRM. An evaluation of US humanitarian structures ordered by Madeleine Albright after the Kosovo experience brought to light the disjointed decision-making apparatus around humanitarian crises:

> Except when extraordinary steps are taken in the midst of worsening crises to vest power in high-level interim appointees—the pattern in Mitch and Kosovo—humanitarian crises are normally handled by several officials below Subcabinet rank who interact without assignment of lead responsibility or formal procedures for coordination. . . . [D]ecisions on when and how to deploy the U.S. military for humanitarian purposes are often made in an ad hoc, cumbersome fashion which has led to costly delays. . . .[55]

This lack of centralized leadership, arguably, allows for the humanitarian agenda to take hold in the way it has in situations where there are no clear national strategic or economic incentives for the US government to be seized with the crisis. Some, however, including Andrew Natsios, see the mid-level of government foreign policy apparatus as a potential stumbling block for action. Diplomats require stability and access to do their jobs, and hence humanitarian emergencies are anathema. Natsios postulates that because of natural resistance of career diplomats and military officers to US military intervention in a humanitarian emergency in an area outside of the US sphere of interest, direct interventions by the Congress or the president will be required to overcome opposition to US action.[56] In other words, the message coming up from the NGOs through OFDA will have to skip some rungs in the decision-making ladder. Indeed, some crises have been known to accelerate and telescope the policy decision process, as when President Bush instructed the State Department to be "forward leaning" on Somalia. A July State Department cable by Ambassador to Kenya Smith Hempstone Jr. on a visit to refugee camps on the Somali-Kenyan border, which came to be known as "A Day in Hell," had piqued the president's concern (he reportedly wrote in the margins "this is very, very upsetting. I want more information").[57] Bush's request for information was passed from the NSC staff to Andrew Natsios and Herman Cohen, the assistant secretary of state for African affairs, who were armed with the information on humanitarian conditions provided by NGOs on the ground in Somalia. In the summer of 1992, when the NSC meetings were not reaching consensus on action for Somalia, the president decided to take the matter forward, and met with Cheney, Scowcroft, and Baker to decide on a plan to bolster UNOSOM and provide a major airlift of US-donated food aid in August.[58]

The Airlift Decision

Throughout the summer of 1992 voices for action in Somalia were growing louder in the administration and in Congress. OFDA director Jim Kunder made his second visit to Somalia together with Senator Nancy Kassebaum (R-Kansas), and in the same month Senator Paul Simon (D-Illinois) also made a trip to the region. The high-profile visits drew attention to the dire situation of Somalis, and the senators returned calling for an armed UN intervention in Senate resolutions. Kassebaum's testimony included special mention of each of the NGOs and ICRC working in Somalia and her commendation of their "courageous work . . . under extremely dangerous and difficult conditions."[59] Her call for military intervention pointedly rejected the notion of a peacekeeping or stabilization force, but rather proposed a military component to aid efforts. In her words, "The mandate would be simple: to provide protection for relief workers and guard relief supplies in route to those most in need."

On July 26, the Security Council passed Resolution 767 authorizing an emergency airlift to provide relief to southern Somalia. On August 13, with the number of dead in Somalia estimated in the tens of thousands, and the predicted deaths without the rapid infusion of aid estimated at 2 million, the US government pledged an additional 145,000 metric tons of food and announced US military support of the airlift and transport of food supplies. Prior to the initiation of the airlift, OFDA's Westcott and Garvelink brought NGOs and ICRC to the Department of Defense, and this group "spent a good deal of time briefing DOD officers on the famine and the situation in Somalia."[60]

OFDA's August sitrep noted the airlift and added, "Relief planners agree that the airlift is only an emergency measure, and that massive quantities of food will have to enter Somalia through the roads and ports, including through commercial channels, to prevent thousands of dying of starvation."[61] In other words, the borders, ports, and interior of the country would have to be militarily secured to allow the food to reach the people who needed it.

In hindsight, the airlift known as Operation Provide Relief begat the military deployment dubbed Operation Restore Hope. By providing badly needed food to Somalia, it set the stage for the subsequent decision to send troops to enable the aid workers to deliver that food to starving Somalis.

CARE and Philip Johnston

Speaking at an event in 1993 marking CARE's forty-seventh anniversary, Secretary of State Warren Christopher made particular mention of CARE's critical role in pushing the US decision to send troops to Somalia: "CARE lighted the way for one of the proudest moments in American foreign policy—a military mobilization for a mission of mercy, saving the people of Somalia."[62]

Many have credited CARE with a large role in pushing the administration to send troops to Somalia, and Philip Johnston in particular for both his back-channel efforts with the US government and his efforts to draw media attention to the crisis. It is a reputation for which CARE has also received criticism, particularly from European NGOs who felt the agency had violated humanitarian principles by advocating a military solution, and by others who thought the mission had been ill-advised, particularly after the US troops were pulled out following the "Black Hawk Down" incident in Mogadishu.

CARE had established itself as the foremost relief agency in Somalia back in 1981, due to its organizational strengths in logistics of food aid delivery. During that period of hunger crisis, the food aid arriving by ship was rotting in ships' holds due to agencies' lack of coordination. The UN High Commissioner for Refugees designated CARE to establish a distribution system to supply the thirty-five refugee camps and the other NGOs working in Somalia, effectively placing CARE in charge of managing others' relief programs as well as its own, and negotiating the terms with the government at the time.[63]

CARE continued to have a large presence and a leadership role among the NGOs during the 1991–92 crisis. Arrangements were made whereby the World Food Programme had the responsibility of shipping the food supplies to Somalia, and CARE held primary responsibility for receipt and distribution from that point onward. When WFP committed to raise the level of food imports to thirty-three thousand tons per month, CARE used its own staff to lead an assessment of Somalia's roads required to plan the massive relief distribution by truck convoy. In that CARE's road assessment was the only such information available, it was later seized on by planners in the US government and military. "Andie [Stovall, CARE worker]'s report became a blueprint for building a realistic food delivery system. The information also became extremely attractive to US officials later that fall as they envisioned a military intervention that wouldn't happen until December."[64]

By the summer of 1992, CARE's president Phillip Johnston had taken an intense personal interest in what he called the largest humanitarian tragedy yet seen—outstripping the Ethiopian famine of 1984–85 and the Biafra civil war of 1967–70. Upon return from a field visit to Somalia, he met with UN undersecretary-general for humanitarian affairs Jan Eliasson, and proposed that he be designated as manager of the UN's proposed "100-day action plan for accelerated assistance to Somalia." Eliasson agreed, reportedly enthusiastic at the opportunity to circumvent the UN politics of appointments and give the job to a representative of the UN's primary operational partners. Johnston took a leave as CARE president to return to Somalia in the fall of 1992 at the peak of the crisis.

Within a week of Johnston's return to Mogadishu, the SRSG resigned after public friction with the secretary-general, and shortly after that the humanitarian coordinator, David Bassiouni, was forced to flee the country when Aideed threatened his life. (Bassiouni continued in the position after evacuating, but how effective he was able to be in the role of humanitarian coordinator while sitting in Nairobi is hard to imagine.) With the UN humanitarian presence in Somalia still very thin and disorganized, Johnston became the UN humanitarian coordinator in Somalia de facto, and was later formally appointed to the position. With the introduction of an NGO chief to the main international position, the high-level side began picking up. Johnston was able to engage the media and administration officials as an expert of the situation who had a strong vision of what needed to be done.

In his book *A Bed for the Night*, David Rieff remarks on the NGO leader's influence. "Johnston's own role in the humanitarian crisis in Somalia was extraordinarily important. Some aid workers believe that he was the driving force behind the militarization of the humanitarian aid effort in the country and the eventual decision by the U.S. government to send in military forces."[65] Alex de Waal, in his highly critical account of the Somalia aid response, also credits CARE and Johnston's role in pushing policy.[66] He also cites incidents of CARE's aggressive mode of convoy operations instigating unnecessary clashes at roadblocks and, in so doing, adding to the perception of humanitarian obstruction—a compelling theme that would be repeated in the run-up to both the Bosnia and the Kosovo interventions.

Interestingly, Johnston himself credits the media primarily for inspiring government action. In contrast to Strobel's and others' findings on the media reporting of Somalia, in his book *Somalia Diary*, Johnston recalls steadily increasing news coverage from September 1992: "In September, a trickle of television reports and newspaper stories had become a steady stream of news coverage. By October the number of stories became a wave of media attention that lifted Somalia to a new level of international awareness and concern. The media helped the world community care about Somalia." Rieff takes up this line: "[T]he same media trajectory could be traced in terms of Bosnia, Rwanda, Kosovo and East Timor."[67] However, not only do the media analyses show media attention spiking after the decisions were made—and accounts of congressional and NSC activity on the issue, spurred by dogged efforts by USAID efforts in Washington, show the policy wheels were already well in motion from earlier in the summer—it would also appear that CARE and Johnston already had the ear of the US government by the time he first took up his managing role in Somalia.

In September 1992 CARE's East Africa program manager Kevin Henry testified before the House Foreign Affairs Committee on the political and humanitarian conditions in Somalia. By his account Congress by this time had already seized the issue, and CARE and other NGOs had briefed congressional staff numerous times prior.[68] Other senior US NGO staff have attested that by the time an issue reaches the point of formal testimony, it is typically for display, not educational purposes. Congress uses the testimony to highlight issues it is concerned with and to try to move the administration. Additionally, the larger NGOs have informal relationships with mid-level officials at USAID, and attend the larger meetings with USAID and other departments. According to one senior US NGO representative, "By the time you are invited to a formal panel your organization will have spent many prior hours talking to them informally."

Unquestionably, the policy process in government was moving slowly, and CARE clearly saw the value of using the media to push the case, as well as garner public support and donations for their own efforts. In media appearances Phil Johnston and others drove home the same message that by now had reached a pitch of utmost urgency in the sitreps— that of starving people and thwarted relief efforts. In September and October Johnston made appearances on the *MacNeil/Lehrer News Hour* and *Charlie Rose* programs, where he announced that while Somalia needed sixty thousand tons of food a month, only seven thousand were being offloaded from ships docked in the port because of the security constraints on the humanitarian effort. He further reported that 20 percent of what was offloaded was then being systematically stolen between the harbor and the first feeding stations in the city.[69] He was also unabashedly political in his prescriptions, calling for the UN to take over Somalia as it was a nonfunctional state, and hence no sovereignty issues applied.

In November, six CARE workers had been killed in a robbery of food supplies, but the organization remained operational and stepped up its media outreach efforts. That same month, CARE arranged a tour for journalists in Somalia.[70] Jane Perlez of the *New York Times* along with BBC and VOA reporters flew with CARE's Philip Johnston and Rick Grant to Bardera, where they saw the CARE food aid operation there, which had stalled due to the fighting.[71] Jane Perlez reported the starvation in Bardera in a detailed and emotional article that day. Later, a *Boston Globe* reporter being hosted by CARE field staff was caught in the crossfire during an attack on a village and the storming of CARE's office by armed bandits in a dramatic, harrowing story that highlighted both the perils of relief work in Somalia and the brave actions of the CARE staff members with an almost action-movie quality.[72]

Also during this time CARE USA chairman Peter Bell and CARE International president (and former Australian prime minister) Malcolm Fraser agreed on an advocacy strategy to prod the United States into action. Their aim was not to appeal for an external military solution to the Somalia civil strife, but more specifically, military protection for their humanitarian efforts. In the nonconfrontational counselor mode of advocacy favored by CARE and other Wilsonian NGOs, their plan was to "try to influence key players within the Bush administration and the UN to support the US taking leadership within the Security Council in the area of adequate security for the humanitarian effort."[73] Their efforts involved calling the deputy chief of the US mission to the UN, Alexander Watson, to appeal for the United States to "show leadership, including the willingness to send troops, in order to protect the international relief effort in Somalia, all within the framework of the UN."[74] According to Johnston's account, the calls were very effective, and led to more off-camera lobbying at the National Security Council and the White House, while other national CAREs began lobbying their governments as well "for greater protection of humanitarian assistance."[75]

Johnston and Fraser met with Secretary-General Boutros Boutros-Ghali, proposing their idea for the United Nations to send fifteen thousand troops to protect and assist in the food delivery effort. The secretary-general was open to the idea, if Fraser could mobilize the international donor community for the money and the troops. Fraser then took the case to acting US Secretary of State Eagleburger. Johnston also lobbied Eagleburger and Jan Eliassan at the United Nations, calling for specific actions to be taken, including for the United Nations to declare null and void its agreements with warring factions, and to change the rules of engagement for the thirty-five hundred troops so that they may be deployed as and where needed to protect the humanitarian operations.

Further, his identical letters stated, "The United States should agree to transport the troops and equipment into Somalia as part of its contribution to the humanitarian effort. . . . [T]he majority should be deployed to Mogadishu and assigned to secure the port and airport and provide protection for convoys of food for the starving around the country." The letters concluded, "The relief program is not working, and it will not work unless the security issue and related issues are addressed."[76]

Though Johnston had no knowledge of it at the time, by November the US military had already begun contingency planning for an intervention, most likely started before the August airlift. According to his memoir, Johnston and others at CARE were queried by USG officials on particulars of the humanitarian situation as part of the contingency planning process:

> When they began I have no idea, but I do know that on November 19 I spoke to officials at the U.S. State Department who asked me a lot of questions concerning the relief program and what I viewed as constraints. I provided firsthand information on the practicalities of the 100-day plan and why it had stalled. I had no sense that American troop deployments were imminent. However, by then it was clear to me that unless military troops arrived in Somalia, the humanitarian effort was not going to work.[77]

Somalia Emergency: From "Tar Baby" to "Proudest Moment"

In November, the NGOs were reporting through OFDA that one quarter of the children under five in Somalia had died already. In addition the Washington, DC–based consortium of NGOs, InterAction, sent joint appeals to President Bush "detailing the extensive problems that relief groups were facing in Somalia without any security from roaming bandits. InterAction requested that the United States increase its support for the UN to provide security for relief operations."[78]

Joint Chiefs Chairman Colin Powell visited Somalia in October, an event that some speculate had an influence on his acquiescence to the military option.[79] But it is possible that this reversal had already occurred, as Pentagon planning for Somalia most likely began sometime earlier. By the end of November, when the NSC was meeting four times in one week about Somalia, "the previous opposition by the Pentagon had been replaced by quiet internal contingency planning."[80] Of the three options being considered—stepping up US support to the UN mission, providing nonpersonnel funding and logistical support, or leading a second Desert

Storm–type coalition with US troops—Powell recommended and the president chose "the strongest option."[81]

Secretary-General Boutros-Ghali sent a letter formally requesting this option to President Bush, after which the secretary-general took on the task of selling it to the Security Council, which passed Resolution 794 on December 3. The Security Council authorized the US-led Unified Task Force (UNITAF) in December 1992,[82] a Chapter VII arrangement whereby the United States would lead a coalition force (having made clear that it would not allow its soldiers to serve under a UN command).[83] The United States dubbed the UNITAF mission "Operation Restore Hope." On December 9, the advance force of thirteen hundred U.S. Marines landed in Mogadishu.

The effect of NGO information may not appear terribly strong when considering the gap of over a year between the first sitrep and the US decision to act. But those involved on the NGO side at the time maintain that they themselves were slow in explaining the direness of the Somalia situation. In fact it wasn't until the summer and fall of 1992, when aid deliveries were increasingly thwarted or attacked and Somalis began dying in greater numbers, that the cables and the sitreps begin pushing explicitly for US military intervention to protect the food deliveries. Kevin Henry, CARE's regional management team leader for East Africa at the time, recounts that even CARE, which was playing the leading role as the largest NGO presence and chief partner of the United Nations for logistics and delivery, was too slow at focusing on the problem and sounding the alarm. The ICRC, according to Henry, was on top of it much earlier and sending senior delegations to talk about the situation with CARE and the US government. However, in their strictly apolitical stance, the ICRC was not calling for specific policy actions as a Wilsonian NGO might do, nor shaming governments in the press a la the Dunantist NGOs. Importantly, neither were they self-referential about the problems facing the relief effort as were the humanitarian NGOs in Somalia—who were essentially asking political actors to help *them* to help the people.

When it came down to support for a military intervention, the Wilsonian-Dunantist divide became clear among NGOs operating in Somalia, even those within the same federations. Oxfam America and Save the Children US were among those supporting the military operation, while Oxfam GB and Save the Children UK stood with other Dunantist organizations in opposing it. Even the US and British offices of Human Rights Watch were split on the issue.[84]

From the standpoint of those at USAID at the time, the US NGOs were pivotal in the decision. William Garvelink believes that the message of the

NGOs as relayed by USAID to the rest of the administration was what drove the policy. What was implied in the sitreps was expressed directly to him and Natsios at OFDA: NGOs were telling them frankly that they needed protection, that they had reduced their staff in Somalia and would be forced to leave altogether if security conditions didn't improve. On November 25, CARE, IRC, and Oxfam America repeated in a public press conference what they had been warning US officials privately: that unless they could be provided with more security, they would withdraw their programs from Somalia.[85] OFDA followed up in meetings and made it clear to the rest of the government that the NGOs simply could not be allowed to leave; it would be utter disaster for Somalis. Garvelink maintains that at one point they even took the step of having Save the Children represented at a higher-level government meeting to say firsthand that the NGOs "needed troops to protect us and our work."[86]

Garvelink is adamant that the internal lobbying of OFDA, using the NGOs' field-based information, was crucial in moving government decisions to do the airlift and later to send troops. He recalls laughingly that he and Natsios "didn't even realize we were out of the mainstream" when they were pushing for troops. At the time, he said, they were not aware that State and DoD wanted no part of a Somalia operation. Rather they thought everyone shared their view of the problem and what was needed, and merely required a push to get the bureaucratic ball rolling. They only found out from later accounts how influential they actually were.

The Centrality of Humanitarian Operations in the Mission Mandates

The strongest evidence of the NGO influence over the Somalia intervention was not that the mandates were constructed as humanitarian, but that they so closely resembled the view of the problem through the NGO operational lens—not the interclan politics and fighting, the abundant supply of small arms flooding the country, or the coercion of populations by bandits and warlords, but rather the looting of warehouses and attacks on relief convoys.

Resolution 794 of the Security Council, which cleared the way for the US-led intervention, represented the first time that the humanitarian consequences of a civil conflict were conceived as constituting a "threat to international peace and security." The resolution is centered on the humanitarian crisis and the inability of relief workers to do their job (the word "humanitarian" appears forty times). Partial text of the resolution's preamble (with emphasis added) follows:

Determining that the magnitude of the human tragedy caused by the conflict in Somalia, further exacerbated by the obstacles being created to the distribution of humanitarian assistance, constitutes a threat to international peace and security,

Responding to the urgent calls from Somalia for the international community to take measures to **ensure the delivery of humanitarian assistance** in Somalia,

Expressing grave alarm at continuing reports of widespread violations of international humanitarian law occurring in Somalia, including reports of **violence and threats of violence against personnel participating lawfully in impartial humanitarian relief activities; deliberate attacks on non-combatants, relief consignments and vehicles, and medical and relief facilities; and impeding the delivery of food and medical supplies** essential for the survival of the civilian population,

Dismayed by the continuation of conditions that **impede the delivery of humanitarian supplies to destinations within Somalia, and in particular reports of looting of relief supplies destined for starving people, attacks on aircraft and ships bringing in humanitarian relief supplies,** and attacks on the Pakistani UNOSOM contingent in Mogadishu. . . .

President Bush echoed the humanitarian operational view of the problem when he announced his decision to send troops to Somalia on December 4 in a televised address, saying the United States had offered to "lead a coalition to get the food through."[87] Indeed, the mission statement for Operation Restore Hope is squarely focused on assisting the humanitarian workers to get their job done: "When directed by the NCA, USCINCCENT will conduct joint/combined military operations in Somalia, to secure the major air and seaports, key installations and food distribution points, to provide open and free passage of relief supplies, to provide security for convoys and relief organization operations, and assist UN/NGOs in providing humanitarian relief under UN auspices." The mission's overall goal being the creation of a "secure environment for the delivery of relief supplies in southern Somalia."[88]

Even before the August airlift the hypothetical military response was becoming conflated with the aid response. Early calls were for a dual-track solution: increased relief aid delivery plus a peacekeeping/stabilization force focused on the warring parties. A report issued by Human Rights Watch in March 1992 made this argument and noted the evolution of the Security Council resolution on the airlift into a more narrowly framed humanitarian venture:

> It is therefore essential that political and humanitarian initiatives are taken simultaneously. On March 17, 1992, the Security Council, under the presidency of Venezuela's Permanent Representative to the United Nations, Ambassador Diego Arria, adopted a resolution on Somalia. The differences between the draft resolution of March 12 and the final document are significant. According to the draft resolution, "[The Security Council] strongly supports the Secretary-General's decision to urgently dispatch a technical team to Somalia to prepare an operational plan for a monitoring mechanism to guarantee the stability of the cease-fire." Under insistence from the U.S., the final resolution omitted any references to the need to monitor the ceasefire. Instead, it merely "strongly supports the Secretary-General's decision urgently to dispatch a technical team to Somalia, accompanied by [a humanitarian] coordinator"[89]

The Somalia emergency predated the "human security" movement in the international humanitarian community, which seeks to centralize humanitarian issues, and the protection of civilians, in the UN security agenda. Human security principles have been reflected in recent years in the Security Council resolutions on the protection of civilians and children and armed conflict.

For the senior leadership in the US government, undoubtedly the Somalia case brought multiple pressures to bear on the interests side of the policy equation—the need to take the pressure off for a US response to Bosnia, the president's concerns for his legacy as he approached the end of his term, as well as the honest desire to help the Somalis whose suffering was being broadcast on television. At a more fundamental level, however, these players' basic understanding of the problem and its urgency was structured by the NGO experience in the field. Without that field presence, it is doubtful that Operation Provide Hope would have occurred. USAID's William Garvelink has asserted bluntly, "If humanitarian actors had not been on the ground [hindered] by armed elements, the US would never have sent its Marines."

Advocacy after the Fact?

How much did formal NGO advocacy—direct and concerted appeals to US interests in an effort to change policy—influence the decision? There were formal advocacy efforts going on, mostly on the part of human rights organizations, but also by the humanitarian NGOs. Andrew Natsios noted that "when President Bush appeared on national television to announce the military intervention in Somalia, he held up a letter signed by 11 American NGOs which urged him to support military intervention through the UN to end the chaos so people could be fed."[90] This particular letter, dated November 19, 1992, came fairly late in the decision-making process, however, and was assuredly not a determinant so much as a way of explaining to the American public the rationale for the decision. Countless other advocacy letters and joint statements have been sent by US NGOs to presidents and other senior government officials that have not resulted in any action taken. In terms of effect on the interest side, as traditional NGO advocacy is directed, it was arguably more effective in the awareness-raising efforts with the media, such as the Jane Perlez story that CARE facilitated. Here again, the NGOs take on a role not so much as advocates but as educators and experts and key actors on the ground, which help to frame the media story.

Consequences and Reversal of the Decision

Colin Powell, though he was ultimately supportive of the decision for a US-led coalition force, reportedly worried about how the eventual turnover to the United Nations would proceed.[91] Indeed, it was in the turnover from UNITAF (Operation Provide Hope, with its high concentration of US Marines) to the follow-up mission of UNOSOM II where the mission is perceived to have gone awry. Without a preexisting strategy to defuse the interclan warfare that led up to the humanitarian crisis, violence escalated again. In all, 140 UN and 44 US soldiers were killed, and in the end the United States was widely perceived as having abandoned its mission.

In June 5, 1993, Aideed's forces attacked the UN troops, killing 22 Pakistani soldiers. At that point Aideed became the target of the mission, which culminated in the disastrous October 3 raid of US Rangers on Aideed's top officers in Mogadishu. The hourlong firefight ended with the bodies of US soldiers being dragged through the city streets to cheering throngs. US politicians and the members of the public who had strongly favored a mission for humanitarian purposes now confronted what had become a US intervention in a complex civil war—not what they had signed on for. Four days after the Mogadishu incident, President Clinton announced that all US troops would be withdrawn by March 31 the following year.

For those involved in the early crisis response in Somalia, a common reading holds the initial operation UNITAF as a success, with UNOSOM II beginning in May 1993 constituting a change in the mission that added nation-building to the mandate (and the US political lexicon). Along with this interpretation of events grew up certain myths. It is not true, for instance, that the Rangers were under UN command during their ill-fated mission. The directive to "get Aideed" came directly from US commanders. An alternate interpretation sees the problems that the mission fell into as following logically from the initial intervention,[92] which had postponed the difficult decisions in an effort to, as Lawrence Eagleburger put it, "feed and get out." Disarmament of the clan militias would have been a crucial step in the restoration of order and stability, but the US troops did not attempt this. Rather, they only insisted that warlords move their weapons out of Mogadishu and other intervention sectors. The message received by the warlords was simply to wait it out. By August 1993 the United States was realizing the vital need to disarm the warring clans and roving bandits, but by this time the thirty-thousand-strong UNITAF was long gone, and UNOSOM II had to rely on the twelve-hundred-member Quick Response Force and several hundred Rangers. After the hunt for Aideed went awry the forces were switched to a defensive posture and essentially told to hunker down until the March 1994 deadline that Clinton set for withdrawal.

In the CARE president's memoir, the US troops had initially wanted to secure Mogadishu and reach desired troop strength before moving out further, as had been their original timetable. However by December 15 they had acquiesced to the demands of NGOs in Baidoa who were being harassed and attacked by marauders, and where at least fifty Somalis were dying each day. "Months later in January and February the military would still believe their problems in Mogadishu were the result of not following the original timetable and securing Mogadishu before going on to Baidoa."[93] According to James Dobbins of Rand, the international response to the Somalia crisis amounted to "an egregious failure in command,"[94] with the United Nations and the United States each looking to the other to assume overall responsibility. As Dobbins sees it, "A relatively small military operation and limited operational setback became a strategic defeat for the Clinton Administration."[95]

Within the NGO community, CARE has received a fair bit of postmortem criticism for its role in Somalia, particularly from the Dunantist organizations who held this situation up as an example of why NGOs have no business calling for military solutions. CARE representatives remain somewhat defensive over their role in calling for the military intervention, pointing to postmission evaluations that show that regardless of the ultimate failures, the intervention saved huge numbers from starvation. CARE was also in an atypical and critical position, as the organization running the port and effectively responsible for the delivery of the entire international community's food aid response. At the same time it admits that it might go about things differently today, and that NGO "advocacy was not developed at that time."[96]

In a pattern that NGOs would see repeated in subsequent humanitarian interventions, their influence dropped off sharply once US forces and civilian officials were on the ground and they were no longer the sole channel of information.[97] As we will see in other case illustrations, the cooperation between the military and NGOs in the Somalia case went fairly smoothly, but even so, the NGOs were no longer listened to as attentively either on the ground or in Washington.[98]

The Lessons and Legacy of Somalia: Did the Message in NGO Information Lead to Bad Policy?

The presence of NGOs on the ground in Somalia was crucial to the US policy decision to intervene. NGO information defined the problem and suggested a solution that centered around protecting and facilitating the relief operations. The narrowly constructed mission, focused on protecting the humanitarian effort without plans for disarming the warring parties or achieving political stabilization, set the stage for future problems and a perceived failure. The specter of Somalia is often cited as a reason the United States was reluctant to intervene in the Rwanda genocide, an intervention that may have prevented close to a million deaths.

Jan Westcott writes, "The decision to send troops was not discussed with relief personnel working in the field prior to their arrival. In my opinion other options were not considered. . . . Unemployed young gunmen created the biggest security threat to relief workers and effective delivery of assistance. Rather than foreign troops escorting food convoys, the troops should have been training, equipping, and supervising Somali escorts in preparation for the military's eventual withdrawal."[99]

The conflation of military and humanitarian goals encapsulated in the much-maligned term "humanitarian intervention" was perhaps the key flaw in the Somalia operation. While it is natural and appropriate for humanitarians to focus on the immediate imperative of saving lives, these short-term relief objectives cannot constitute the sum total of a political or military intervention that must consider long-term peace building and stabilization. It follows that the problem with the Somalia intervention was not that the mandate was enlarged after the troops were on the ground, but that it was not large enough at the outset. Writing about Somalia in 1994, shortly after the United States withdrew, authors Clarke and Herbst concluded, "This much is manifest: no massive intervention in a failed state—even one for humanitarian purposes—can be assuredly short by plan, politically neutral in execution, or wisely parsimonious in providing 'nation-building' development aid." [100] In other words there is no such thing as a simple humanitarian intervention; no reasonable strategy to "feed and get out."

No mission that saved hundreds of thousands of lives can be justly called a failure, but it is clear that the original mission's narrow parameters of protecting the humanitarian deliveries created serious problems that the follow-up operation was unable to resolve. The message of the NGO information—help us deliver the food—was too shortsighted. The NGOs got what they asked for, but it was a short-lived victory as far as the Somali civilian population was concerned. When seized upon by political actors seeking a quick and easy operation, it sowed the seeds for failure. Today Somalia remains anarchic and in need—the archetype of that sad oxymoron known as the "chronic emergency." Its fate may not be the fault of the NGOs, but should be a cautionary tale about how to look at a situation and communicate it to governments.

Notes

1. M.G. Freeman, D. Waldo, USA; Capt. Robert B. Lambert, USN; LTC Jason D. Mims, USA, "Coalition Humanitarian Operations: Operation Restore Hope—A CENTCOM Perspective," draft of internal USAID document, July 15, 1993.

2. Jon Western, "Press Coverage and the War on Terrorism, 'The CNN Effect': How 24-Hour News Coverage Affects Government Decisions and Public Opinion," Brookings Institution/Harvard Forum, January 23, 2002, http://www.brookings.edu/comm/transcripts/20020123.ht (hereafter, Brookings Institution/Harvard Forum).

3. In his book *Famine Crimes* (Bloomington: Indiana University Press, 1997), Alex de Waal quotes an unnamed UN official who calls the Somalia response "the greatest failure of the UN in our lifetime" for its effective absence during the worst of the famine in 1992 (179).

4. There are differing accounts of the origin of this term. To some it referred to the artillery-mounted vehicles, to others the armed guards

themselves. One version has the term originating in the NGOs' funding proposals. Unable to budget for armed guards explicitly, as donor regulations would not permit this, the NGOs would add a line item for "technical consultants," hence "technicals."

5. Jan Wescott, "The Somalia Saga, 1990–1993" (author's draft), 24. A March 1992 report has a similar take: "The almost total absence of the United Nations (U.N.) since Barre was ousted in January 1991 has put the entire burden of meeting the needs of civilians on the ICRC and the small NGO community in the country" (Human Rights Watch, "Somalia. No Mercy in Mogadishu: The Human Cost of the Conflict & the Struggle for Relief," Africa Watch and Physicians for Human Rights, March 26, 1992, http://www.hrw.org/reports/1992/somalia/.

6. Phillip Johnston, *Somalia Diary* (Atlanta: Longstreet Press, 1994), 37.

7. Ibid., 41.

8. UNOSOM I was created under UN Security Council Resolution 751 of April 24, 1992. Originally limited to Mogadishu, its mandate was later extended and its forces enlarged under Resolution 775 to provide protection to humanitarian deliveries throughout Somalia.

9. Johnston, *Somalia Diary*, 49.

10. Keiko Oizumi, "The United Nations and the Multinational Force in the Somalia Conflict," wwwsoc.nii.ac.jp/psaj/05Print/e_newsletter/1999/oizumi.html.

11 Newspaper columnist Marianne Means, quoted at the Brookings Institution/Harvard Forum.

12. Warren P. Strobel, *Late-Breaking Foreign Policy: The News Media's Influence on Peace Operations* (Washington, DC: US Institute of Peace, 1997). The argument is also made by Jon Western; Lyn S. Graybil, "CNN Made Me Do (Not Do) It," *Sarai Reader* (2004), http://www.sarai.net/journal/04_pdf/22lyn.pdf); and others.

13. Other research on the issue shows similar findings. As quoted in Lyn S. Graybill, "'CNN Made Me Do (Not Do) It' Assessing Media Influence on U. S. Interventions in Somalia and Rwanda," *Sarai Reader* 2004: Crisis/Media, 170–183, 171 (http://www.sarai.net/journal/04_pdf/zzlyn.pdf).

> Jonathan Mermin's analysis of television coverage of ABC, CBS, and NBC points to very low coverage of Somalia from January through June, an increase in July, and extensive coverage in August and September, a sharp drop-off in October, and

a recovery in November. Three full stories occurred on January 5th, February 27th, and March 2nd with grim predictions of numbers who would starve without relief. Mermin argues, however, that these stories, broadcast five to seven months before Bush's decision to take charge of the airlift, could have had little impact on his decision (Mermin, Jonathan, "Television News and American Intervention in Somalia: The Myth of a Media-Driven Foreign Policy," *Political Science Quarterly*, vol. 112, no. 3 [1997] pp. 385–403).

14. Steven Livingston, quoted at the Brookings Institution/Harvard Forum.

15. Andrew Natsios held the position of director of the Office of US Foreign Disaster Assistance at the beginning of the Somalia crisis, and in 1992 was made assistant administrator of USAID for Food and Humanitarian Assistance.

16. Steven Livingston, Associate Professor of Political Communication and International Affairs, George Washington University, quoted at the Brookings Institution/Harvard Forum.

17. Andrew Natsios, *U.S. Foreign Policy and the Four Horsemen of the Apocalypse* (Westport, CT: Praeger, 1997), 130.

18. Andrew Natsios, "Illusions of Influence: The CNN Effect in Complex Emergencies," in *From Massacres to Genocide: The Media, Public Policy, and Humanitarian Crises*, ed. Robert I. Rotberg and Thomas G. Weiss (Washington, DC: Brookings, 1996).

19. Ibid., 154.

20. Valerie Lofland, "Somalia: U.S. Intervention and Operation Restore Hope," in *Case Studies in Policy Making and Implementation*, ed. David A. Williams, 6th ed. (Newport, RI: Naval War College, 2002), 57.

21. Comments by Claus Kleber, at the Brookings Institution/Harvard Forum.

22. Kleber, at the Brookings Institution/Harvard Forum.

23. Kouchner's advocacy/publicity seeking was largely responsible for the rift with his MSF colleagues, which led him to leave the organization and found Médecins du Monde.

24. Westcott, "Somalia Saga," 43.

25. Donald M. Snow, *Distant Thunder: Patterns of Conflict in the Developing World*, 2nd ed. (Armonk, NY: M. E. Sharpe, 1997).

26. Brookings Institution/Harvard Forum.

27. Jon Western, "Sources of Humanitarian Intervention: Beliefs, Information, and Advocacy in the U.S. Decisions on Somalia and Bosnia," *International Security* 27, no. 1 (July/August 1999): 30–47.

28. Freeman et al., "Coalition Humanitarian Operations," 3.

29. Natsios, "Illusions of Influence," 154.

30. USAID/OFDA Situation Report No. 1, July 17, 1991 (OFDA archives, Washington, DC).

31. Natsios, *U.S. Foreign Policy and the Four Horsemen of the Apocalypse*, 127.

32. Janice Wessel (nee Westcott), USAID Haiti, interview with author. December 2, 2004.

33. An official cable to Washington from the US Liaison Office in Mogadishu (February 1994) states that Westcott's reports "helped bring the Somali catastrophe to the attention of policy makers in Washington and embassies in the region; that in turn stimulated food airlifts and ultimately, Operation Provide Hope" (E.O. 12356; Subject: Aid Officer Westcott Service in Somalia).

34. Natsios, *U.S. Foreign Policy and the Four Horsemen of the Apocalypse,* 132.

35. A small Austrian NGO called SOS Kinderdorf, headed by an intrepid doctor, was the only international organization that did not evacuate Mogadishu during the peak of the coup violence in early January.

36. Westcott, "Somalia Saga," 2.

37. Ibid., 9.

38. Ibid.; Natsios, *U.S. Foreign Policy and the Four Horsemen of the Apocalypse*; Jan Westcott and William Garvelink, interviews with author. June 15, 2004.

39. USAID, *Front Lines*, September 1992, quoted in Westcott, "Somalia Saga."

40. Westcott was gradually able to extend her stays inside Somalia, though it often entailed a bizarrely circular approval system wherein the State Department would first obtain approval for her trip requests from the designated official in the region—Westcott herself.

41. Wescott, interview with author.

42. Unclassified cable from American Embassy in Nairobi, "Subject: Somalia Relief," May 13, 1992.

43. USAID/OFDA, Somalia Situation Report No. 9, May 7, 1992.

44. USAID/OFDA, Somalia Situation Report No. 10, June 23, 1992.

45. USAID/OFDA, Somalia Situation Report No. 11, August 14, 1992.

46. Ibid.

47. USAID/OFDA, Somalia Situation Report No. 14, October 1, 1992.

48. USAID/OFDA, Somalia Situation Report No. 17, December 17, 1992.

49. Natsios, "Illusions of Influence," 132.

50. Ibid.

51. William Garvelink, USAID/DCHA, interview with author.

52. Strobel, *Late-Breaking Foreign Policy*, 135.

53. Douglas Hunter, U.S. Department of State, Bureau for Population, Refugees and Migration, interview with author (April 22, 2002).

54. US government internal report, "Interagency Review of U.S. Government Civilian Humanitarian and Transition Programs" ("Halperin Report"), 12. Copy of report, US Dept. of State, January 2000. Released under FOIA, obtained from the National Security Archive, George Washington University (http://www.gwu.edu/~nsarchiv/NSAEBB/NSAEBB30/index.html/#doc).

55. Ibid.

56. Natsios, *U.S. Foreign Policy and the Four Horsemen of the Apocalypse*, 128.

57. Cited in Strobel, *Late-Breaking Foreign Policy*, 132.

58. Jeff James of the State Department (in NSC during Somalia) is quoted as follows:

> [The President] wanted something done and gave the crisis increased focus. He also instructed the State Department to be forward leaning on Somalia and told the national security advisor, Brent Scowcroft, to begin exploring an enhanced airlift effort. At about the same time, I started attending NSC interagency meetings and it soon seemed apparent to me that a consensus on an airlift effort was not going to happen. When the president found out the interagency working group process was not cutting it through reports from the national security advisor, he decided to get a food airlift operation going despite the haggling. (Lofland, "Somalia," 57)

59. Senator Nancy Kassebaum, "The Humanitarian Crisis in Somalia," Statement before the Senate Foreign Relations Committee, July 22, 1992.

60. Wescott, "Somalia Saga," 53.

61. USAID/OFDA, Somalia Situation Report No. 11, August 14, 1992.

62. US Dept. of State, "93/05/14 Statement of CARE's 47th Anniversary," Office of the spokesman (http://dosfan.lib.uic.edu/ERC/briefing/dossec/1993/9305/930514dossec.html).

63. Johnston, *Somalia Diary*, 14.

64. Ibid., 41.

65. David Rieff, *A Bed for the Night* (New York: Simon & Schuster, 2002), 34–35.

66. Alex de Waal, *Famine Crimes: Politics and the Disaster Relief Industry in Africa* (Oxford: James Currey with Indiana University Press, in association with the International African Institute, 1997).

67. Rieff, *Bed for the Night*, 40.

68. Kevin Henry, CARE, interview with author.

69. Johnston, *Somalia Diary*, 62.

70. Other NGOs and agencies in Somalia were hosting journalists as well. Jan Westcott recalls "at one point in August MSF/France had 17 journalists staying at their compound and the UN had about 40" ("Somalia Saga," 43).

71. Johnston, *Somalia Diary*, 58.

72. Wil Haygood, "Death, Bullets Sear Somali Night: Journalists Caught in Attack on Village," *Boston Globe*, October 18, 1992.

73. Johnston, *Somalia Diary*, 61.

74. Ibid.

75. Ibid.

76. Ibid., 65.

77. Ibid.

78. Western, "Sources of Humanitarian Intervention," 135.

79. Lofland, "Somalia," 59.

80. Robert B. Oakley, "An Envoy's Perspective," *JFQ Forum* (Autumn 1993): 45.

81. Ibid.

82. Security Council Resolution 794 (December 3, 1992).

83. The resolution took the unprecedented step of defining a humanitarian emergency as a security threat, thus justifying Chapter VII action: "Endorses the recommendation by the Secretary-General in his letter of 29 November 1992 (S/24868) that action under Chapter VII of the Charter of the United Nations should be taken in order to establish a secure environment for humanitarian relief operations in Somalia as soon as possible."

84. Natsios, *U.S. Foreign Policy and the Four Horseman of the Apocalypse*, 68.

85. De Waal points out that of the three, only CARE had significant programming under way in Somalia, but notes the press conference made a big impact with the administration.

86. William Garvelink, USAID, interview with author.

87. Transcript of December 4, 2002, address in *New York Times*, December 5, 2002, quoted in Johnston, *Somalia Diary*, 67.

88. Freeman et al., "Coalition Humanitarian Operations," 6.

89. Human Rights Watch Report, "No Mercy in Mogadishu: The Human Cost of Conflict and the Struggle for Relief," March 1992, http://www.hrw.org/reports/1992/somalia/.

90. Natsios, *U.S. Foreign Policy and the Four Horsemen of the Apocalypse*, 57.

91. Oakley, "Envoy's Perspective," 45.

92. See, for example, Walter Clark and Jeffrey Herbst, "Somalia and the Future of Humanitarian Intervention," *Foreign Affairs*, March/April 1996, 70–85.

93. Johnston, *Somalia Diary*, 84.

94. James Dobbins, John G. McGinn, Keith Crane, Seth G. Jones, Rollie Lal, Andrew Rathwell, Rachel Swanger, Anga Timilsina, *America's Role in Nation-Building: From Germany to Iraq*, Rand, 2003 (http://www.rand.org/publications/MR/MR733/), 69.

95. Ibid.

96. Kevin Henry, CARE, interview with author, July 28, 2004.

97. The same can be said of the US government aid agencies. Westcott reports Marines avoiding, ignoring, or laughing off her advice, such as when she recommended strongly that they not enter Somaliland, as the Somaliland authorities and public did not want them there ("Somalia Saga," 55).

98. For example, NGO personnel involved in Somalia at the time recall a meeting they had with Admiral Howe some months before the Mogadishu raid, where they "strongly advised him against" taking that particular future course.

99. Westcott, "Somalia Saga," 53–54.

100. Walter Clarke and Jeffrey Herbst, "Somalia and the Future of Humanitarian Intervention," *Foreign Affairs* (March/April 1996), vol. 25, no. 2, 70–85: 71.

CHAPTER FOUR

BOSNIA

This chapter and the one that follows examine two other pre–September 11, 2001, complex crises in the developing world, both with prominent humanitarian components, and ultimately resulting in US-led international interventions. These chapters contend that, as in Somalia, NGOs not only played a key role in "humanitarianizing" the conflicts' problematique, but created a policy momentum in Washington that tilted inexorably toward full-ultimate-throttle engagement in the crises. Twice again, the US government's participation in the humanitarian efforts preceded muscular diplomatic and military action. And twice again, faced with a US-backed aid effort, heroic but futile even in its successes, the United States ultimately took the reins of the international political/military response. Unlike Somalia, of course, the Balkans represent Western Europe's backyard, the testing ground for the NATO alliance, the birthplace of the First World War, and the focal point for nightmare scenarios of future intracontinental conflict. The Balkans crises therefore naturally present a less stark demonstration of NGO information influence than the Somalia case. As this chapter shows, however, a small core group of NGOs on the ground in the early phase of the conflict played a similar role in framing the issue and feeding the information-hungry policymakers in Washington with field-based reporting; through the OFDA, this information moved the debate and shaped policy.

"Ethnic Quagmire" and the Evolution of a Humanitarian-Centered Mandate

High spirits engendered by the dismantling of the Berlin Wall and the Soviet power structure along with it, buoyed further by a decisive victory in the Persian Gulf over Iraqi aggression, led to optimistic proclamations of a "New World Order" in the early 1990s. This optimism quickly sank in face of resurgent ethnonationalist violence and state fragmentation throughout the remainder of the decade.

When the predominantly Muslim government of Bosnia-Herzegovina announced its secession from Yugoslavia, following on the heels of Slovenia and Croatia, the Bosnian Serb and Croat populations were suddenly faced with the prospect of becoming minorities in a new nation under Muslim leadership. Acting on historical fears and resentments, and, in the case of the Serbs' particularly, encouraged and equipped by their "home governments," these groups took up arms and initiated civil war against the Bosnian government and their own neighbors. The ensuing three years of war witnessed atrocities against civilians that evoked memories of the horrors of World War II, driven home by the combatants' use of the term "ethnic cleansing" to describe the forced removal of large groups of people from occupied areas.

Throughout Bosnia, Muslim refugees fleeing Serb forces in the countryside attempted to seek refuge in cities and larger towns, and faced siege conditions once they arrived. As the war progressed, the world began hearing reports describing the wholesale destruction of villages by invading paramilitary forces, Nazi-style concentration camps where Muslims were being forcibly detained, mass killings, systematic rapes, and torture. All told, it is estimated that 250,000 were killed and nearly 2 million displaced during the war.[1]

Several months passed before the United States overcame its initial reluctance to take action in Somalia once the humanitarian crisis became apparent. According to accounts from those inside the administration at the time, the United States was facing an even more unattractive proposition in the case of Bosnia, and the strong desire, on the part of the Bush administration, to leave it to Europe to attend to its own problems and manage the international response.

In large part this was due to the "quagmire" mind-set with which many in the US and other governments viewed the Balkans. Western policymakers interpreted the conflict in Bosnia as the playing out of centuries-old ethnic hatreds, set loose by the collapse of the old regime.[2] Such a perspective views all parties as more or less equally culpable, and inclines third parties not to intervene. By the time the United States became actively involved, however, the paradigm had shifted to one of mainly Serb aggression against Bosnian Muslims and Croats. In the previous chapter it was suggested that the humanitarian crisis in Somalia received US military attention first because of the information and the messages of urgency emanating from Western NGO actors on the ground.[3] While the ICRC and a core group of international NGOs were present in Somalia and communicating directly to government through the OFDA pipeline, very few relief and development NGOs had a presence (or indeed any prior experience) in Eastern-bloc countries, where authorities tightly constrained access. Yugoslavia, moreover, was one of the more developed and economically well off of the communist countries, so there would have been little reason for an international NGO programming presence prior to the outbreak of war. The lack of a significant operational humanitarian presence on the ground in the early stage of the conflict helps explain why the image of the crisis seen by the West was dominated by the fighting and ethnonationalist politics and not, as in Somalia, the humanitarian need and response.

As the conflict raged on and the humanitarian effects worsened, more NGOs became operational on the ground and began feeding information to the US and other governments through the implementer-donor relationship. Humanitarian problems, such as how to help Bosnians survive the winter in besieged Sarajevo, moved to the fore. The eventual US military response took on similar characteristics to Somalia, in that it began as a mission driven by and focused on humanitarian concerns, and only later transformed into peacekeeping with politico-military objectives. Also, as in Somalia, one US-based NGO (in this case, the International Rescue Committee) played a particularly important role in setting the stage for the US response through its partnership with the US humanitarian donor agency USAID/OFDA.

UNPROFOR

The United Nations Protection Force (UNPROFOR) had been on the ground in Croatia since March 1992, having been originally established to keep the peace between Serb and Croat forces in Croatia for the time it took to negotiate an overall peaceful resolution to the crisis in Yugoslavia. After fighting broke out in Bosnia-Herzegovina, UNPROFOR's mandate was extended and enlarged to deploy military personnel in parts of that republic, specifically to facilitate and protect humanitarian assistance efforts.[4]

Having failed to provide a disincentive to Serb-Croat hostilities in Croatia (both sides had violated the UN Protected Areas and taken back their weapons), UNPROFOR sights were set considerably lower in Bosnia, focusing initially on preventing fighting around the Sarajevo airport so humanitarian supplies could get through. Some in the international community thought of the humanitarian mandate as a way of buying time until a political settlement could be attained. In hindsight, others say the focus on the humanitarian action was both a mask for lack of political will and an attempt to stem the tide of asylum-seekers headed for Western Europe. In any event, from the beginning UNPROFOR's small deployment in Bosnia (one hundred military and civilians staff initially) was to protect humanitarian operations rather than quell the violence or demilitarizing factions. In calling for the mandate extension, the secretary general highlighted the urgency of beefing up the mission "the better to protect UNHCR and its relief efforts."[5] Security Council Resolution 757 (1992) imposed sanctions on the Federal Republic of Yugoslavia (Serbia and Montenegro) in response to the Yugoslav People's Army (JNA) support of the rebel Bosnian Serbs, and "demanded that all parties create the conditions necessary for unimpeded delivery of humanitarian supplies to Sarajevo and other destinations in Bosnia and Herzegovina, including the establishment of a security zone encompassing Sarajevo and its airport."[6]

Insufficient troop deployments continued to cripple UNPROFOR in each of its mandated tasks,[7] even though these were mostly limited to protecting the humanitarian efforts. When UNPROFOR failed in its efforts to secure the Sarajevo airport and provide safe passage for humanitarian aid deliveries, its mandate was extended again, and again with humanitarian aid as the prime objective. Resolutions 770 and 776 (1992) used the strongest possible language in peacekeeping mandates, but toward humanitarian rather than peace enforcement ends. Invoking the spirit of Chapter VII's collective security provisions, Resolution 770 called for "all measures necessary"[8] to be used to facilitate the delivery of humanitarian aid to Sarajevo and other parts of Bosnia. All told, every one of the forty-six Security Resolutions on the conflict taken between May 1992 and November 1995 "deals either explicitly or implicitly with measures aimed at alleviating civilian suffering."[9]

UNPROFOR's new mandate was to support the humanitarian aid operations of the UNHCR and to provide military protection for these operations upon UNHCR's request. (The mandate to protect humanitarian operations, not Bosnian civilians, was repeated by UNPROFOR commanders like a mantra according to David Rieff.[10]) UNPROFOR troops were enlarged and deployed in five new zones, with each zone's headquarters to have civilian staff specifically for liaison with UNHCR, and a separate UNPROFOR command was established for Bosnia. Like many UN peacekeeping missions, UNPROFOR's mandate was approved only for six months at a time, and required regular renewals. By September 1993 the continued noncooperation by the parties and criticism of UNPROFOR for failing to achieve what it was not equipped, staffed, or, in fairness, mandated to do, the secretary-general announced in September 1993 that he was "sorely tempted" to recommend to the Security Council that it pull the plug on UNPROFOR altogether.[11] This never did happen, however, and UNPROFOR remained in Bosnia and Croatia for more than two years beyond that until the Dayton Peace Accords were signed. Boutros-Ghali had reasoned that pulling the troops out would only lead to more and bloodier conflict. Not spoken of but perhaps just as important, after troop buildups and dispersion throughout the country over the previous years, there were now very real dangers associated with evacuation, not to mention the disgrace it would bring. UNPROFOR thus continued on its by now largely humanitarian mission until the US-brokered cease fire and Dayton peace agreement of November–December 1995.

UNHCR, the Red Cross, and NGOs:
The Humanitarian Effort in Bosnia

Most accounts of the humanitarian response to the crisis in Bosnia-Herzegovina focus primarily on the leading role of the UN High Commissioner for Refugees. In Bosnia the United Nations indeed played a much stronger and more central role than it had in Somalia. As violence erupted and spread across the Bosnian republic, and humanitarian response became the focal point of international engagement in the crisis, UNHCR was designated by the secretary-general as the lead humanitarian agency in the region. In this role UNHCR would work in partnership with the ICRC and coordinate the efforts of the other UN agencies and the NGOs. This was a watershed moment for the United Nations' refugee organization, representing both a newly operational role in internal conflicts and a new prominence among the constellation of humanitarian agencies. The change came on the heels of its leadership in the northern Iraq Kurdish crisis, in which UNHCR had reluctantly and late in the game accepted a lead role in aiding the displaced Kurds.[12] UNHCR approached the ex-Yugoslavia mandate more energetically, willingly donning the mantle of the United Nations' major player in humanitarian emergencies.

The humanitarian needs in Bosnia were considerable. Ethnic cleansing had resulted in 2.6 million Bosnians being forcibly displaced in under three months since the hostilities began in April 1992. By the time the Dayton Peace Accords were signed in November 1995 the number of internally displaced and refugees had risen to 3 million—more than half the population of Bosnia-Herzegovina.[13] In Sarajevo and other enclaves, residents faced prolonged siege conditions. Although UNHCR traditionally handled cases of refugees proper—that is, those who have fled across an internationally recognized border—the humanitarian crisis in the disintegrating Yugoslavia was clearly related mainly to forced migration, and so fell more within the mandate and capacities of UNHCR than any other UN agency. In February 1992 UNHCR and ICRC agreed on a division of labor whereby UNHCR would handle relief deliveries to noncombat areas in Croatia and Serbia while ICRC would focus on the areas of active violence. After the shooting death of one of its delegates in May, however, ICRC temporarily withdrew from the country, leaving UNHCR with the additional responsibilities. UNHCR was thus placed for the first time in the role of direct service provider in a conflict, delivering aid to IDPs and nondisplaced war victims alike.[14] UNHCR's role ultimately encompassed the primary responsibility for all food deliveries inside Bosnia until after Dayton in 1995, when the Word Food Programme at last took over.[15]

Accustomed to working in noncombat areas, across borders from the fighting that their refugee clientele had fled, and with the cooperation of host-country governments, the UNHCR was taking on a vastly different mandate in the Balkans. Its resources were stretched, as they were responding to refugee situations in Ethiopia, Malawi, Pakistan, and Sudan, and continuing the Kurdish operation in northern Iraq. Unlike the ICRC it had no experience working in areas of active fighting, and it lacked emergency preparedness measures or contingency plans for such an operation in Europe.[16]

Aside from the ICRC, every humanitarian organization running programs within Bosnia implemented its programming under the "UNHCR umbrella," meaning they cleared their planned relief deliveries with UNHCR, were registered by and carried UNHCR ID cards which could be helpful when dealing with local parties, and received some logistical support (such as buying low-cost fuel for their vehicles at UNHCR-designated pumps). For the multitude of local organizations and NGOs delivering assistance, UNHCR acted as coordinator, facilitator, disciplinarian, and in some cases funder of NGO assistance activities. UNHCR issued humanitarian ID cards to three thousand staffers of 250 organizations.[17] In addition, some two thousand vehicles from over 150 organizations had UNHCR plates.[18]

There is disagreement in the literature and case evaluations on UNHCR's and ICRC's reporting roles. Their own internal reports emphasize as pivotal their information-gathering and -sharing function, as in the reports they provided from Serb-held areas. As the only international bodies present, they maintain, the two organizations helped reveal crucial information on ethnic cleansing that would otherwise not have reached the media.[19] Others argue that the two bodies' concern for not offending the Serbs and thus jeopardizing the entire humanitarian program led them to "balance" their public statements in a way that reinforced the ethnic quagmire mind-set among the international community, particularly in the early months of the war.[20]

One is reluctant to pass judgment on the organizations that were working under extreme hazards and without a script in order to provide some aid to civilians amid the chaos of war. Nonetheless, their early statements did appear to deliberately spread the blame around in equal measure. ICRC's August 13, 1992, statement quoted by the BBC lambasted "all sides" for being "guilty of the systematic use of brutality . . . [and] forced population transfers on a massive scale, the so-called ethnic cleansing."[21] To their critics, such as author Gregory Kent, this illustrates how the organizations fostered a sense of moral equivalence, even to the point of misrepresenting the actions and capacities of the Bosnian government, which had no means to effect massive "forced population transfers." Kent points out that "the ICRC statement gave no mention of the special and overwhelming responsibility of Serbian forces and authorities, a critical omission," while at the same time implicating the Bosnian government's side "on the flimsiest of evidence"[22]

Even more damning was UNHCR's decision a few months earlier to soft-pedal information of the massacres at Zvornik in April 1992. The aftermath of the atrocities, committed by Serb paramilitary forces under the notorious Arkan, were witnessed by a UNHCR official, Jose Maria Mendiluce, the High Commissioner's special representative. "He saw the corpses of slaughtered children being piled onto trucks. He was caught up in crowds of civilians fleeing in panic and horror as Serb forces shelled them."[23] According to NGO colleagues who spoke with him upon his return, Mendiluce forthrightly expressed his outrage over what he had witnessed to all who would listen, yet his accounts were softened and downplayed in UNHCR's official reports from Geneva, presumably so as not to create a political storm and damage UNHCR's standing with Serb authorities. UNHCR Geneva's report did not describe a massacre and rout of the population by Serb militias, but rather referred generically to "refugees" fleeing war-affected areas "citing fighting and lack of food."[24] Kent argues that the media was likewise misled in an example of UNHCR's "gatekeeping," or withholding of information contrary to the dominant frame.[25]

UNHCR and ICRC, unable to provide physical protection to civilians, hoped their presence would provide a passive protection by discouraging acts of violence in the sight of international observers. Failing this, their accounts emphasize that they served the end by "bearing witness" where there was no one else to do so. The media and UNPROFOR, for example, were denied permission to enter large parts of Bosnian Serb territory as well as Bosnian Croat enclaves such as East Mostar. UNHCR and ICRC were the only international organizations present to bear witness to the atrocities and communicate them to the outside world. But there is much disagreement as to whether the political tightrope they were forced to walk permitted them to be successful in this role. Kent implies, to the contrary, that the media caught on to the death camp story through Bosnian Muslim and NGO sources, despite ICRC and UNHCR's gatekeeping.

Ultimately, while both agencies "regularly denounced, each in its own way, forcible displacement and violations of human rights and humanitarian law,"[26] the picture they painted at the beginning was of a humanitarian crisis created by chaotic violence stemming from all sides.[27] This picture was the best argument noninterventionists could make for not taking decisive action in the conflict. Ironically, this made UNHCR's role in Bosnia even more untenable. An evaluation asserts that UNHCR initially perceived its role as "buying time for a political solution":

> As time passed, that solution failed to materialize, and humanitarian activities remained the centre-piece of UN efforts in Bosnia-Herzegovina. The gap between the deterioration in events and the lack of international political or military responses became acute, and UNHCR was left struggling in the vacuum.[28]

Once it was clear that providing "aid in situ" would not provide the passive protection that is often hoped the humanitarian presence infers, and that political intervention was not forthcoming, UNHCR in 1992 made the controversial but in hindsight the only possible choice: to help evacuate populations from their home communities in advance of ethnic cleansing forces.[29]

As lead agency, UNHCR had to grapple with the always difficult role of "coordinator" for agencies over which it had no management authority, and lead negotiator with local authorities with which it had no political standing. A common problem for the United Nations in countries experiencing crisis or pre-crisis conditions, the designated UN authority must juggle the roles of liaison with warring parties and advocate for their victims. An unhappy compromise often results. The NGOs—most of which are usually clamoring for a strong coordinator to establish a rational, unified structure for coordination during emergencies—stress the importance of an independent humanitarian coordinator who is free from political constraints and can advocate aggressively for humanitarian concerns. So it was with the NGOs in Bosnia, who owed much to UNHCR's logistics and communications systems in Bosnia, but were among its fiercest critics.

Local political considerations were not the only factor affecting the potency of UNHCR's informational role. Others were the institutional interests of UNHCR within the UN system of agencies and the nature of the donor relationship. As a large UN agency with a specific humanitarian mandate, UNHCR inhabits a different type of "agent" role in the principal-agent relationship with donors than do the NGOs. Its large budget comprises regular, assessed contributions from an Executive Committee of government donors, and does not function, like most NGOs, on a grant-to-grant basis.[30] This situation gives UNHCR both more independence and latitude in programming, and more responsibility to do things right. Its failures bring into question the appropriateness of the mandate and the competence of the whole agency. Though often seen to represent the entire UN system, UNHCR is forced to compete with its other agencies. It is an unfortunate but natural tendency, therefore, for its spokespeople and senior management to burnish the image of the agency while ignoring the bleak bigger picture. As is done by the World Food Programme in other cases, UNHCR's statements in Bosnia tended to stress procedural accomplishments, such as metric tonnages delivered per province. Richard Holbrooke observed caustically in this regard that "in its press releases, UNHCR boasted about the amount of food it had brought in, not the inadequacy of the system or the rising death toll."[31] Essentially the UNHCR officials were trying to prove themselves capable of handling the impossible task that was set before them, when in truth they were understaffed, stretched thin, and according to other organizations on the ground, "completely out of their depth."[32] Roy Williams, head of programming for IRC at the time, has said that in Bosnia UNHCR was in a situation so far outside its usual refugee protection mandate that "events contradicted its very essence."[33] Therefore, he said, the organization was forced to focus on matters of logistics, communications, and the mechanics of aid deliveries—counting the number of trucks getting through, for example—simply because it couldn't do anything else under the circumstances. David Rieff and other critics have noted that by highlighting the "little successes" of the effort, UNHCR, and the UN more broadly, inadvertently helped to "obscure the fact that no real progress was being made."[34]

The internal US government accounts of the Bosnia crisis and response depict the UNHCR operation particularly in the early years, in a very unflattering light, as do the cables and sitreps from the field at the time. Specifically, the US government was dissatisfied with UNHCR's inability to monitor the distribution of its food deliveries to ensure they were getting to the people most in need, its "slow and awkward" method for sub-granting and expending donor funds, and its inability to provide effective coordination for the other humanitarian implementers.[35] OFDA remained highly critical of UNHCR's performance once it established an office in the US Embassy in Zagreb, and early relations between the two bodies were strained.[36] Several OFDA cables to Washington criticize UNHCR's staffing, policies, and performance, one of which found its way to Geneva and further alienated UNHCR from OFDA.[37]

While UN narratives stress the importance of UNHCR's witnessing and reporting in ultimately inciting policymakers to action, the only US government entity actively engaged with the crisis at that time—OFDA—found it had little use for UNHCR's information for decision-making purposes. An evaluation commissioned by OFDA reported that "UNHCR did not serve as a good source of centralized information or experience on which to base funding strategy." In fact, the report continues, UNHCR demonstrated fairly poor communication with rest of the humanitarian community and was overly focused on establishing a massive humanitarian infrastructure to keep adequately abreast of the changing humanitarian scene. UNHCR's "ignorance about the environment and developments" was matched, in the OFDA's estimation, by UNPROFOR's "absolute ignorance of what was happening on the ground." Instead, OFDA relied heavily on its NGO implementing partners, and one in particular.[38]

OFDA's New Go-To NGO:
IRC and the Information Pipeline from Bosnia

The crisis in the former Yugoslavia brought the international NGOs into Europe, most of them for the first time, excepting those few that had their origins in the aftermath of World War II, long before any of the current personnel or programming modalities. There was trepidation in many NGO headquarters at first, not knowing how their expertise based on the paradigm of Southern developing countries could translate in the very different sociopolitical context and environmental conditions of this crisis.

The New York–based International Rescue Committee (IRC) was one of the few international NGOs to get on the ground very early on in the Yugoslavia crisis, and was in fact present before the first hostilities erupted in Bosnia. They did so through an unprecedented arrangement with the Office of US Foreign Disaster Assistance, which sought an operational partner to set up a presence in the field in advance of any humanitarian operations to provide information on the growing conflict, in order "to help [OFDA] get closer to the action on the ground."[39] In December 1991 a team comprising USAID and embassy staff, together with IRC personnel, toured Bosnia, Croatia, Vojvodina, and Serbia to assess humanitarian needs. IRC produced the report from the assessment mission, and shortly thereafter accepted funding from OFDA to set up offices in three republics.[40] In what was the first and only formal arrangement of its kind between the donor agency and a humanitarian NGO, IRC's presence constituted what OFDA hoped would be a "humanitarian trip wire" enabling the timely infusion of US relief aid in the event of a major crisis.[41] Roy Williams, head of IRC programming at the time, had embraced the idea, likening it to the case of South Sudan the year before where "a group of us NGOs had badgered [then head of OFDA] Julia Taft into getting involved." On the ground in the former Yugoslavia IRC field officers behaved very much like journalists, traveling around the region, interviewing locals and culling local press accounts, and preparing detailed reports for submission to OFDA in Washington, and later Zagreb. Referred thereafter in some official documents as "the lead U.S. PVO working in the former Yugoslavia,"[42] IRC maintained a key role with the US government and among the international humanitarian community that grew up during the Bosnia crisis.

Although the administration of President George Bush had remained determinedly on the political sidelines of the Yugoslavia crisis, which it felt was Europe's to solve, OFDA had become involved even before the spread of violence to Bosnia in anticipation of a US humanitarian response. In this case, information gathering was more than an important aspect of the donor-NGO relationship; it was the very crux of the issue. In fact in the beginning IRC's sole function was to funnel information to OFDA on what was happening on the ground. As US government employees subject to security restrictions, neither OFDA nor any embassy staffers were free to move around in the war affected areas. As Fawcett and Tanner reported, "By helping IRC set up a ground presence, OFDA ensured it had a trusted partner on hand in the event it decided to launch any widespread humanitarian operation—a lesson culled directly from Northern Iraq. Finally, given the fluidity of the situation, OFDA correctly figured that IRC's field based information and analysis would assist its decision making."[43]

At the time, IRC saw itself as prepositioning in anticipation of setting up operations that would be funded by the United States, enhancing its organizational capacity to operate in a context so unlike the African and Asian settings they were accustomed to, and generally facilitating their future work. IRC and other US NGOs at that time were especially "naïve about politics"[44] and had no particular agenda beyond delivering aid. The concept of humanitarian NGO advocacy was still underdeveloped, and the IRC had no institutional strategy or agenda for influencing the United States or other governments.[45]

The IRC-OFDA relationship was close and congenial, nevertheless representing the classic case of mutual dependence—the NGO dependent on government funding to get operational, and the government dependent on the NGO to be their eyes and ears as well as the implementers of their official assistance. The IRC's Gerald Martone has referred to it as a "reluctant symbiosis,"[46] stressing the extent of the reliance on operational humanitarian NGOs by government (and other organizations such as those with a human rights focus) on everything from accommodations to transportation and logistics to travel permits in country.

Another important NGO-USG link came in the person of Richard Holbrooke. A member of the board of directors of IRC, Ambassador Holbrooke had made two fact-finding trips to the former Yugoslavia in his IRC capacity before accepting the position in the Clinton administration that made him the point person for the Dayton peace negotiations that ultimately ended the war. After leaving IRC's board (as required when accepting a government position), Holbrooke retained close ties with the organization, and consulted as well with other US-based NGOs operating in the former Yugoslavia. On his trip to Croatia and Bosnia in 1992, Holbrooke was hosted by IRC, and was taken around to refugee camps by an IRC worker who also translated the heartrending stories of the refugees. He spoke to British UNPROFOR about the prospect of lifting the arms embargo on Bosnia, saying "there are ways around" the UN sanctions, as were found in Pakistan (where he was the US ambassador during the time the Mujahadeen fighters in Afghanistan were being supported by the United States).[47] During the same trip the head of Refugees International, Lionel Rosenblatt, toured with Holbrooke through Bosnia.[48] Holbrooke became the most forceful advocate in the Clinton administration for strong US action in the Balkans, and his appointment to undersecretary of state for European and Canadian affairs represented the start of assertive US diplomatic engagement in the crisis. In his book on the subject he recounts how much of his time in country was spent amid the international community of relief workers, for whom he professes a deep admiration.

When the war began in Bosnia, IRC reported on a daily basis to OFDA's operations center in Washington.[49] The reports and assessments included the movements and needs of displaced populations, reports on where fighting and forced displacements were taking place, political information about the various factions in the regions, economic developments, UN activities, and general political and security conditions. OFDA staff would share these reports with other government offices, including faxing them directly to the State Department, where the "refugee program bureau found the information invaluable."[50] A senior US humanitarian official recalled that IRC reporting began simply as "a few faxes a week, then the people in State couldn't live without it," particularly the bureaus "least informed about our [OFDA's] type of work."[51] Many US officials involved in the crisis reportedly did not realize that IRC was being funded by OFDA and saw their presence and extensive reporting as a signal of the gravity of the developing emergency. "In a classic case of an assessment that is correct for the wrong reasons, Ambassador Zimmerman concluded that 'something really big was happening' when IRC's head of operations Roy Williams arrived in Yugoslavia."[52] By helping IRC set up its field presence and disseminating its field reports, OFDA helped draw attention to the growing humanitarian crisis in the Balkans within the broader US government. And for its part, IRC's informational role not only raised its prominence with the US donor, which deferred to it on humanitarian assessments and proposals with complete trust, but also inferred upon it "the depth and breadth of view to advise other organizations, including UNHCR and other NGOs."[53]

IRC Information and the First Sarajevo Airlift

The conventional history of the US role in the Bosnia conflict holds that the Bush administration remained staunchly anti-interventionist (in the famous words of James Baker, "We don't have a dog in this fight"[54]) and that Clinton reversed the policy. Nevertheless, the humanitarian activities under the Bush administration had set the policy ball in motion. The OFDA-IRC connection became a symbol for growing US concern and a triggering device for more vigorous policy action. If US humanitarian action began as a fig leaf, it in fact turned out to be the spear tip of US intervention. One case in point is the often overlooked first airlift to Sarajevo undertaken unilaterally by the United States over two days in April 1992, some six months before Clinton was elected. For three months prior, the IRC staffer in Bosnia had been submitting reports on growing incidents of violence throughout the region, links between the Serb paramilitaries and the Yugoslav National Army, and the circle of roadblocks tightening around Sarajevo. In March 1992 the IRC representative recommended to the US embassy in Belgrade that an airlift be organized into Sarajevo.[55] The US State Department and Pentagon agreed, based on the same information from IRC. UNHCR was "initially reticent,"[56] but IRC and US officials obtained their agreement as well as that of the other NGOs, the Bosnian government, and the Yugoslav Army. The airlift was organized by IRC in Bosnia, and the military C-130s that flew the supplies in also carried the US ambassador to Belgrade, Warren Zimmerman, and a senior State Department official, Ralph Johnson.

Interviews with OFDA officials reveal that their thinking at the time was to use US military assets, particularly air power which had special significance so soon after Desert Storm, to send a signal to the Serbs to back down, and at the same time hoped that it would create momentum for more active US government involvement.[57] "They . . . reasoned that the airlift might provide the thin end of a wedge that would get US policy more directly involved in Bosnia."[58]

After some months IRC began implementing aid projects, and so moved out of the strictly information-provision function and into a more operational role. However, IRC continued to be a crucial information source for the US government via OFDA, and by now had an air of veteran expert with the US government and among other NGOs, even though they had only preceded most other international organizations on the ground by a few months. For the first few years of the Bosnia aid response, OFDA was not directive of its NGO-implementing partners but willingly followed their lead in programmatic decisions and funded NGOs freely according to NGO determinations of what should and could be done.[59]

In December 1992 OFDA fielded a Disaster Assessment and Response Team (DART) to the region, which afforded it a somewhat closer view of the field. Although based in the US embassy in Zagreb, the DART officers made frequent trips into Bosnia. To their great frustration their movements were constrained by security regulations, and most trips were confined to twenty-four hours at a time. Typically on these trips the OFDA staff would stay at the IRC facilities and be taken around by IRC staff. Much of the information that was passed by IRC and other NGOs during this time was informal, "over a beer," and lent the feeling of OFDA and its NGO partners being part of a team.[60] Though no longer in an exclusive informational arrangement, IRC and OFDA's working relationship remained close, and IRC continued to win the praise and pride of USAID and other parts of government. In the report of the 1993 Humanitarian Assessment Team dispatched by President Clinton into Bosnia, IRC is singled out for accolades: "IRC is probably the most important NGO active in Bosnia. . . . The courage of IRC personnel, their creative drive to stimulate local production, their enormous credibility, and their success in organizing and supporting HCR logistics requirements are outstanding. They reflect the American can-do attitude in a measure few others match."

Moving the Debate:
Humanitarian Information's Hidden Hand

In the spring of 1992, staff from the State Department's Eastern Europe bureau and PRM had joined together with OFDA, the Department of Defense, and the National Security Council in a Humanitarian Working Group on the crisis in Yugoslavia, which was chaired by State. As the name (perhaps deliberately) implies, humanitarian aid remained the focus of the US government's response to the crisis, but the engagement of the political actors from State as well as DoD and NSC signaled higher-level policy concerns. All of these actors were hungry for information, which they were evidently not receiving from the US embassy in Belgrade and consulate in Zagreb, or any field intelligence sources. NGO field information continued to flow to OFDA "and hence to a wider US audience."[61]

Once on the ground, thought it still lacked the freedom of movement to personally assess conditions in many areas, the OFDA/DART office maximized the NGO information pipeline and began processing the NGOs' information into their sitrep format and providing them to Washington, where they were widely read throughout the US government. Once DART staff were occupied with the funding of NGOs in relief efforts, they relied even more heavily on the NGOs to feed them information, despite the fact that they now had staff in the field. Unlike sitreps in some other cases that could be summaries of several months' worth of information, these thrice-weekly reports had an up-to-the-minute feel to them and "provided a morning 'look-good,' smart pill to the reader dealing with Bosnia on a daily basis [and] often provided the fresh layer of detail upon which key decisions were made."[62]

> The information collected by IRC flowed into the great Washington information maw. This in turn fed and further stimulated the hunger for information in Administration circles. Hence one of the major flows of information into Washington had a humanitarian slant to it. . . . OFDA's senior management saw that information was an invaluable currency in the Yugoslav crisis. In a context of information hunger, the new reporting triggered a growing demand for OFDA reports, which in turn provided a bureaucratic incentive to gather more information. OFDA's involvement on the ground increased and its reputation was enhanced.[63]

Though members of Congress are not "slugged" on the recipient list of the embassy cables as are the White House, State, other embassies, and the

Pentagon, interested members of Congress were also avid readers of the reports out of Bosnia. The prevailing attitude at OFDA and State regarding this information was to "spread it around" as much as possible.[64] Congressional allocations for the relief effort greatly increased during this period. In June 1992 the United States had committed $33 million to the former Yugoslavia, and by November 1992 the amount had increased to $92 million.

The ripple effects of the field reporting seen during the Somalia case were repeated in Bosnia. Several times the sitreps were quoted verbatim in State Department briefings and statements from White House and congressional staff.[65] According to the US government review of the response, the usefulness of OFDA's reporting vastly outstripped that of the intelligence agencies in terms of offering an understanding of what was really happening on the ground. In fact, those in OFDA and the NGO community at the time attest there were no other significant sources of intelligence on the ground in Bosnia. According to OFDA staff, the CIA was getting much of their information from OFDA and the NGOs. One IRC staff member recounted, "Once in a while you saw a US military officer, or someone at a meeting who it's not clear who they work for in the government (so everyone assumes CIA), but they weren't energetic in intelligence gathering."[66]

The sitreps and cables conveyed a sense of urgent need, underscored the difficulty in getting the aid through, and made quite clear that political forces were to blame for the crisis and that political solutions were necessary. "Within these assessments BHR OFDA and the DART sided with the victims and pushed for solutions that addressed the root causes of the suffering."[67] The official OFDA/DART mandate was "to study current US and international humanitarian assistance efforts in B-H with the purpose of making recommendations on ways the USG could improve and augment its own contributions or render the larger international effort more effective . . . to consider alternatives unconstrained by prior policies toward commitment of U.S. resources in the region."[68] Indeed, the DART's reporting frequently spilled into direct policy prescriptions, as in these examples from an internal OFDA (DART) report on East Bosnia:

> UN Security Council resolutions mandating UNPROFOR's mission in B-H fail to address important specifics of UNHCR coordination except that UNHCR has the lead in determining the need for security. **Recommend State initiate immediate discussions within the UN Security Council to better define the relationship between UNPROFOR and UNHCR.**

UNHCR indicated some difficulty in integrating military personnel with their civilian humanitarian aid operations and may be reluctant to accept further US military support. **Recommend State champion the increased participation of more NGOs and PVOs in those areas that can further aid UNHCR's overall logistics operation.**

* * *

Besieged enclaves in Eastern Bosnia should be designated "safe havens," protected by sufficient international military force to ensure an end to the shelling of civilians.

If the international community is unwilling to create safe havens, the international community should immediately begin to evacuate besieged civilian populations.

If the security situation continues to decline within Serbia, Montenegro, and Eastern Bosnia, the international community should allow more refugees and displaced civilians whose security is threatened to immigrate.

Although framed in the context of relief efforts, the substance of the OFDA report carried candid political import:

Continued and augmented relief effort is entirely dependent on secure and unimpeded access to central B-H. An attempt by Serb forces to seize additional territory or additional skirmishes between HVO and BIH would force relief agencies to withdraw with tragic consequences. Both of these developments are considered likely in the relatively near future unless preventive measures are taken immediately. This situation deserves priority attention in policy consideration and ongoing international and regional negotiating efforts and initiatives. . . . The Serbian forces in BIH depend on resupply from Serbia. The USG should explore diplomatic and economic initiatives to encourage HVO cooperation and to discourage Serbian aggression, thereby enabling the international community to continue the relief effort. (Internal OFDA document Central Bosnia Group 2)

Often the daily cables made vaguer but no less political recommendations. As one cable reporting on the humanitarian situation in Gorazde
concluded, "Finally, and obviously, something should be done to stop
Bosnian Serb shelling of innocent civilians in Gorazde."[69] When interviewed today, IRC and OFDA representatives don't lay claim to any conscious political agenda to influence US government policy, but rather
stress they simply wanted to address humanitarian issues. Nevertheless
more than one sitrep found its way to the *New York Times* and other US
media, featured in stories on Sarajevo that were later credited in adding to
the pressure for policy change. Interviews with US and NGO workers
involved at the time frequently raise one cable in particular that was especially strong in its language, and caused a great deal of rumbling in Washington. Sent on August 19, 1993, and excerpted below, the cable cites UN
and NGO reports of drastically declining nutrition, health, and shelter
conditions in Sarajevo that would become deadly as winter approached:

UNCLASSIFIED

OFDA 08/19/93

....

SUBJECT: TFSR01: SARAJEVO—THE END IS AT HAND

_____

SUMMARY

_____

1. SARAJEVO IS ON THE VERGE OF COMPLETE COL-
LAPSE...THIS IS AN URGENT CALL FOR ACTION

...

6. ONE YEAR AGO SARAJEVO WAS IN VERY SERIOUS
CONDITION. NOW THE SITUATION IS CRITICAL. PEO-
PLE DEVOTE THEIR DAILY ACTIVITIES TO COLLECT-
ING WATER AND FOOD. SARAJEVO APPEARS MORE
LIKE AN AFRICAN REFUGEE CAMP IN THAT PEOPLE
CARRY ANY TYPE OF CONTAINER TO COLLECT
WATER.

...

11. THE DETERIORATION OF PEOPLE'S PHYSICAL HEALTH WILL MAKE THEM MORE VULNERABLE TO THE EFFECTS OF WINTER. THE TEAM BELIEVES, AND RELIEF ORGANIZATIONS OPERATING IN SARAJEVO CONCUR, THAT A MAJOR PUBLIC HEALTH CATASTRO-PHE IS IMMINENT.

After several recommendations involving the infusion of fuel, food, water purification units, and other relief supplies, the cable concludes:

18. ACCESS – THIS IS THE SINGLE MOST IMPORTANT RECOMMENDATION. ALL LAND ACCESS MUST BE OPENED. HVO MUST BE REQUIRED TO ALLOW COM-MERCIAL TRAFFIC FROM THE COAST AND THE SERBS MUST BE REQUIRED TO ALLOW TRANSPORT FROM THE AIRPORT TO THE CITY, AND ALL RELIEF ROUTES OR CONVOYS MUST BE AFFORDED ADEQUATE PRO-TECTION FROM GROWING LAWLESS ELEMENTS IN CENTRAL BOSNIA.

POSTSCRIPT

---

19. THE 'JOKE' NOW CIRCULATING SARAJEVO GOES AS FOLLOWS. QUESTION: 'WHAT IS THE DIFFERENCE BETWEEN AUSCHWITZ CONCENTRATION CAMP AND SARAJEVO?' THE ANSWER: 'AUSCHWITZ HAD GAS.'

GALBRAITH##

Reminiscing on the Somalia case, senior OFDA staffer William Garvelink observed how he and Andrew Natsios had not realized at the time how OFDA was moving the debate with its field information. Like-wise in the Bosnia case, the internal review of OFDA's activities states, "It is interesting to note that OFDA information professionals did not seem to realize the extent of their influence."[70]

The Frame Changes: Death Camps, Winter, and the Beginning of Assertive US Involvement

Analysts mark a turning point of the understanding of the conflict in the summer of 1992 when the focus shifted to what appeared more and more as a coordinated campaign of violence against Bosnian Muslims orchestrated with Belgrade's tacit approval and support.[71] In various parts of the US government the prevailing mind-set of Bosnia as a morass of ethnic violence had begun to lose ground to the alternative frame of Serb aggression. IRC had by this time been reporting from the ground for six months, detailing incidents of Serb violence against the outgunned Bosnians, and in April had triggered the US airlift to Sarajevo. The Humanitarian Working Group on Bosnia, comprising State, DoD, USAID, and NSC personnel, had started meeting a couple of months prior. Still, some in the US State Department along with many of the foreign offices in Western European governments continued to hold the old line, as embodied in the statement by UNPROFOR's Cedric Thornberry, "There are no innocent parties in Bosnia."[72] The OFDA internal review reported that higher-level State Department officials had not yet become very familiar with the ground-level issues, had not framed the problem in humanitarian terms, and "reverted to a gut sense of the problem."[73] Reportedly it was junior and mid-level officers, the main consumers at State of the NGO/OFDA field reports in the beginning, who were generally more in favor of strong US action.[74]

In another parallel to the Somalia case, while some officials at State and the Pentagon were seeking to avoid a potential Bosnian quagmire, the issue was of growing interest in Congress, certain members of which had seized of the situation since the first days of the breakup of Yugoslavia. Congress grew still more active over Bosnia in the summer of 1992.[75] On August 2, 1992, Roy Gutman of *Newsday* broke the first news stories about the "death camps" that Bosnian Serbs were using to imprison Muslims. His interviews of witnesses from Omarska caused a huge stir in the US media, and a subsequent BBC television report on the camps added to the worldwide indignation. (According to a practitioner who was there at the time, Gutman was initially steered toward the Omarska witnesses by humanitarian workers who wanted the story out.) The newly focused public attention may have provided a decisive push for the Senate Foreign Relations Committee to enact Resolution 330 four days later that cited "horrible atrocities being committed by Serbian-backed forces" and "acts of genocide," and called for the United States to promptly consider the use of force.[76] The resolution also decried the fact that "much needed supplies of food and medicine are being repeatedly blocked." Again as in Somalia, although congressional action appeared to follow press reporting, on closer inspection it becomes clear that policy action on the Hill had preceded the spikes in media coverage. The Congressional Record shows at least forty formal statements and resolutions prior to August 1992 calling for stronger US action in Bosnia. Many congressional delegations traveled to the region as well, where they would attempt to gather information firsthand from local officials, UN representatives, and NGOs. When Senator Daniel Patrick Moynihan (D-NY) visited the region, he was hosted by IRC and accompanied by Peter Galbraith, the future US ambassador to Croatia.

The outcry among the public and some members of Congress at this stage did not, however, lead to a decision on the part of the executive branch for decisive new political or military action. Criticism of the Bush administration's handling of Bosnia was mounting as the election approached, and the president held an emergency meeting in his vacation home on August 8, but senior officials were not prepared to consider using force in the region. Both the White House and the State Department focused instead on supporting the UN mandate for the delivery of humanitarian assistance. European peace negotiations were faltering, and humanitarian response presented itself once again as the only viable path, whereas the diplomatic track appeared to be going nowhere.

The US government made three major allocations of funding for humanitarian organizations during 1992, increasing the international agency presence on the ground. With the increase in humanitarian grants, greater numbers of government officials were brought into the backstopping of the humanitarian efforts, and consequently a greater government investment in the enterprise, which some have suggested created a humanitarian aid–driven policy momentum[77] that ultimately had a greater effect than public opinion and media pressure.[78]

Despite his campaign calls for Bush to take stronger measures against the Serbs, President Clinton showed similar ambivalence during his first year in office. Thus, whereas news reports of death camps, systematic rapes, and other human rights abuses in Bosnia may have had a lot to do with changing the public's perception of the war, they weren't sufficient by themselves to get the US government more actively involved politically or militarily. The question then emerges: Was it more the death camps or the obstructed aid convoys that ultimately moved the United States to action? Was it the newly received wisdom of Serbs as the bad guys per se, or Serbs as bad guys blocking food?

Even Bill Clinton in his campaign speeches cited aid obstruction specifically, and "urged air strikes, supported by the United States if necessary, against the Serbs *if they continued to block the delivery of humanitarian goods* to people trapped in Sarajevo."[79] US Senate resolutions in August 1992 and January 1993 also cite the blocking of international aid efforts as an egregious contravention of and justification for stronger US and international action against the Serbs.[80] The theme of humanitarian obstruction was also sounded repeatedly in the media.[81] Indeed, despite ostensible protection by UNPROFOR, the humanitarian aid convoys in Bosnia repeatedly met with major obstacles, including roadblocks, land-mines, and hostile fire. Several Security Council resolutions made special note of the obstruction of humanitarian aid by the combatants, "deplored" and "condemned" these actions, and repeatedly demanded the unhindered movement of relief supplies. The United Nations reported that despite these problems a total of 34,600 tons of relief supplies were delivered to eight hundred thousand beneficiaries in 110 Bosnian locations during the winter of 1992–93. The Serbs proved particularly adept at using humanitarian access as a pressure release valve, repeatedly tightening their stranglehold and then relenting before international pressure and momentum built up too much against them. This explains why one sees repeated declarations in US cables (including three during August–December 1993) that unless access improves, "a humanitarian (crisis/catastrophe/disaster) is imminent,"[82] followed by cables reporting that access had improved somewhat in some areas and X amount of aid supplies had been delivered to Y number of provinces. Perhaps if the aid coming in had been blocked and stolen even more flagrantly as had been the case in Somalia, if there were never any successful convoys, and if the opposing forces had been as anarchic and intransigent as those in Somalia, the military response would have come sooner. But aid workers were allowed to go about their jobs with enough efficacy (in August 1993 the United Nations reported that the food pipeline was meeting 93 percent of Bosnia's needs[83]) that the massive humanitarian disaster never quite arrived. People were dying from snipers' bullets and mortar shells, not lack of donated food.

The idea that "humanitarian obstruction" ultimately begets the strongest government response would lead one to the ironic conclusion that humanitarians in fact were too successful in Bosnia and so prolonged the emergency. According to an OFDA review of the "Cuny Water Project" (the subgrant issued to IRC by UNHCR out of a large grant from George Soros), Fred Cuny reasoned that if the Serb authorities allowed the water treatment plant to be set up in Sarajevo, then Sarajevans would have potable water needs met. If they blocked it at the airport, "then Cuny had a highly visible and tangible instance of humanitarian obstruction with which to lobby the US and other Western governments for firmer action."[84] The lack of water in Sarajevo in the summer was reported in a

DART document that was obtained by the *New York Times*, "and was said to have significantly raised the tempo towards air strikes."[85] The Cuny plant succeeded beyond expectations, providing up to 90 percent of the city's water needs, and remains a testament to effective humanitarian assistance. Ironically, as noted, its success may have prolonged the war.

A 1993 OFDA briefing book prepared for US officials arriving in the region painted a picture of a stalemated mission and growing humanitarian crisis needs:

> UNHCR has been attempting to carry out a comprehensive land convoy aid delivery program, but renewed fighting, in the face of signed ceasefires and UN Security Council resolutions, has resulted in blocked roads, destroyed bridges, a general breakdown in security, increased thefts of humanitarian cargo and increased attacks on relief workers. A cut-off of commercial cargo traffic into Bosnia, by the Croatian forces in Bosnia (HVO), has further increased the pressure on relief agencies to meet relief needs.[86]

As in Somalia, there was another threat implied by the humanitarian obstruction: If the aid organizations continued to face obstacles and worsening security conditions, they would pack up and leave, and the resulting humanitarian conditions would be disastrous. As a June 1993 internal OFDA report, entitled "Security Problems Increasing Threat to Relief Workers and Bosnians," described:

> The result of the breakdown in security is increased attacks on civilians working for UNPROFOR, UNHCR and NGOs, as well as UNPROFOR military personnel. Money, equipment and personal property is also being taken. According to [program officer for Bosnia, UN Center for Human Rights in Zagreb] Thomas Osorio, the deteriorating security situation in central Bosnia is making a difficult logistics problem even worse, as more areas become inaccessible, the flow of aid slows, essential international drivers quit, and the existing food stocks diminish, with little hope of replenishment through commercial means. If international organizations cannot or choose not to operate under these conditions, vulnerable populations are likely to suffer heavy losses.[87]

Reports from the humanitarian personnel in the field seemed also to put the last nails in the coffin of the "ancient hatreds" theme. The US government humanitarian assessment team report from the field had this to say: "The team was often told that there are no 'good guys,' but to imply equal culpability is a distortion of reality and a travesty of the enormous suffering inflicted on the Bosnian Muslims. Wherever the team went, it saw clear evidence that the Muslims are the overwhelming victims of the war in Bosnia-Herzegovina."[88]

The report later bluntly admonishes that the United States should not delude itself into thinking that humanitarian assistance was in any way an adequate response to the Bosnia crisis.

> The current international relief effort, even if it is saving some lives and relieving some human suffering, cannot be called effective or successful as long as the killing and displacement of the population and the destruction of property, indeed an entire economy, is allowed to continue. While augmented relief efforts recommended below and in the body of the report are essential to the international community's efforts of reducing human suffering, these proposed projects are a band-aid on a patient requiring intensive care.[89]

Winter Scare, 1993–94

The prospect of winter in besieged Sarajevo had the humanitarian aid community casting dire warnings of the massive mortality to come. Fall 1992 began the "first in a long series of Balkan 'winter-scares,'"[90] but it was the approaching winter of 1993 that saw the most dire and vocal consensus on the looming danger. Accustomed to meeting emergency needs only in southern developing countries, NGO and UN humanitarian workers were not experienced in northern climates, or the impact of cold on urban industrialized populations. Having no idea what to expect, they assumed the worst and turned out to be wrong. Official US intelligence reports also flagged the potential for large numbers of deaths, predictions that were repeated in the media,[91] but these were accepted wholesale from the relief organizations "with little or no critical analysis from the intelligence agencies themselves."[92] The hundreds of thousands of predicted deaths did not occur; as Fred Cuny (one of the few at the time) was reported to have observed, in cold weather "people die from exposure"— in other words, they don't die in their apartments. Sarajevans' access to resources, support networks, and various coping mechanisms to get them through the long siege were repeatedly and vastly underestimated. In hindsight, NGOs admit to providing bad information, and they chalk it up to one part NGO ignorance and one part deliberate alarmism in hopes of moving politicians to action. An example of this approach can be found in a survey performed in 1993 on the effects of winter on the morbidity and mortality of Sarajevans by the American affiliate of Médecins du Monde (Doctors of the World—DOW) and the Francois-Xavier Bagnoud Center for Health and Human Rights at Harvard. Prior to traveling to Bosnia, the team met in Cambridge, Massachusetts, hosted by Francois-Xavier Bagnoud Center director and DOW board member ex-officio Jonathan Mann. Some team members expressed reservations that the survey's scope and methodology did not seem capable of reaching definitive conclusions about the impact of winter on health indicators. Dr. Mann replied that the larger objective of the study was to draw attention to the humanitarian plight in order to move governments to action, and not to do a scientifically rigorous survey. The survey's findings were reported in a journal article entitled "Bosnia: The War Against Public Health," which, while acknowledging its methodological limitations, presented a powerful and wide-ranging treatise of the impact of violence on society, and testified to "crimes against public health" being committed in Bosnia.[93] The cause of winter was taken up at USAID as well. In a letter to Acting Secretary of State Eagleburger, assistant USAID administrator Andrew Natsios urged that "immediate and massive action must be taken now to avert a tragedy by the onset of the winter season."[94]

Throughout 1993 the US military involvement was limited to enforcing the no-fly zone and the maritime ban, and the military would not take further steps toward forceful engagement until spring of the following year. As had the previous administration, Clinton used humanitarian action as the US point of entry into the conflict. In February 1993, Clinton decided to withdraw support of the faltering Vance-Owen peace plan,[95] and obtained the agreement of the UN secretary-general and British Prime Minister John Major to do humanitarian airdrops in Bosnia. Also that month, Clinton dispatched the "humanitarian assessment team" composed of State Department, USAID, Centers for Disease Control, and Department of Defense personnel, along with IRC and other NGO representatives. As part of Clinton's "Six Point Plan" to reform US policy towards the conflict, the team's explicit objective was to "examine constraints on the relief effort."[96] Further, in addressing the humanitarian obstruction and other problems on the ground, the team was "free to consider alternatives unconstrained by prior policies toward commitment of U.S. resources in the region."[97] The team's report in April indeed went far beyond discussing the technicalities of the humanitarian relief program, but rather, as mentioned above, lamented the futile, Band-Aid nature of humanitarian aid in the face of the conflict, and urged US military intervention.

At this point the collective wisdom in the US government no longer shared the initial European take on the conflict as an inevitable eth-nonationalist conflagration that needed containment, but had clearly formed a picture of the aggressors and victims in Bosnia. However the military, still under the chairmanship of General Colin Powell, remained reluctant to be drawn in, and Clinton repeatedly stated that US forces would be sent in only in the context of a peace agreement, not to support the current UNPROFOR mandate.[98] Clinton also worried that a unilateral US action against the Serbs would create problems in the NATO alliance.[99] What remained to be launched then was a strong US initiative to engineer a peace agreement between the warring parties.

Richard Holbrooke recounts that, at this point, the pressure from the reports out of Bosnia, the press coverage, and the critical attitude in Europe toward US policy in Bosnia "reached into the highest levels of the government"[100] and spurred the reorganization of the State Department, with Strobe Talbott promoted to deputy secretary in the fall of 1993. In early 1994, with an eye on Bosnia as a priority issue, Talbott asked Holbrooke to take over the Bureau of European and Canadian Affairs. Preferring to continue in his job as ambassador to Germany, Holbrooke at first declined but in May relented when President Clinton personally added his voice to the request.

Holbrooke, who was first introduced to Bosnia on a humanitarian assessment trip as an IRC board member, had never approached the conflict with a realpolitik amorality, but felt that what was at stake was nothing less than genocide. In a January 13, 1993, memorandum to the Clinton administration, before his appointment, he recommended four objectives for the USG in Bosnia: "first, 'to save as many lives as possible in Bosnia'; second, 'to make containment of the war a top priority'; third, 'to punish the Serbs for their behavior'; and fourth, to use this crisis as an opportunity to strengthen the UN system."[101] At that time the administration had still not summoned the will to act so assertively. Colin Powell was strongly against involvement, and Tony Lake, the national security advisor, was defensive about exactly what Clinton had promised to do during the campaign. Although the following month Secretary of State Warren Christopher announced the administration's intent to negotiate and enforce a peace agreement, it would be some time still before this process was launched.

In February 1994 the international public was galvanized by a fresh outrage with the Sarajevo marketplace shelling that killed thirty-four civilians. The images from the "marketplace massacre" did not instigate a policy reversal in the US government, but rather "accelerated and catalyzed a policy evolution that was already under way."[102] When policymakers in government take action, it is based on the information they have, and in most cases the media is not telling them things they do not know (rather, that is what NGOs are doing). The media can, however, add to the impetus by making it more in the government's interest to act for public opinion reasons.

In a significant step toward direct engagement and diplomatic leadership in the Bosnia crisis, the United States spearheaded the formation of the Contact Group on Bosnia, which consisted of the United States, Britain, Russia, France, Germany, and Italy. The European Community and United Nations were now no longer the focus of diplomatic efforts, and the United States had significantly more invested in the outcome.[103] By the fall of 1994, the United States had begun planning with NATO for an eventual peacekeeping force for Bosnia that would secure a peace agreement.[104] The NATO planning exercises started in earnest at this point, and considered "a variety of military actions, including extraction of UN peacekeepers and various air strike options."[105]

In July 1995 the Serb forces moved on Srebrenica, one of the "safe havens" for Bosnian Muslims, and subsequently massacred approximately seven thousand Bosnian men and boys under the noses of UNPROFOR troops who stood by helplessly. This at last moved the international community to agree to remove the "dual key" authority for military reprisals, shared by UN and NATO, placing the responsibility in NATO's hands alone. The US government took the reins of the peace negotiation process, and Richard Holbrooke's shuttle diplomacy mission began the following month. Holbrooke had pushed for air strikes both within and without the US government since before Srebrenica, and now had an unfettered mandate to attempt to bring an end to the fighting. (He also had motivation from a different source. Holbrooke's twenty-five-year-old son Anthony was working for humanitarian NGOs, and in July was with Refugees International interviewing refugees emerging from Srebrenica. Holbrooke recalls in his book how his son called him from the field and demanded he "get my ass in gear"[106] to do something about it.)

The Waning Influence of NGOs in Bosnia Post-Dayton

The peace negotiations began in Dayton, Ohio, in early November, and culminated in the signing of the Dayton Peace Accords on November 21. IFOR, the NATO force to succeed UNPROFOR, would, unlike its predecessor, have the right to go anywhere in Bosnia, and have an unequivocal mandate to use force if necessary. It was to be composed of sixty thousand

NATO troops, one third of which would be Americans. In his televised speech of November 27, 1995, President Clinton used humanitarian language to sell the proposed US involvement in Bosnia to the American public. The president cited the need to "protect civilians" before the national security interests of "stabilizing a region." Clinton emphasized that US leadership in the peace-building efforts in Bosnia is, for humanitarian reasons, "the right thing to do."

Despite Clinton's humanitarian rationale, and despite the policy stimulus that NGO information had provided along every step of the Bosnia crisis, the NGOs saw a discouraging and familiar pattern in the way their status with the US government seemed to drop once the military was deployed. With other USG entities including the military proliferating on the ground, policymakers in State and elsewhere no longer eagerly sought out NGO information and advice. Even OFDA's attitude toward the NGOs changed after Dayton. Whereas before, OFDA had followed the NGOs' lead and encouraged them to be innovative in their programming, OFDA now became much more hands-on as a donor and directive with NGO projects to the point of micromanagement.[107] Instead of funding NGO projects as they came in, OFDA began designing reconstruction-oriented aid programs and telling NGOs where they could fit within them.[108] NGO personnel interviewed today recount how some organizations by 1995 had developed considerable field-based knowledge, expertise, and nuanced understanding of the Bosnian context, yet were completely ignored once the United States was engaged militarily. The irony of this, they point out, is that in the beginning of the conflict, when they were listened to intently by the government, they were by their own admission completely naïve.

Conclusions: Humanitarian Information as Policy Lever

Holbrooke insists that there were no compelling US interests at stake in Bosnia beyond the "nightmare scenario" of the conflict spreading to Greece and Turkey and tearing NATO asunder, which most people regarded as highly unlikely. Rather, it was simply an urge to help people, a goal that ultimately required intense diplomatic maneuvering backed by military resolve.[109] Another view of the matter, taken by many analysts of the conflict, accuses the US and other Western governments of using the "humanitarian alibi" to mask their inaction in a deliberate attempt to avoid becoming involved in the conflict. David Rieff has accused the US and Western powers of using aid as a means of crisis containment, insisting these governments "chose to do *anything but* intervene. Instead they mounted one of the largest and most heroic humanitarian relief efforts in modern history . . . while pursuing decidedly unheroic diplomatic negotiations."[110]

The initial reluctance to intervene militarily cannot be disputed. However, at least on the part of the US government, on which this study has focused, there is also no evidence of the deliberate use of humanitarian aid for such obfuscation.[111] On the contrary, as internal reviews quoted here suggest, humanitarian action was used by US government officials working on Bosnia not as a fig leaf, but rather as the "thin edge of the wedge" to bring in the political muscle. US government officials working on Bosnia (whose numbers increased concomitantly with the humanitarian effort on the ground) increasingly advocated a stronger policy stance in Bosnia, and "used humanitarianism until policy could catch up with us."[112] Bosnia was perhaps the most striking example of how OFDA can use its relatively autonomous mandate within the US government to launch a proactive aid response that may later be leveraged for a political response.

Looked at more broadly, humanitarian assistance in Bosnia, as in Somalia, preceded military intervention when the exigencies of the political and military situation thwarted the humanitarian effort. In the Bosnia case, UNPROFOR was essentially part of the humanitarian intervention, charged with protecting and facilitating the humanitarian efforts. When this arrangement proved unworkable, bigger guns were finally brought in.

Gregory Kent said the humanitarian emphasis contributed to the prolongation of the war. By allowing Britain and other European powers to lead on Bosnia for the first three years of the conflict, he claims, the United States contributed to the longevity of the "ethnic template" of the war, which made intervention seem pointless and humanitarian aid the only appropriate response.[113] "Military escorts for humanitarian aid to stop besieged civilians dying from starvation and injuries from sniper and shellfire seemed, in this light, perfectly appropriate to the problem of Bosnia, setting up its people for years of sustained conflict and low-level slaughter and the eventual massacre at Srebrenica."[114]

There is some validity to the charge that humanitarian action without accompanying political action can be counterproductive. The concept behind the tragic experiment of the "safe areas" is essentially a humanitarian notion—providing safe haven and assistance for civilians fleeing a war is taken for granted. Yet the NGO information channeled up through the US donor body did not display this reasoning. Quite the reverse, at nearly every stage the message aid workers were sending was that something more than they were capable of doing needed to be done.

There is little doubt that the humanitarian organizations, and IRC in particular, played an important role in the evolution of US policy. From

the first IRC field reports that triggered the initial airlift to their prominent participation on Clinton's humanitarian assessment team, NGOs
were treated as expert advisors, and their opinions carried weight. The
information-gathering and -reporting role fed the policy machine and
moved it forward, even when all US actions remained in the realm of assistance. IRC and the other major US NGOs (who received the bulk of the
US assistance during the conflict) went into Bosnia "naively, with no political agenda," let alone an advocacy plan. It is interesting to consider what
might have been different vis-à-vis their policy influence had they been
pursuing a deliberate political strategy.

Finally, though the humanitarian effort in Bosnia had many
important successes to show for it, it also had deficiencies. One of these
was in the area of information. As the winter scare demonstrated, though
it may have been compelling, the NGO information was not always accurate or thorough. Surveying and other rigorous methods of assessing needs
and evaluating projects was done haphazardly, and only in part because
of security conditions. An internal OFDA/DART memo in 1993, not for
the first time, made reference to this fact: "No organization has consistently done market surveys of food prices in Bosnia over the past year
which would give us an early warning indicator of serious food insecurity
leading to widespread severe malnutrition or deaths from starvation."[115]
The lack of good hard data detracts from organizations' credibility and
leads to the continued and somewhat justified impression that NGOs are
prone to crying wolf.

Notes

1. US government (USAID/BHR/OFDA), World Bank, and UNHCR
reports.

2. Richard Holbrooke attributes the groupthink at the State Department, which framed the conflict as a boiling over of ethnic tensions (a
quagmire best avoided) rather than Serb aggression, to past analyses
such as Kaplan's *Balkan Ghosts* and even Rebecca West's classic *Black
Lamb and Grey Falcon* (Holbrooke, *To End a War* [New York: Random
House, 1998], 22).

3. In Jon Western's take on the Somalia case, he posits in a similar
vein that Somalia received US military attention before Yugoslavia, in
large part because of the "initial information and propaganda advan-
tages" of "liberal humanitarianists" in NGOs and their audiences in
government (Jon Western, "Sources of Humanitarian Intervention:
Beliefs, Information, and Advocacy in the U.S. Decisions on Somalia and

Bosnia," *International Security* 27, no. 1 [July/August 1999]).

4. "In June 1992, as the conflict intensified and extended to Bosnia and Herzegovina, UNPROFOR's mandate and strength were enlarged in order to ensure the security and functioning of the airport at Sarajevo, and the delivery of humanitarian assistance to that city and its environs. In September 1992, UNPROFOR's mandate was further enlarged to enable it to support efforts by the United Nations High Commissioner for Refugees to deliver humanitarian relief throughout Bosnia and Herzegovina, and to protect convoys of released civilian detainees if the International Committee of the Red Cross so requested" (UN Department of Public Information, "United Nations Peacekeeping: Former Yugoslavia—UNPROFOR" [August 31, 1996]).

5. William Shawcross, *Deliver Us from Evil* (New York: Simon & Schuster, 2000), 149.

6. United Nations, "Information Notes: United Nations Peacekeeping," DPI/1306/Rev.4, February 1995, 70.

7. The troops to enforce the sanctions regime along the border were not forthcoming, so it remained an unresourced mandate (Shawcross, *Deliver Us from Evil*, 149).

8. UN Security Council Resolution 770, August 13, 1992.

9. Mark Cutts, "The Humanitarian Operation in Bosnia, 1992–95: Dilemmas of Negotiating Humanitarian Access," Working Paper No. 8, New Issues in Refugee Research, Geneva, UNHCR, May 1999.

10. David Rieff, *Slaughterhouse: Bosnia and the Failure of the West* (New York: Simon & Schuster, 1996).

11. United Nations, "Information Notes: United Nations Peacekeeping," DPI/1306/Rev.4, February 1995, 81.

12. John Fawcett and Victor Tanner, "Fighting Ethnic Cleansing with Humanitarian Action? A Report to USAID's Office of Foreign Disaster Assistance (Part of the OFDA Former Yugoslavia Review 1991–1997)" (Unpublished draft, internal OFDA document, Washington, DC, 1999).

13. Kirsten Young, "UNHCR and ICRC in the Former Yugoslavia: Bosnia and Herzegovina," *International Review of the Red Cross* 843, September 30, 2001, 781–805, 783.

14. UNHCR was responsible for the delivery of 950,000 tons of food to various parts of Bosnia, by truck and air transport, including the largest and longest-running humanitarian airlift to Sarajevo between July 3, 1992, and January 9, 1996; coordinating the delivery of 160,000 tons of food and other aid supplies; and the medical evacuation of more than

1,100 war casualties. See ibid. and Cutts, "The Humanitarian Operation in Bosnia."

15. World Food Programme, "WFP Intervention in Bosnia Herzegovina '92–'97, An Internal Evaluation," http://www.ennonline.net/fex/05/ev24.html.

16. "WFP/UNHCR Joint Evaluation Mission: Emergency Food Assistance to Returnees, Refugees, Displaced Persons and Other War-Affected Populations in Bosnia and Herzegovina," Rome: WFP, Geneva: UNHCR (November 1997); Fawcett and Tanner, "Fighting Ethnic Cleansing with Humanitarian Action?"

17. Young, "UNHCR and ICRC in the Former Yugoslavia," 787.

18. Cutts, "The Humanitarian Operation in Bosnia," 4.

19. For example, as one report states, "UNHCR reports of appalling conditions in Bosnian Croat-run detention camps in the Mostar region in August 1993, which received heavy coverage in the international media, led to Western political pressure on the Croatian authorities in Zagreb, the main sponsors of the Bosnian Croats. This in turn resulted in the Bosnian Croats agreeing to grant the ICRC full access to the camps (which had until then been denied for almost six months), and to allow UNHCR to resettle the detainees to third countries" (Young, "UNHCR and ICRC in the Former Yugoslavia," 785).

20. Gregory Kent, "Humanitarian Agencies, Media, and the War against Bosnia: 'Neutrality' and Framing Moral Equalisation in a Genocidal War of Expansion," *Journal of Humanitarian Assistance*, (August 2003), http://www.jha.ac/articles/a141.pdf.

21. Quoted in ibid., 17.

22. Ibid., 18.

23. Fawcett and Tanner, "Fighting Ethnic Cleansing with Humanitarian Action?"

24. UNHCR/UNICEF/WHO, *Emergency Report: Displacement in Former Yugoslavia*, June 2, 1992.

25. Kent, "Humanitarian Agencies, Media, and the War against Bosnia," 12.

26. Young, "UNHCR and ICRC in the Former Yugoslavia," 785.

27. In fairness, the balancing act gave way to more assertive statements in the latter half of the conflict. In August 1993 when UNPROFOR said there was no siege of Sarajevo and that the Serb forces outside the city were merely deployed "in a tactically advantageous position around the city," UNHCR and ICRC, along with the rest of the humani-

tarian community, publicly refuted the statement. The previous month the High Commissioner Sadako Ogata had spoken out most forcefully, saying, "I condemn the actions of those who are blocking the delivery of food, medicine, fuel, water, power, gas, and other humanitarian assistance in a cowardly attempt to starve and kill innocent victims (Commander Barry Frewer speaking at UNPROFOR press briefing in Sarajevo, August 16, 1993); UN High Commissioner for Refugees Sadako Ogata remarks in Geneva, July 9, 1993; United Nations, "Final Report of the United Nations Commission of Experts Established Pursuant to Security Council Resolution 780 (1992): 'Annex VI—part 7/10 Chronology of the battle and siege of Sarajevo.'"

28. Young, "UNHCR and ICRC in the Former Yugoslavia," 788.

29. Fawcett and Tanner, "Fighting Ethnic Cleansing with Humanitarian Assistance?"

30. It also receives large infusions of additional relief funds for specific emergencies, and the Yugoslavia crisis resulted in an enormous financial influx to the organization. By August 1992, the USG alone had already contributed $9 million to UNHCR's operation in the country. All told, donors had given $152 million to UNHCR (figures cited in Fawcett and Tanner, "Fighting Ethnic Cleansing with Humanitarian Assistance?").

31. Holbrooke, *To End a War*, 48.

32. John Fawcett, interview with author, February 3, 2005.

33. Roy Williams, interview with John Fawcett and Victor Tanner, March 26, 1998 (author's notes).

34. Rieff, *Slaughterhouse*, 120.

35. OFDA cables beginning December 1992; John Fawcett and Victor Tanner, "Breaking the Siege by Water: Fred Cuny in Sarajevo" (unpublished document, 1999).

36. An OFDA cable dated August 23, 1993 reveals how OFDA by summer 1993 was pressuring UNHCR to do better monitoring, noting in a confidential cable that "probably no more than 20 percent of food aid to the GOBH-controlled portion of (Sarajevo) goes astray, but to date, no monitoring has been allowed in Serb-controlled areas." In a meeting with Tony Land, the UNHCR chief in Sarajevo, the OFDA cable notes he was defensive of UNHCR, pointing out the low levels of malnutrition as a result of UNHCR's deliveries, but acknowledged that UNHCR "owes it to the donors" to ensure aid is not wasted or misappropriated. According to a former IRC staff member, UNHCR HQ initially offered a contract to IRC to do food aid monitoring for UNHCR

in order to stem diversions, but the expatriate UNHCR representative responsible for the region was comfortable with the system as it was, accepting diversions as the cost of doing business and maintaining access. HQ did not overrule the field staffer, so the monitoring never happened. OFDA officials were very frustrated by that episode. (Interview with author, February 2005).

37. OFDA representative in Bosnia, interview with author; background materials for Fawcett and Tanner report. John Fawcett and Victor Tanner, "The Political Repercussions of Emergency Programs, A Review of USAID's Office of Foreign Disaster Assistance in the Former Yugoslavia (1991–1996)," a report to USAID/BHR/OFDA (Washington, DC: Checchi Consulting and Co., 2002).

38. Ibid., 46.

39. John Fawcett and Victor Tanner, "The Political Repercussions of Emergency Programs, A Review of USAID's Office of Foreign Disaster Assistance in the Former Yugoslavia (1991–1996)," a report to USAID/BHR/OFDA (Washington, DC: Checchi Consulting and Co., 2002), 24.

40. Ibid., 25.

41. Fawcett, interview with author.

42. Internal OFDA documents prepared by team members of the US Interagency Humanitarian Assessment (February/March 1993).

43. Fawcett and Tanner, "The Political Repercussions of Emergency Programs," 25.

44. Williams, interview with author.

45. Gerald Martone, interview with author, December 10, 2004.

46. Ibid.

47. Fawcett, interview with author.

48. Holbrooke, *To End a War*, 45–47.

49. Fawcett and Tanner, "The Political Repercussions of Emergency Programs," 26.

50. Ibid.

51. Notes from interview with senior OFDA official. Background materials for Fawcett and Tanner, "The Political Repercussions of Emergency Programs."

52. Fawcett and Tanner, "The Political Repercussions of Emergency Programs."

53. Ibid., 20.

54. Holbrooke, *To End a War*, 27.

55. IRC internal documents; US Department of State cable, April 14, 1992.

56. Fawcett and Tanner, "The Political Repercussions of Emergency Programs."

57. Interviews with senior OFDA staff; background materials for Fawcett and Tanner, "The Political Repercussions of Emergency Programs."

58. John Fawcett and Victor Tanner, "Birth of the Aid Juggernaut in Former Yugoslavia (1991–1992): Humanitarian Plot or Unintended Consequences?" OFDA "Former Yugoslavia Review" (1991–1997) (unpublished draft, Washington, DC, 1999).

59. In all, OFDA ended up funding three hundred separate grant agreements to approximately fifty NGOs from nine countries, for a total of $200 million. Of this, IRC received the largest share—$40 million in seventy grants, followed by Catholic Relief Services and Mercy Corps, which received twenty grants totaling over $20 million each (OFDA, Bosnia Situation Reports).

60. Fawcett, interview with author.

61. Fawcett and Tanner, "Birth of the Aid Juggernaut in Former Yugoslavia," 40.

62. OFDA, "Former Yugoslavia Review," draft, December 22, 1998, 25–26.

63. Fawcett and Tanner, "Birth of the Aid Juggernaut in Former Yugoslavia."

64. Senior OFDA official, interview with author; unpublished background documents, Fawcett and Tanner, "The Political Repercussions of Emergency Programs."

65. OFDA, "Former Yugoslavia Review" (1991–1997).

66. IRC staff member, interview with author.

67. Fawcett and Tanner, "The Political Repercussions of Emergency Programs," 71–72.

68. Internal OFDA document.

69. State Department cable, April 23, 1993.

70. OFDA, "Former Yugoslavia Review," 26.

71. See Kent, "Humanitarian Agencies, Media, and the War against Bosnia"; Warren P. Strobel, *Late-Breaking Foreign Policy: The News Media's Influence on Peace Operations* (Washington, DC: US Institute of

Peace, 1997); Western, "Sources of Humanitarian Intervention."

72. Britain's Cedric Thornberry was head of civil affairs for UNPRO-FOR. Quoted in Rieff, *Slaughterhouse*, 192.

73. OFDA, "Former Yugoslavia Review," 7.

74. Ibid.

75. Ibid.

76. United States Senate Resolution 330—Original Resolution Reported Relating to Authorization of Multilateral Action in Bosnia-Hercegovina (August 6, 1992).

77. "Additional personnel were devoted to the problem. More people meant that more information was needed. With the establishment of the Humanitarian Working Group chaired by State, the importance of humanitarian aid as a component of U.S. foreign policy to the former Yugoslavia increased" (Fawcett and Tanner, "Birth of the Aid Juggernaut in Former Yugoslavia").

78. Strobel also points at this juncture in the Bosnia conflict to argue that the Bush administration was not swayed by media-driven public pressure, and posits that the media's influence dissipates over time if the government does not take action despite the coverage (*Late-Breaking Foreign Policy*, 153).

79. Holbrooke, *To End a War*, 41.

80. United States Senate Resolution 330—Original Resolution Reported Relating to Authorization of Multilateral Action in Bosnia-Hercegovina, August 6, 1992; Resolution 11—Relative to Bosnia-Herzegovina, January 21, 1993.

81. E.g., the *New York Times* reported on the aid blockages and the humanitarian officials appeals "to Western governments, including the United States, to take decisive new steps to ensure that relief supplies get through" (John F. Burns, "Relief Director in Bosnia Calls for Tougher Action," *The New York Times*, February 15, 1993).

82. Cables: August 19, 1993; November 4, 1993; and December 14, 1993.

83. WFP quoted in OFDA cable, August 20, 1993.

84. "Breaking the Siege by Water: Fred Cuny in Sarajevo," in OFDA, "Former Yugoslavia Review."

85. Ibid.

86. USAID/OFDA, "Briefing Book DART-Zagreb," internal OFDA document, June 15, 1993.

87. Internal OFDA document, June 3, 1993.

88. Humanitarian Assessment Team, Sarajevo Report, internal OFDA document, 1993.

89. "Country-Wide Findings and Recommendations for B-H: Security and Access," Humanitarian Assessment Team, internal OFDA document, March 9, 1993.

90. Fawcett and Tanner, "Fighting Ethnic Cleansing with Humanitarian Action?" 23. Western, "Sources of Humanitarian Intervention," notes that "Central Intelligence Agency analysis estimate that as many as 250,000 Bosnian Muslims might die from starvation and exposure was leaked to the press even before it was briefed to the National Security Council (NSC)," 131.

91. Michael Gordon, "Winter May Kill 100,000 in Bosnia, the C.I.A. Warns," *The New York Times*, September 30, 1992.

92. Fawcett and Tanner, "Birth of the Aid Juggernaut in Former Yugoslavia," 49.

93. In Jonathan Mann, Ernest Drucker, Daniel Tarantola, and Mary Pat McCabe, *Medicine and Global Survival*, vol. I, no. 3, 1994.

94. Letter quoted in Western, "Sources of Humanitarian Intervention."

95. In his autobiography, Clinton says his decision not to endorse the Vance-Owen plan stemmed from his conclusion that European support for the plan, combined with the arms embargo, had "weakened Muslim resistance to the Serbs." He realized the airdrops would do nothing "to address the causes of the crisis" but saw this period as when his administration began to make progress toward that end (Bill Clinton, *My Life* [New York: Knopf, 2004], 511).

96. OFDA Sitrep No. 9, March 19, 1993.

97. OFDA internal memo.

98. "I have said since February of 1993—since February of 1993—constantly, for more than two and a half years now, that the United States should participate in implementing a peace agreement. We should not have ground troops on the ground, under the present U.N. mandate. We should not have ground troops on the ground in combat" (President Clinton's remarks at press conference, September 26, 1995, Clinton Presidential Library online archives, http://www.clintonfoundation.org/legacy/092695-presidential-statement-on-bosnia-negotiations.htm).

99. Clinton, *My Life*, 513.

100. Holbrooke, *To End a War*, 56.

101. Ibid., 52.

102. Strobel, *Late-Breaking Foreign Policy*, 155.

103. David T. Buckwalter, "Madeleine's War: Operation Allied Force," in *Case Studies in Policy Making and Implementation*, ed. David A. Williams, 6th ed. (Newport, RI: Naval War College, 2002).

104. NATO had already made its first (albeit limited) air strikes, at Holbrooke's urging, in November 1994, against the Serbs' airfield in Ubdina, a Serb-controlled area of Croatia, for the Serbs' violation of the no-fly zone. They were derisively referred to as "pinpricks" by the news media.

105. Buckwalter, "Madeleine's War," 96.

106. Holbrooke, *To End a War*, 70.

107. Interviews with NGO representatives.

108. OFDA Review.

109. Holbrooke, *To End a War*, 52.

110. Rieff, *Slaughterhouse*, 13.

111. One could argue, however, that the White House and State Department public statements highlighting humanitarian successes evidenced a desire to spin the US actions in the most favorable light.

112. Internal background documents for OFDA, "Former Yugoslavia Review."

113. Kent, "Humanitarian Agencies, Media, and the War against Bosnia."

114. Ibid.

115. "Countrywide recommendations," internal OFDA document.

CHAPTER FIVE

KOSOVO

The massive international aid response to the Kosovo crisis ranks among the most exhaustively studied and evaluated of all humanitarian endeavors.[1] The vast majority of these studies focus on the period beginning in winter–spring of 1999, just as the humanitarian community fled the region in advance of the NATO air strikes in March 1999, followed by floods of refugees, in numbers that were much greater than anticipated. Most of the humanitarian evaluations examine agency performance and coordination in meeting the needs of the refugees in Macedonia and Albania, and in assisting with the return and reintegration three months later under a NATO military presence. During this period Kosovo was awash with NGO projects and donor money (a per capita rate of 526 aid dollars per annum[2]—one of the highest ever[3]), and many of the problems had to do with NGO overpopulation and duplication of efforts. This chapter does not retrace this well-trod ground but focuses rather on the two years prior to the refugee crisis and the run-up to international intervention in the conflict, led this time by an assertive and proactive US policy. Only a small handful of NGOs were operating in Kosovo during these years, when there were few if any other sources of information to Western governments, and through their ground presence and local contacts they again provided the information basis on which policy decisions were made, for good or ill.

Introduction: An Altered Field

The crisis in Kosovo brought NGOs back to the Balkans at the end of the decade in a fairly changed operational environment. As described in chapter 1, the Rwandan refugee crisis in Goma 1994–6 had crystallized the critiques that had been swirling around the assistance community, and touched off a collective crisis of conscience among the major humanitarian actors. NGOs now thought deeper and differently about their roles and responsibilities in political contexts, had "professionalized" their ranks and set common standards for performance, and were more actively coordinating and communicating with their fellow organizations both in the field and through headquarters-based consortia like InterAction in the United States and ICVA and SCHR in Europe. The ICRC Code of Conduct had been widely adopted, at least in principle, and NGOs now adhered to or were at least aware of a set of norms for provision of aid in emergencies. Politically, there was an attempt to become savvier and to take into account the bigger picture when planning relief interventions, even to use the aid presence as a catalyst for peace building. At this time the major NGOs, including the heretofore pragmatic and technically oriented US-based ones, began establishing "policy and advocacy" departments in their organizations, cultivating political expertise to supplement their programming knowledge base. While the Wilsonian-Dunantist differences remained regarding relations with government, at this point the two traditions were getting closer to using the same language. US NGOs no longer viewed the information-gathering role for the home government as innocuously as did IRC during the early years of the Bosnia conflict. Still, the informal information pipeline was still very much in effect in Kosovo, and there were remnants of the team spirit between OFDA and its favored NGO partners.

For their part, government donor agencies had changed as well. USAID, Britain's DFID, ECHO, and others had become much more closely involved in project design, a trend that continues today, and had instituted stricter guidelines to their grantees for showing measurable results.[4] Donors seldom rubber-stamped NGOs' proposed projects anymore. A project proposal now went through many more iterations between the donor and the potential grantee, often in the field, before the donor was satisfied that it met their requirements and reflected their priorities. Additionally, new actors had cropped up in the field as significant players. These included the military, which after northern Iraq, Somalia, and Bosnia had reached a high point of crossing over into humanitarian activities, and private-sector firms, just beginning to get their feet wet.[5]

And finally, for most of the decade the United Nations had been struggling to reform its humanitarian action within its system of aid agencies. A widely perceived crisis in coordination among the UN humanitarian agencies had led to a series of resolutions in the General Assembly, most significantly resolution 46/182 of December 1991 and 48/57 of December 1993, which created the Department of Humanitarian Affairs (later the Office for the Coordination of Humanitarian Affairs, or OCHA), the Consolidated Appeals Process (CAP), the Central Emergency Revolving Fund (CERF) mechanism, and the position of Emergency Relief Coordinator with the status of undersecretary-general. It was also during this period that the United Nations established an executive committee of sorts among the humanitarian agencies known as the IASC (Inter-Agency Standing Committee), which for the first time included the NGO community in a formal, institutionalized manner as participants in the coordination process.[6] Although progress was (and remains) halting, these new structures helped to bring "a degree of manageability to what had become a crowded and complex system for the provision of humanitarian relief, characterized by counter-productive inter-action between actors leading to inefficiencies, gaps, and duplication of efforts."[7] In adopting these measures the UN humanitarian actors had acknowledged the importance of NGOs in humanitarian response, and the reality that the United Nations was not the sole or even the primary international actor in humanitarian assistance, though it endeavored to maintain a central coordinating role.

On the other hand, certain things had not changed. The stampede of international agencies into emergency settings, for instance, which can send local rents and salaries soaring when hundreds of them descend on a small area, was repeated in Kosovo (and several times since). Despite efforts to diversify their funding bases and expand into new private partnerships, the US NGOs had not become any less dependent on public funding at the end of the 1990s. In fact, with the rise of emergencies and subsequent large supplemental allocations through OFDA, many NGOs' budgets were showing higher public-private ratios than before.[8] Kosovo's "humanitarian circus,"[9] as David Rieff has called it, showed that some familiar problems with the aid enterprise persisted, and were magnified by the enormity of the response. Any message that the NGOs as a community would have wished to send to governments in the interests of humanitarian concerns was precluded by their competition, the excessive flag-flying of their donors, and the closeness with which the NGOs associated their programming with the political agendas of their home governments. The circus Rieff describes took place after the refugee exodus into Macedonia and Albania and their subsequent return. In the run-up to the crisis that this chapter focuses on, the field was smaller. One finds that the NGOs provided their information to the donor partners with more circumspection, and with more sophisticated linkages to advocacy efforts in their headquarters, but the information was confused, incomplete, and without an advisory objective. Like in

Somalia, a humanitarian impetus was the trigger for government action, but the action was inappropriate for the crisis, and not what the humanitarian actors would have hoped for.

The Last Tinder Box in the Balkans: The Kosovo Conflict in Brief

The province of Kosovo had been disputed territory for centuries. Part of historical Serbia, Kosovo held an important place in Serbian nationalist identity since the fateful battle against the Turks in 1389, when the kingdom of Serbia fell to five hundred years of Ottoman domination. It was in Kosovo, on the site and anniversary of that historic battle, that Milosevic in 1989 made his speech appealing to Serbian unity that many say touched off the Serb nationalist movement in Bosnia.[10] Nonetheless, in 1998 it was home to approximately 2 million ethnic Albanians and fewer than two hundred thousand Serbs. Concerned over secessionist sentiment among the majority Albanian population, Serbian President Slobodan Milosevic abrogated the province's autonomous status in 1989 and Belgrade assumed direct control over Kosovo's governance. A great many Albanians in government and public-sector positions were forced out or left in protest, and were replaced by Serbs. A parallel system quickly emerged, where Belgrade ran the official government structures and the Albanians made use of private professionals, an underground Albanian school system, and networks of health and social services provided by an indigenous NGO called the Mother Theresa Society (MTS). The Albanian underground "government," led by Ibrahim Rugova and his LDK party, was so well organized that it was able to extract taxes, in the form of a levy on the remittances of Albanians who worked outside the country.[11]

For nearly ten years the situation in Kosovo was tense but mostly peaceful. The mission of the Organization for Security and Cooperation in Europe (OSCE) that had been monitoring the situation in Kosovo in 1992 was "disinvited" by the Serbs the following year, and as a result no international body had been undertaking human rights monitoring or other international information-gathering/reporting since 1993. After the status of Kosovo was left off the agenda at Dayton, frustrated militant elements of the political underground quietly began to grow in membership and mobilize. In 1997, state collapse and ensuing chaos in neighboring Albania provided a large and readily available supply of arms and munitions, and sporadic episodes of violence occurred between the guerrillas known as the Kosovo Liberation Army (KLA)[12] and Serb police (paramilitary forces). KLA attacks on police were followed by violent police actions against towns and villages suspected of harboring the KLA. In turn, the KLA rapidly surged in membership, assisted by Kosovo's population and unemployment rates—the highest in the region.[13]

Despite the fact that most Americans were unfamiliar with Kosovo, it was already on the radar screens of many officials in the US government, as well as in European governments, and elicited a much quicker international reaction than in the previous cases described. In February–March 1998 the crackdown of Serb police forces resulted in the first massacres of men, women, and children in remote Kosovo villages, and raised the concern of the US and European governments. NATO, backed up by UN resolutions, issued a series of condemnations and warnings to Belgrade that year, culminating in an ultimatum in September to find a peaceful solution and withdraw the growing Serb forces from the province, or face NATO military reprisals. Richard Holbrooke, the US negotiator who brought about the Dayton Agreement, was again the lead diplomat in brokering a deal with Milosevic in October to achieve the withdrawal of Serb forces. Two months later OSCE monitors were on the ground to verify Serb compliance with the October agreement. In February 1999, after seeming compliance and then noncompliance by the Serbs, and additional episodes of violence, the United States engineered the Rambouillet Accords to bring the conflict to a peaceful resolution. NATO forces began air strikes as the warned result of Serbs' flouting of the Rambouillet accords.

By May/June 1998 the policy momentum in Washington was well under way. The NSC was discussing the use of air strikes against the Serbs (for which NATO had already begun planning the month prior[14]) and Holbrooke had begun a new diplomatic initiative to get an agreement between Belgrade and the Kosovars. Therefore the beginning of assertive US engagement, which culminated in NATO's military intervention, could be said to begin at the point that Holbrooke engineered the October agreement. Prior to October, a still small but growing number of humanitarian NGOs constituted the main international presence in Kosovo. The OSCE Kosovo Monitoring Mission did not become operational until December 1998, as a result of the October agreement, and there was only a sparse presence of human rights organizations on the ground. The humanitarian NGOs' feeding of information through the human rights organizations and directly to the US government through the donor relationship helped raise the alarm that set the Kosovo diplomatic initiative in motion.

Before the Eruption: The International Presence in Kosovo

In the years before the violence began brewing, only a few international NGOs were operating in Kosovo, most of them US-based. Catholic Relief Services (CRS) got on the ground in 1994 running relief item distributions and education programs. Doctors of the World (DOW)—the US affiliate of Médecins du Monde—had been running health projects in both the public and Albanian parallel system since 1992, and established a long-term mission presence in 1994. Mercy Corps International became involved in Kosovo in 1996, working closely with the local Mother Teresa Society in health and nutrition projects. MSF Belgium had a team of volunteers working on health care and clean water projects in Kosovo since 1993. A British NGO, Children's Aid Direct, also had a sporadic programming presence during the period.[15]

The NGO footprint in Kosovo in the mid-1990s, though small, was larger than that of the United Nations. Because Kosovo was a part of sovereign Serbia, and a point of particular political sensitivity with Belgrade, the United Nations could not deploy in Kosovo to the extent it may have wanted, given the relative poverty and need in the area. UNHCR was on the ground to oversee a group of ten thousand Serb refugees from the Krajina region of Croatia, who had not been resettled and reportedly were directed to the Kosovo region against their will by Belgrade. Since much larger numbers of Serb refugees were being housed elsewhere in Serbia, UNHCR's presence in Kosovo before the refugee crisis was small, and they did not play a strong coordinating role for the NGOs.[16] UNICEF had a staff person based in Kosovo as well, as part of a FRY-wide public health assistance program.

Throughout the evolving and early crisis period, this small group of international NGOs led the international humanitarian response. DOW in particular became important as the touchstone of the US government humanitarian office, OFDA, which relied on DOW staff for information, accommodations, and launching the first relief response to the violence. DOW became involved in Kosovo at the initiative of one of its physician board members, Alan Ross, who was also a scholar of the region and took a personal interest in Kosovo. Mercy Corps' CEO, like Ross and other key NGO personnel involved in Kosovo, had the sense that the Serb-Albanian dispute in that region was a piece of "major unfinished business coming out of Dayton."[17] And while there was no humanitarian crisis as yet, there was certainly need enough to keep a handful of NGOs in assistance projects.

The poorest and most underdeveloped Balkan province for decades, Kosovo's population was now especially vulnerable due to the breakdown in public services. Although no major humanitarian emergency was yet apparent, maternal mortality was high and TB rates were soaring as patients fell through the cracks of an underresourced public health system.[18] Other public health crises loomed as Albanian parents feared having their children vaccinated by Serb-run immunization programs, suspecting an attempted genocide, such was the level of mistrust and rumor mongering that pervaded the public discourse. The NGOs, through partnerships with MTS, were providing public health and nutritional supports to the Albanians who would not or could not access the official government system. Food aid, which was provided to the poorest families, reflected the resources available to donors and aid agencies more than the objective needs of the population at large. Because international economic sanctions were still in force against Serbia, only "emergency" aid funding was allowed to flow to Kosovo. Hence for these projects the NGOs were receiving the majority of their grant funding through OFDA (the emergency wing of USAID), and secondarily, the European Community Humanitarian Office (ECHO). At times this arrangement led to awkward convolutions of project proposals as NGOs took pains to spin their public health infrastructure inputs and other more development-oriented programming as "emergency response." At the same time, OFDA's engagement in the region through its NGO implementers smacked of both a preparedness measure and a preemptive humanitarian presence.

The latter half of the 1990s had seen NGOs embrace the spirit of new humanitarianism, a rights-based approach to aid, and the idea that NGOs had a responsibility to be politically astute—if not actively in pursuit of peace-building objectives—in their programming. The NGOs that had established a presence in Kosovo shared the sense that a crisis was simmering under the surface and could erupt into a Bosnia-type conflict. Some of them, such as Mercy Corps, framed the problem as Serb repression of Albanians, and worked exclusively with MTS and its partners. Others, like DOW and CRS (and later IRC when it started working in Kosovo in 1997), worked with both the Serb and Albanian communities and attempted to use their projects as a forum to bring the two sides together (for instance, physician training and public health outreach efforts involving both Serb and Albanian doctors) but were often frustrated in their efforts. Despite the raised political consciousness these NGOs tried to bring to bear on pre-crisis Kosovo, ultimately their ground-level information networks left them feeling confused at the time and somewhat manipulated in retrospect.[19]

For the most part, the international NGOs in Kosovo had only vague awareness of the KLA and its activities by 1997. Accustomed to working with the social sector of the popular and well-organized pacifist movement LDK, many echoed their Albanian contacts' doubts as to whether the KLA even existed. Even as the first KLA attacks began, many suspected the Serbs had invented the group to justify brutal tactics and further subjugation of the Albanian Kosovar population. Those who knew the KLA to be real still felt it was more a red herring used by the Serbs than a serious political or military force. In a region where strong family and social networks made it seem that everyone knew everyone, it was hard for Kosovars and by extension the international NGOs they worked with and for to imagine a group with whom no one they were acquainted belonged. Awareness began to grow by early 1998 as KLA membership had swelled to several thousand, albeit in decentralized and fragmented cells.

OFDA and the NGO Information Channel in Kosovo

OFDA had maintained its DART structure in the US embassy in Belgrade and had begun funding activities in Kosovo while the war in Bosnia was still raging. The first congressional earmark for aid to the former Yugoslavia was made in October 1992 for $20 million; of this, $5 million was designated for Kosovo. OFDA granted this money for projects run by CRS and Mercy Corps.[20] Kosovo was given $5 million again in 1993 and 1994, as DOW was becoming operational and beginning to receive a share of the money for its health-care projects. In 1995 OFDA expenditures in the former Yugoslavia rose to $40 million, and the Kosovo programs' share grew to nearly $7 million, with the same three agencies as primary grantees.

At the end of 1997 most of the humanitarian relief projects in Bosnia had given way to rehabilitation and repatriation/reintegration of returning refugees and displaced persons. The DART in Belgrade was overseeing a $25 million Emergency Shelter Repair Program to rebuild housing in war-damaged areas, and funding relief efforts in pockets of need around the former Yugoslavia. Chief among these was Kosovo, where Serb refugees remained housed in collective centers and where NGOs had identified upwards of fifty thousand "extremely vulnerable families" among the ethnic Albanian population.[21] The frequency of OFDA/DART's reporting to Washington had declined from one or more sitreps per week at the height of the Bosnia conflict to one every several months. In the sitreps for July and December 1997, the passages that stand out for the urgency of their tone have to do with Kosovo. In these reports the DART warns that decreasing donor assistance for ex-Yugoslavia may spell future trouble for

Kosovo in particular: "Significant needs remain, particularly for Krajina refugees housed in collective centers (CCs) and among ethnic Albanians in Kosovo. In a time of decreasing donor assistance, overall conditions in Kosovo may worsen with the return of ethnic Albanians to Kosovo from Western Europe."[22]

Although DOW was a new and untested partner of OFDA when it first began programming in Kosovo, by 1997 it had become a primary point of contact for OFDA/DART personnel, similar to the role played by IRC in the early years of the Bosnia crisis. Over the next year, along with frequent phone and fax communication with the NGO field office, USAID/OFDA teams made several assessment visits to Kosovo (under fairly heavy security detail), each time staying at the DOW house—the only place they were cleared to spend the night.[23] These visits allowed for hours of informal discussions in which DOW staff shared what they knew of the escalating situation on the ground from their local staff and other contacts, often fielding questions well outside the realm of aid operations, such as "How many [KLA fighters] do they think are out there?" DOW and the other NGOs were also invited up to Belgrade for strategic planning meetings with USAID and State Department regional personnel.

A Quicker Trigger: US and International Policy Reaction on Kosovo

The United States did not lead the military intervention in Somalia until after nearly two years of conflict and hundreds of thousands of deaths, and the emergency in Bosnia went on for three and a half years before NATO boots were on the ground. The Kosovo conflict received much quicker attention and action. Already engaged in the Balkans, and united in the perception of Serbian culpability, the international community was long on the alert for possible problems in Kosovo. This included the "preventive deployment" of a contingent of US Marines in Macedonia under the UNPROFOR mandate quietly installed in 1993.[24] Unlike in Bosnia, the United States did not hang back to let Europe lead Western policy towards Kosovo. Chastened by the experience in Bosnia, and uncomfortable with dealing with Milosevic while his role in that conflict went essentially unpunished, the United States and its NATO allies were arguably much more ready for a fight this time around.[25]

Western European governments had the immediate concern of the prospect of refugees flooding across their borders, particularly Germany, which already had a large number of Kosovar economic migrants. And, as ever, there existed the looming, worst-case-scenario threat of a war in

Kosovo expanding to Macedonia and bringing in Greece and Turkey, thus imperiling NATO. From the beginning of the Serb crackdown, US Secretary of State Madeleine Albright was a strong voice calling for assertive US involvement. It was during one of the many tense exchanges over Kosovo with Joint Chiefs Chairman Colin Powell that Albright made her famous remark, "What's the point of having this superb military you're always talking about if we can't use it?"[26] Last but not least, Albanian Kosovars also had strong advocates in the US Congress, including Senator Bob Dole, who held a personal interest in the Balkans predating his political career. Dole had traveled to the region a few times, including in 1990 when he was an eyewitness to the Serb authorities' violent suppression of Albanian protestors in Kosovo's capital, Pristina. Dole spearheaded an informal contact group on Kosovo that included other senators and House members with sizeable Albanian American constituencies.[27]

For its part, NATO, now under command of General Wesley Clark of Holbrooke's negotiating team for the Dayton Accords,[28] was proactive and determined to play a big role. NATO issued its first statement in March and by July had conducted air exercises and made contingency plans for a series of scenarios, ranging from an enforcement of a peace agreement to "forced entry subjugating all of the FRY."[29]

As a result, the wheels of policy and military planning seemed to move much faster than in the prior cases, and the time between the initial outbreak of fighting and the US-led military action was just a little over a year. Throughout that year the humanitarian presence grew from only a few NGOs to a sizeable operation running aid convoys and mobile clinics out to affected areas. A large part of the information on ground-level developments came from those involved in the humanitarian effort, who signaled not only outbreaks of fighting and displacements of villagers, but also increasingly the security risks and obstructed access they themselves began to face as their operation grew.

The Villages Are Burning:
Urgent Messages and Uncertain Needs

The scattered violence that began occurring in parts of Kosovo in 1998 was and remained fairly low-level by most measures of armed conflict.[30] The killings were nonetheless horrific, and inspired heightened fears and ethnic polarization throughout the region. In late February, after a series of KLA attacks on police outposts, the Serbian police raided villages in Drenica that were suspected strongholds of KLA fighters. The raids were designed not only to rout the enemy but also to terrify would-be supporters, with homes burned and the children and other family members of suspected militants slaughtered wholesale by police forces.

Many of the NGO personnel who were working on or in Kosovo during this period confess to being caught off-guard by the progression of events. Although, as one senior staff member said, "All of us were aware of the Albanian diaspora funneling money and arms to Kosovo,"[31] the NGOs nevertheless were as surprised as any outside observer by the rapidity of the KLA's rise and the ferocity of the Serbs' campaign against them. The Drenica massacres of February–March 1998 occurred when many Albanians were telling their international NGO contacts and employers that the KLA was a Serb pretext for violent suppression of the majority Albanian population in Kosovo. An NGO worker who attended the funeral for the victims was somewhat stunned, as were many of the Kosovars in the crowd, when uniformed KLA soldiers appeared and made a speech about their impending liberation of Kosovo.[32]

The massacres were followed by mass protests in Kosovo's capital Pristina, which were put down by police using tear gas and water cannons. Throughout 1998, fighting and raids on villages caused displacement of thousands of Albanians, some of whom took refuge with host families, while others hid out in forests. Those who fled their still intact houses would sometimes sleep in the open air at night to be safe from nighttime raids and return to the village during the day to keep watch over their property.

Spring and Summer 1998

During the first few months of the relief operations, the NGOs were not able to determine definitive numbers of the displaced population (which changed on an almost daily basis as more villages were affected and others returned to their homes or were absorbed by host families), and they had an even fuzzier picture of needs. Many of the towns and villages in question were very remote, and as the fighting and Serb police presence made access difficult, NGO personnel could not get out to visit each one to make assessments. They relied on MTS, who had the largest web of contacts and workers throughout the region, and their own local staff members' contacts, to advise them on which villages had been affected, and reported what they heard to the DART personnel in Zagreb and at times directly to Washington in telephone calls. The small group of NGOs that had been distributing food parcels and other relief items to targeted needy households before the Serb crackdown decided to speed up the pipeline from their suppliers in order to run aid convoys out to the affected villages. Through their communications with the primary donor, USAID/OFDA, the organizations received sufficient indications that US funding for these emergency deliveries would be forthcoming. At first these convoys consisted of just DOW and Mercy Corps; a few weeks later CRS joined. The convoys went out two to three times per week to whichever villages MTS had advised needed help and where the roads were passable. On at least one of these early convoys, the NGOs were joined by television cameras as the media picked up on the developing crisis in Kosovo. Interviews with NGO staff involved in the convoys reveal differing perspectives on the urgency. Some attest that on arrival they would find the humanitarian needs were far less than thought, and the convoys were often a pointless sideshow. Others point out that in hindsight the plight of the Kosovars was worse than anyone had known at the time. Many people were terrorized into silence—afraid to tell of Serb actions in their community for fear their families would be next. Along with the Serb police forces, "Arkan's Tigers," the infamous paramilitary group from the Bosnian war, were reportedly moving about Kosovo committing similar atrocities. Of course, the NGOs were in no position to provide protection to the victims of violence. The convoys were an example of the humanitarian organizations, again the face of the international community in country, directing the only means at their disposal (food and soap and plastic sheeting) toward a problem rooted in politics and violence.

A few months later these convoys were joined by the UN agencies UNHCR and the World Food Programme. Though in the beginning they did not have aid supplies or many staff of their own in Kosovo, WFP provided extra trucks to transport NGO aid supplies, and UNHCR provided vehicles for convoy "escorts." Thus the UN imprimatur was given to the operation, and the low-level assistance program in Kosovo transformed into a wartime emergency humanitarian relief convoy operation similar to that in Bosnia, though on a much smaller scale.

The deliveries were haphazard and often constrained, as the Serbs were tightening their restrictions on NGO movements inside Kosovo (and preventing others from getting visas to come in) and often turning back vehicles from checkpoints. More than once NGO personnel arrived at their warehouses to load up for a convoy, only to find they had been padlocked. The convoy would then be delayed until they could negotiate with Serb authorities for access to their own goods. The humanitarian obstruction as reported by NGOs, with its echoes of

Bosnia, became a particular point of concern to Western policymakers. In May, NATO's North Atlantic Council of Foreign Ministers issued a statement that emphasized this issue in the first paragraph: "It is particularly worrying that the recent resurgence of violence has been accompanied by the creation of obstacles denying access by international observers and humanitarian organizations to the affected areas in Kosovo."[33]

A few other NGOs were able to set up operations inside Kosovo during the spring period, but their total numbers remained small. Of all the international NGOs working in Kosovo, only DOW had formally registered with the Belgrade government and had letters of authorization from the Ministry of Health to conduct projects in Kosovo, which helped them move around somewhat more freely in Kosovo and have visas granted quicker than the others could.[34] However, DOW had only a few dozen staff members, and like the other NGOs, relied on MTS and local groups to do the bulk of the village-level deliveries, some of which were so far out of the way that parcels were delivered on donkey-back.

Back in Washington, the humanitarian information from NGOs reached open ears in the US government, including those at a higher staff level than in previous cases. H. Roy Williams, the vice president in charge of programming of IRC during the Bosnia crisis, was now head of OFDA. Another such crossover was Julia Taft, formerly the president of the US NGO consortium InterAction, and now installed as head of the humanitarian wing of the State Department, the Bureau of Refugees, Population, and Migration (PRM). (Even though PRM is mandated to provide most of its funding to international organizations like UNHCR and the Red Cross, Taft came to the position with a strong bias toward NGOs and pushed the office to become more involved with them.[35]) With Williams and Taft heading up the two primary channels for US humanitarian action and funding, there were voices higher up that were not simply repeating and utilizing NGO information from the field, but were actively pushing for greater NGO involvement in interagency discussions and joint planning meetings within the broader US government. Largely at Taft's initiative, State/PRM, OFDA, and the NGO consortium Interaction began cosponsoring monthly joint planning meetings on the Kosovo situation. The forum, which brought NGOs together with State Department and OFDA staff as well as representatives from the military and other parts of government, continues today.

Also in Washington, DC, humanitarian NGOs were holding weekly roundtable meetings with human rights organizations to share information and discuss complementarity in field programming—meetings that were duplicated, on a less frequent basis, in New York. The operational humanitarian NGOs were cautious about going public with their evidence of rights abuses, and preferred to transfer it to the human rights NGOs. The human rights NGOs for their part had few monitors of their own in the field, and so relied on the humanitarians not only for the information but also for their help with logistical matters such as visas, accommodations, and transportation. Human rights workers were increasingly using the humanitarian frame and citing humanitarian obstruction in their advocacy, as in this statement by Human Rights Watch:

> Human Rights Watch is dismayed that despite the mounting evidence of widespread humanitarian law violations in the region, the international community has repeatedly failed to follow through on warnings to Yugoslav President Slobodan Milosevic. . . . Humanitarian aid organizations, journalists, and human rights researchers have been denied access to the region between Pec and Dakovica. Although information on human rights and international humanitarian law violations therefore remains incomplete, there is substantial and credible evidence that serious violations of humanitarian law are taking place.[36]

Less than two months after the Drenica massacres, as the humanitarian response to the emergency was gearing up in country, Madeleine Albright called a National Security Council principals' meeting on the subject. The US Special Envoy Robert Gelbard proposed that the United States threaten Milosevic with NATO air strikes, which the alliance had been planning since the previous month. Those present did not agree to go forward since there was no Plan B for NATO if the air strikes didn't work, but the option was clearly on the table.[37] The six-nation Contact Group (United States, Russia, Britain, France, Germany, and Italy) that the United States had convened to coordinate international policy during the Bosnian war also took a role in the Kosovo crisis. The group met in April 1998 and issued a strong statement that, while explicitly not endorsing an independent Kosovo, called on Belgrade to "cease repression" of Kosovars, readmit OSCE monitors into Kosovo, and take immediate action toward a negotiated solution.[38]

State Department briefings, as they had before in Bosnia, tended to underscore the humanitarian effort that the United States was supporting.[39] Madeleine Albright also emphasized the aid dimension in her public statements, and she began explicitly describing US humanitarian assistance as a foreign policy tool—one of "three tracks" (diplomatic, humanitarian, and military) that the United States was pursuing to resolve the Kosovo crisis.[40]

Ambassadors Richard Holbrooke and Chris Hill (ambassador to Macedonia) from the Dayton negotiations were charged with the diplomatic initiative to settle the conflict. Holbrooke managed to arrange a meeting with Milosevic and LDK leader Ibrahim Rugova, who was also granted a meeting with President Clinton the following month,[41] but realizing that power, credibility, and loyalties were shifting to the KLA in Kosovo, Holbrooke and Hill began talks directly with the insurgents in Geneva, Switzerland, in late June.

On the diplomatic front, things at first seemed to be progressing. Over the summer, Milosevic agreed to sit down in meetings with Holbrooke and later with Russian President Boris Yeltsin, where he was warned of the seriousness with which increasing violence in Kosovo would be handled. For a short time afterward the Serbian leader displayed more willingness to negotiate with Kosovars and eased off on the police crackdown in the region. During the abatement, however, the KLA moved to lay claim to large swaths of territory within Kosovo, and the prospect of a KLA victory over the province began to emerge as a real possibility. In the face of the KLA gains the United States and NATO made clear in public statements that a rebel seizure of Kosovo was not what they had in mind,[42] and Belgrade again stepped up their offensive in the province. In August the tide of violence reached the humanitarian community, when three local humanitarian workers attached to MTS were killed while delivering NGO food parcels. In the following month an ICRC doctor was killed and others were injured when their vehicle struck a land mine.

Fall and Winter 1998: A New Winter Scare, Intensifying Humanitarian and Diplomatic Initiatives

The Serbs' "summer offensive," consisting of shelling villages and implementing raids with small armed patrols, forced an estimated three hundred thousand Kosovar Albanians from their homes. Somewhere in the neighborhood of fifty thousand were thought to be surviving in the open air, hiding in the forest with little or no shelter. Humanitarian workers, unable to access many of these IDPs or get an accurate fix on their numbers, sounded the alarm about the impending humanitarian crisis. "The prospect of tens of thousands of Kosovars starving or freezing during the coming winter, in the words of one pundit, 'concentrated the minds in Washington and elsewhere.'"[43] The winter scare can be seen as directly responsible for ratcheting up the anti-Milosevic rhetoric and moved the Contact Group to push through UN Security Council Resolution 1199 in late September, which demanded a ceasefire and action toward a negotiated settlement, upon which Richard Holbrooke based the "October Agreement" which he persuaded Milosevic to sign the following month:

> The Security Council,
>
> . . .
>
> *Deeply concerned* by the rapid deterioration of the humanitarian situation throughout Kosovo, alarmed at the impending humanitarian catastrophe as described in the report of the Secretary-General, and emphasizing the need to prevent this from happening,
>
> . . .
>
> 1. *Demands* that all parties, groups, and individuals immediately cease hostilities and maintain a ceasefire in Kosovo, Federal Republic of Yugoslavia, which would enhance the prospects for a meaningful dialogue between the authorities of the Federal Republic of Yugoslavia and the Kosovo Albanian leadership and reduce the risks of a humanitarian catastrophe;
>   . . .[44]

Also invoking the humanitarian warnings of the winter threat, the US secretary of state declared that "President Milosevic's flouting of UN resolutions and international norms has led Kosovo to the brink of a humanitarian catastrophe."[45] On the same day President Clinton released a statement saying, "With more than 250,000 Kosovars displaced from their homes and the cold weather coming, Milosevic must act immediately. . . . The resolution places responsibility squarely on President Milosevic to take the concrete steps necessary to prevent a major humanitarian disaster and restore peace in the region."[46] (Clinton's citing the figure of 250,000 IDPs may have been technically correct as the estimate went, but the vast majority of these displaced peopled were sheltered in other homes. His statement gives the impression that a quarter of a million people were exposed to the elements.)

The urgent humanitarian warnings throughout the run-up to the war, as it turns out, overstated the humanitarian assistance needs of the population. That winter, for instance, most of the IDPs who had been living in the open returned to their homes or found refuge with host families.[47] Many evaluations of the Kosovo response have noted the comparatively good condition (when compared with other emergencies) of the Kosovar beneficiaries. Thanks to extensive family and community networks, MTS services, and various coping mechanisms that the international community had only a limited picture of, the victims of displacement were better equipped to endure their ordeal than expected. Even after the bombing and the exodus across the Macedonian and Albanian borders, it was found that "the refugees were relatively better nourished, healthier and with better access to good resources (including remittances) than those in other emergencies."[48] When the NGO-run mobile health clinics supplied their epidemiological data to the World Health Organization in January 1999, the resulting morbidity report looked not unlike what you might find in a typical stable population at that time of year. The most common diagnosis (accounting for 35 percent of total consultations and 50 percent of diagnoses for children 0–5) was respiratory infection, including common colds.[49] In contrast, the major cause of morbidity and mortality among populations in severe emergencies tends to be diarrheal diseases (caused 70 percent of deaths among Kurdish refugees in northern Iraq and 90 percent of deaths among Rwandan refugees in Goma). Throughout the Kosovo conflict and refugee crisis, malnutrition levels remained low.[50]

The material aid, which even some NGO workers at the time believed was more than necessary, had to be delivered with little or no monitoring of end use, due to security risks. In most cases the convoys would drive out to an affected village where a local entity (typically MTS) would receive the supplies and assume responsibility for distributing them onward to the needy families. In such scenarios some of the aid, not surprisingly, was diverted, and ended up in KLA bunkers and Serb police stations alike.[51] Such diversions are obviously not unique to Kosovo, and it is very doubtful that it could have affected the course of the conflict, but it merely indicates the extent to which the humanitarians were flying blind.

Despite the growing security risk and access difficulties, the aid operations greatly expanded through the fall and winter of 1998.[52] Several other NGOs established offices in Kosovo during this period and began participating in the aid delivery efforts. The French parent organization of DOW, Médecins du Monde (MDM), had arrived, along with MSF France and other health-oriented relief organizations such as International Medical Corps (IMC). These NGOs began running mobile clinics with the purpose of accessing displaced or remote populations who had lost access to health care. CARE International established a mission presence in late 1998, and IRC significantly expanded its field presence and programming (its staff of three had since 1997 mainly engaged in assessments, and it now had over twenty expats, three field offices, a fleet of trucks, and two mobile clinics). Oxfam and Solidarites were among the organizations involved in water/sanitation projects. Many other organizations had arrived in the region and had staff waiting in Macedonia or Albania, but could not establish a mission presence in Kosovo because Serbs were creating long delays in issuing visas for NGO personnel and turning back vehicles and confiscating equipment at the borders. The food pipeline of the World Food Programme (WFP) had kicked in a few months after the agency's arrival in August, and convoys were running at the rate of three to four per day. UNHCR increased its expatriate staff from three to thirty-nine, opened three satellite offices, and in addition to escorting convoys now had a fleet of trucks and supplies of its own to contribute.

As the Serb forces grew increasingly obstructionist and security problems increased in the summer and fall of 1998, the NGOs highlighted the constraints to the humanitarian deliveries in their reports to the donors, as well as the heightening risks to NGO personnel and property. The roadblocks, confiscations, incidents of harassment, and other problems faced by the humanitarian workers were detailed in these reports. At one point, a fairly large amount of discussion and reporting was dedicated to the NGOs' reported "number-one security issue,"[53] which was the Belgrade government's refusal to grant them radio licenses, which they needed to communicate between vehicles and with their personnel in the field. NGO concerns over the risks and obstacles to the humanitarian delivery operations were communicated to the donor, and these in turn became the focus of the sitreps and other embassy communications from OFDA/DART to Washington. A review of the embassy cables containing the Kosovo sitreps shows—with greater transparency than in the Bosnia or Somalia cases—that individual NGO reports were often reproduced verbatim and compiled into the OFDA report, with minimal overlay from the DART officer responsible for preparing the sitrep. Agencies also prepared situation reports of their own for public awareness and advocacy purposes.[54]

The Holbrooke-Milosevic "October agreement," forged under repeated threats of NATO military action, called for a cease fire and for Belgrade to withdraw its forces from the region. It also established the

Kosovo Verification Mission (KVM)—a renewed operation by OSCE whose personnel were to be readmitted to Kosovo to monitor adherence to the terms of the agreement and UN Security Council Resolution 1199.[55] Though the KVM took some months to get up and running, by the end of December 1998, the international actors now possessed a new channel of information on political and military developments outside the NGO community.[56] (However, the slow deployment of monitors, and continued reliance on NGOs to report from certain areas and to signal new developments meant a fairly large degree of overlap between the two sources. OFDA communications to Washington relayed several pieces of information that cited KVM and NGOs as sources.)[57] The fragile truce lasted only until December, when the KLA killed six Serbian youths in a café in Pec, and the Serbs in response redeployed their forces in violation of the October agreement and the supporting Security Council Resolution 1203.

In Washington, planning around the Kosovo crisis had entered a new phase. From October 1998 up until the air strikes, the NSC and the State Department co-chaired an Executive Committee that met twice weekly for joint planning between the relevant political, military, and humanitarian actors in the US government, in order to provide consensus recommendations to the senior staff at the deputies level. Julia Taft of PRM chaired the humanitarian subgroup, which had heavy NGO involvement. At those meetings the NGOs would share the latest information on conditions and raise questions and concerns from their staff in the field. However, according to the authors of an internal review of US humanitarian action, the humanitarian group was excluded from some of the more "sensitive military discussions" and thus hindered from both inserting the humanitarian considerations to the military operations planning, and from developing adequate contingency plans.[58] As one report noted, "These arrangements [for including humanitarian actors] were not adequate. There was no humanitarian input into an initial UN resolution that cited the need for FRY registration of all NGOs who operated in Kosovo. . . . [Later,] daily deputies meetings eclipsed the EXCOM process and humanitarian representatives were no longer regular participants"[59]

Although during the run-up to the Kosovo campaign the NGOs were more formally involved at a higher level of US policy planning than ever before, their voices were already losing influence as the ultimate military outcome of the US policy grew imminent. With the military planning process now in full swing, the humanitarians were in essence already being pushed to the sidelines. (In fact, it was not until after the air strikes and the return of the refugees that humanitarians were given a permanent seat at the planning table with military actors in Washington. The Kosovo Coordination Council [KCC], created under the leadership of a senior civilian humanitarian official, was charged with leading the US humanitarian agenda, "including the military components of relief efforts. Had [such leadership] been incorporated early on into senior Administration deliberations," according to the internal USG review, "we might have seen superior contingency planning for, and later management of the refugee outflow."[60])

January–March 1999: Downward Spiral

From the beginning of the New Year the situation deteriorated rapidly. The Serb forces escalated their attacks, and on January 15 slaughtered forty-five Kosovar civilians in the town of Racak. The Racak massacre drew international attention and outrage and coalesced the resolve within the US government that it was time for a hard line against Belgrade that was backed up by a genuine military threat. From mid-February to mid-March Secretary of State Albright and Ambassador Holbrooke hosted negotiations between Serbs and KLA representatives in Rambouillet, and later Paris. The meetings concluded with the Serbs' refusal to sign the Rambouillet accords and increased escalation of violence in Kosovo. At this time there were a reported two hundred thousand IDPs inside Kosovo and a few thousand who had already fled across borders.

The OFDA sitreps in March detail the increasing incidents of humanitarian workers being targeted for harassment and violence.[61] Road checkpoints had increased, and convoys and assessment missions were more frequently denied access to their target areas. Serb police had taken to the intimidating practice of showing up at NGO offices and residences and demanding information on their activities and aid supplies. Vehicles were being stolen or vandalized, with windows broken and tires slashed. In one embassy cable, OFDA warns that increasing violence, risk to aid workers, and humanitarian obstruction were jeopardizing the humanitarian operations.

> IF THE SITUATION DETERIORATES SUBSTANTIALLY, THE SUPPLY ROUTES INTO KOSOVO COULD BE CUT OFF, SERIOUSLY THREATENING THE ABILITY OF THE INTERNATIONAL COMMUNITY TO MEET HUMANITARIAN NEEDS. SHOULD RELIEF WORKERS BECOME TARGETS IN THE CONFLICT, MUCH OF THE ASSISTANCE EFFORTS WOULD FALTER.[62]

During the latter half of March, NGOs increasingly drew down their staff in the face of increasing security risk, particularly after the departure of the OSCE mission.[63] By March 20 only the skeleton staffs of some ten to twelve NGOs and UNHCR, WFP, and ICRC continued to deliver relief supplies inside Kosovo.[64] On March 22, with NATO air strikes looking like a foregone conclusion, Holbrooke met with Milosevic in Belgrade in a last effort to persuade him to sign an interim peace plan. A day earlier an NGO director in Belgrade received a heads-up telephone call, with the USAID/OFDA warning him, "If Holbrooke leaves without a deal, you don't want to be there."[65] The following day humanitarian operations shut down, UNHCR escorted out the last of the aid workers who were leaving, and the remaining personnel from the UN and NGOs (now only four—Mercy Corps, International Medical Corps, MSF, and MDM) hunkered down in their residences. NATO's seventy-eight-day campaign of air strikes began on March 24.

In hindsight, some NGO staffers who were involved in Kosovo before the air strikes have expressed the feeling of having been "instrumentalized by all sides," Albanian, Serb, and the NATO coalition, and quite unhappy at the outcome. One former NGO worker who had seen the situation evolve said in the end he felt manipulated and helpless to prevent the air war, which was precipitous and made matters (from the humanitarian standpoint at least) much worse. The interviewee reflected, "The sad part is, after all that, Kosovo is now an ethnically pure country."

The Air Strikes and the Humanitarian Consequences of the "Humanitarian Intervention"

Operation Allied Force, NATO's first offensive war in Europe, was launched largely on humanitarian grounds. Secretary-General Javier Solana underscored the humanitarian rationale when he announced that the air operation was "directed towards disrupting the violent attacks being committed by the Yugoslav army and Special Police Forces and weakening their ability to cause further humanitarian catastrophe . . . We must stop the violence and bring an end to the humanitarian catastrophe now taking place in Kosovo."[66] President Clinton sounded the theme in his public statements as well, citing the ongoing humanitarian crisis along with the threat of war spreading in the region as the reason the US and NATO must act.[67] Unfortunately the tactics chosen—aerial bombardment exclusively—had the perverse effect of triggering a massive humanitarian crisis as over half a million Kosovars fled the country. NATO's own postmortem review of the air campaign concluded that ruling out ground forces allowed Milosevic to feel empowered to act in ways that created the crisis that followed. He had likely calculated that Clinton's and NATO's assurances that ground troops were not in the offing afforded his forces the opportunity to wreak havoc inside Kosovo in a last-ditch effort to rid the province of its Albanian population. With no Western troops on the ground and all but a few humanitarian workers evacuated in advance of the air strikes, the Albanians were left with neither protection nor assistance, and completely at the mercy of Serb forces. At the time NATO sought to spin the refugee crisis as evidence of Belgrade's ruthlessness and thus a justification for the air war to stop the violence.[68] However, its own analysis of events in a postmortem review of the Kosovo campaign later concluded:

> The military operation was undertaken with the expectation of a quick air victory, but resulted in a 78-day bombing campaign. Until Belgrade yielded in early June, Operation Allied Force had only a marginal effect on halting the violence against Kosovar Albanians, and Serb fielded forces survived NATO's air war largely intact. Moreover, on the eve of Milosevic's capitulation, U.S. and NATO decision makers faced the prospect of conducting a ground invasion for which they were unprepared.[69]

The focus on air power as the political preference, the report goes on to say, created a "disjoint" within the NATO planning process whereby the air operations were separated from the option of an air-land campaign. Once the air war began, "The absence of a credible joint force option ceded the initiative to Belgrade. Belgrade's decision to accelerate the ethnic cleansing was undertaken in recognition that NATO had virtually no ability to stop it by military means."[70]

The military's strategic miscalculation was matched by a serious humanitarian miscalculation. Though there had been warnings of possible huge refugee movements to the tune of hundreds of thousands,[71] UNHCR had treated this as an unlikely, worst-case scenario, and had made contingency preparations for fifty thousand at most.[72] The exodus of over three quarters of a million refugees[73] into Macedonia over a short time period created a huge strain on the relief actors, the local communities, and the host government. The NGOs were similarly caught short of updated contingency plans, and not one had adequate preparedness measures in place for an operation of that scale.

The humanitarian actors were scrambling to become operational and meet the needs of exhausted and traumatized refugees at the same time. The crowded humanitarian field of now hundreds of NGOs—including those who had evacuated, those who had been waiting in bordering countries, and those who began to arrive in greater and greater numbers—naturally exacerbated the confusion and coordination problems. In addition, national militaries were getting in on the act, deploying in host countries to run the humanitarian operations on behalf of their governments.

In another somewhat ironic twist, US public support for NATO's action increased dramatically after the start of the refugee emergency: "Following the refugee exodus, United States public support for the air war jumped to sixty-one percent (from only forty-three percent in February), and there were even fifty-two percent who supported ground troops should the strikes not work. Europeans were at least as enthusiastic for action as their United States counterparts."[74]

The operation was at risk of failure, however, and NATO was forced to change tack. At the April summit NATO allies agreed to employ all available options to prevail, including a ground invasion. General Clark then directed the updating of land-war plans, which called for 175,000 troops, of which 100,000 would be Americans.[75]

The Serbs finally relented under increasingly intense air bombardment and the growing threat of ground troops after all. On June 2 Milosevic accepted NATO's terms and stood down, and eight days later NATO announced the suspension of the air campaign. The UN Security Council passed Resolution 1244, which created a UN-led interim trusteeship government in Kosovo (UNMIK) under a NATO security umbrella, and left Kosovo's final status undecided for an indefinite period. Kosovars began returning in large numbers shortly after the air strikes ceased.

Epilogue: The Refugees Return, and the Circus Comes to Town

Kosovo has entered the annals of humanitarian response as the textbook case of the large and unwieldy international footprint. The aid organizations (UN agencies as well as NGOs) entered fierce competition over physical and programming space, staff, and donor funding that was staggeringly high relative to the humanitarian need. A bizarrely inflated subeconomy sprang up and flourished around the expatriate presence, as did, reportedly, the regional sex trade. Despite the good work of many organizations, the Kosovo experience left a lingering impression of unprofessional behavior, all the more disappointing as it came after the advances in professionalization and standardization among the main humanitarian providers. A review of the multiple Kosovo crisis evaluations notes that they share the general impression of a field lacking in professionalism, where the recently formalized codes of conduct and operational norms "were either unknown, neglected or denied in the field. Instead, a sort of 'institutional amateurism' ruled."[76]

The donor governments also received a great deal of criticism for adding to the fray, as they took up field-level presence in unprecedented numbers, inserting their own flags and logos to the plethora of humanitarian emblems, and competing for visibility. The "bilateralization" of humanitarian assistance was first recognized as a growing phenomenon in Kosovo, with donors earmarking greater and greater portions of their aid for specific implementers and projects for which they would receive credit, as opposed to pooling funds for multilateral aid efforts.[77]

Regarding civil-military relations between the NATO forces and the humanitarian organizations, opinions were mixed. Some reviews and interview respondents praised the relatively smooth cooperation and turnover of humanitarian responsibilities between the military and NGOs. Others emphasize the marginalization of the humanitarian community once the military was on the ground, and even in the few months leading up to the campaign. Despite the potential many NGOs saw in the joint planning meetings in Washington, they felt steamrolled when they were shut out of higher-level military meetings and when planners took a tour of the region in a mission that did not include the NGOs. As many had found in Somalia and in Bosnia, the NGOs who had been working in Kosovo for a long time and who at one time had been eagerly sought after for their information and opinions by military and political actors before the air strikes now found the military clearly taking over their bailiwick and not setting much store in their opinions.[78] Some of the Wilsonian NGOs may have begun to regret the government attention they had courted before the war. In the most controversial example, CARE Canada accepted a large grant from CIDA to field expatriate personnel (some ex-military and one in fact a serving military officer) to identify and recruit monitors for the OSCE mission who would provide intelligence on troop movements and other politico-military matters. The mission was kept quiet, but word got out early on in Pristina. In addition to the disapproval of many of its NGO colleagues, CARE had to deal with Serb reprisals, including the arrest and detention of three CARE staffers as spies.

But CARE was not the only organization whose members exhibited an uncomfortable closeness with their home government in the Kosovo response. A curious form of humanitarian-military cooperation occurred as NGOs, including national affiliates of the same federation, began to cluster themselves in sectors of Kosovo assigned to troop contingents from their home nation.[79] Neutrality in local politics was an issue of contention as well. DOW (MDM) had friction with Mercy Corps over DOW's policy of working with the Serbs, and giving some of their food to the Yugoslav Red Cross for distribution while Mercy Corps worked exclusively through MTS. MDM France thought MDM USA (DOW) was too cozy with Serb authorities, and both France and USA were opposed to DOW Greece seeming partial to the Serbs when it came in after the exodus of Albanians to help in the Serb-run hospitals.

Some Dunantist agencies like ICRC and MSF had adhered to the strict policies they set for themselves to protect their neutrality by not accepting any military support for their work in Kosovo. (However, one could argue that operating in the Kosovo theater post–NATO air strikes, and in the absence of a genuine humanitarian crisis, was tantamount to endorsing and supporting the NATO action.) It is somewhat surprising how little analysis and policy consideration the major Wilsonian agencies seem to have put into the question of drawing the line between military and humanitarian operations, viewing it mostly in practical terms as to how the military could help with logistics.

A Kosovo review study undertaken by the Humanitarianism and War Project at Tufts University outlined the debate between humanitarians on their appropriate role in engaging with the diplomatic and military initiatives. Along with those who insisted humanitarian actors should remain outside the political realm, it notes, there were many who felt equally strongly that aid organizations had a responsibility to inject the humanitarian dimension into the political discussion, and to proactively "approach military planners with information regarding the likely effects of military action on civilian populations."[80] This debate continues today, and with renewed intensity in light of the US-led occupation of Iraq.

Notes

1. In December 1999 ALNAP (the Active Learning Network for Accountability and Performance in Humanitarian Action) reported that a minimum of twenty-five separate evaluations of the Kosovo response were being conducted, commissioned, or undertaken by various government donor agencies or foreign offices, UN agencies, the Red Cross, NGO consortia, and independent think tanks. In addition, many of the individual humanitarian actors involved in the response did in-house reviews of their own performance in the response. Dozens of retrospec-

tive articles on Kosovo have been written, one noting that the surfeit of studies was "ironically propagating precisely the duplication of resources and lack of co-ordination that is a principal criticism of the original aid programme" (Toby Porter, "The Partiality of Humanitarian Engagement," *Journal of Humanitarian Assistance*, June 2000, www.jha.ac/articles/a057.htm).

2. James Dobbins, John G. McGinn, Keith Crane, Seth G. Jones, Rollie Lal, Andrew Rathmell, Rachel Swanger, and Anga Timilsina, *America's Role in Nation-Building: From Germany to Iraq* (Rand, 2003), http://www.rand.org/publications/MR/MR1753/.

3. Comparative data on per capita aid across crises can be found in the Dobbins report for Rand, as well as Barnett R. Rubin et al., *Building a New Afghanistan: The Value of Success, the Cost of Failure*, Center on International Cooperation, New York University, in cooperation with CARE International, March 2004.

4. In the case of the US government, the insistence on quantitative indicators was not only to justify aid expenditures but also a manifestation of the results-based management movement that had swept through all areas of government under the Clinton administration. See Stoddard, "The US and the Bilateralisation of Humanitarian Response," HPG Background Paper, Overseas Development Institute, London, December 2002 (http://www.odi.uk/hpg/papers/background12us.pdf).

5. Francois Grunewald and Veronique de Geoffroy, "Kosovo: Drawing Lessons from a Disaster," Groupe URD, Lyons, France, RRN Newsletter, Overseas Development Institute (November 1999), available online at http://www.urd.org/publi/kosleson.htm.

6. On the IASC NGOs are represented through the three major consortia: ICVA, InterAction, and SCHR. Although technically "standing invitees" along with the Red Cross, they are treated for the most part as full and equal members.

7. Bruce Jones and Abby Stoddard, "External Review of the Inter-Agency Standing Committee" (New York: OCHA, December 2003), 3.

8. USAID VolAg reports.

9. David Rieff, "Kosovo's Humanitarian Circus," *World Policy Journal* 17, no. 3 (Fall 2000), 25–32.

10. "The lack of unity and betrayal in Kosovo will continue to follow the Serbian people like an evil fate through the whole of its history. Even in the last war, this lack of unity and betrayal led the Serbian people and Serbia into agony, the consequences of which in the historical and moral

sense exceeded fascist aggression." Speech by Slobodan Milosevic on St. Vitus Day, June 28, 1989, marking the six hundredth anniversary of the Battle of Kosovo.

11. David T. Buckwalter, "Madeleine's War: Operation Allied Force," in *Case Studies in Policy Making and Implementation*, ed. David A. Williams, 6th ed. (Newport, RI: Naval War College, 2002), www.au.af.mil/au/awc/awcgate/navy/pmi/oaf.pdf.

12. From the Albanian: Ushtria Clirimtare e Kosoves (UCK). The KLA's first attack was the killing of two Serb policeman in 1993, and it killed another two Serb policemen in 1996.

13. Buckwalter, "Madeleine's War," 100.

14. "Initial NATO planning for both potential ground and air operations began in April 1998. . . . Formal NATO planning for potential ground and air operations against Yugoslavia [either to help enforce peace settlement or in the case a settlement was not reached] began in early June." Bruce Nardulli, Walter L. Perry, Bruce R. Pirnie, John Gordon IV, John G. McGinn, *Disjointed War: Military Operations in Kosovo, 1999*, Rand Corporation, 2002 (http://www.rand.org/pubs/monograph_reports/MR1406/), 13.

15. The faith-based NGO International Orthodox Christian Charities (IOCC) also had a programming presence in Kosovo starting in the mid-1990s, but it was limited to assisting the Serb refugees in collective centers. Handicap International provided inputs to centers for the disabled.

16. NGOs relied on UNHCR, however, for low-cost diesel fuel at UNHCR-designated pumping stations around Kosovo, and for the ID cards which at times helped ease the way with Serb authorities at checkpoints, etc.

17. Nancy Lindborg, Mercy Corps International, interview with author.

18. Doctors of the World, Kosovo reports (internal documents).

19. NGO personnel, interviews with author (February 2005).

20. OFDA FRY Situation Reports.

21. USAID/BHR/OFDA, "Former Yugoslavia—Complex Emergency, Situation Report #2, Fiscal Year 1997" (July 31, 1997), and "Former Yugoslavia—Complex Emergency, Situation Report #1, Fiscal Year 1998" (December 5, 1997).

22. USAID/BHR/OFDA, "Former Yugoslavia—Complex Emergency, Situation Report #2, Fiscal Year 1997" (July 31, 1997).

23. DOW staff, interviews with author (January 2005).

24. In 1995 the Macedonia contingent became known as the United Nations Preventive Deployment Force (UNPREDEP) in FYROM (Former Yugoslav Republic of Macedonia).

25. On December 24, 1992, President Bush sent a one-sentence cable to President Milosevic that became known as the "Christmas warning." Read to Milosevic in person by Acting Secretary of State Eagleburger, the message was, "In the event of conflict in Kosovo caused by Serbian action, the U.S. will be prepared to use force against Serbians in Kosovo and in Serbia proper" (text reproduced in *The Kosovo Conflict: A Diplomatic History through Documents*, ed. Philip E. Auerswald and David P. Auerswald. Kluwer Law International, Cambridge/The Hague (August 2000).

26. Buckwalter, "Madeleine's War," 93.

27. Senator Alfonse D'Amato (R-NY) and Congressmen Elliot Engle (D-NY) were among those in Congress who led efforts to bring attention to the plight of Albanians in Kosovo and to take a hard line against Belgrade on the issue.

28. As the Joint Staff officer responsible for global politico-military affairs and US military strategic planning (1994–96) General Clark led the military negotiations for the Bosnian Peace Accords at Dayton.

29. Buckwalter, "Madeleine's War," 99. Planned military options (and anticipated required troops) included:

"A" Agreed ceasefire, with negotiations for a peace settlement to follow (50,000).
"A-" Enforcement of agreed peace settlement (28,000).
"B" NATO forced entry subjugating all of the FRY (200,000).
"B-" Forced entry into Kosovo only (75,000).

30. The Stockholm International Peace Research Institute (SIPRI), the University of Michigan's Correlates of War Project, Monty Marshall's Center for Systemic Peace, and Ruth Leger Sivard, *World Military and Social Expenditures 1991* (World Priorities, Washington, DC, 14th edition, 1991) generally concur in the definition of "major armed conflict" as "resulting in the battle-related deaths of at least 1000 people in any single year" (SIPRI). In contrast, Kosovo yearly deaths numbered only in the dozens.

31. Mercy Corps staff, interview with author (December 2004).

32. Doctors of the World staff, interviews with author (January/February 2005).

33. North Atlantic Council (NAC) Statement, May 28, 1998.

34. Greg Hunter, interview with author (January 6, 2005).

35. Julia Taft (March 2003) and PRM staff, and interviews with author (April 2002).

36. Excerpt from "Human Rights Watch Statement to the Contact Group," Press release, June 1998, http://www.hrw.org/press98/june/kosvo610.htm.

37. Buckwalter, "Madeleine's War," 99.

38. "Statement on Kosovo adopted by the members of the Contact Group, Rome, 29 Avril 1998," *Le Monde Diplomatique*, www.mondediplomatique.fr/cahier/kosovo/contact-290498-en.

39. Daily press briefings by Department of State deputy spokesman James Foley, August 1998.

40. Remarks by Secretary of State Albright to the OSCE Permanent Council, Vienna, September 3, 1998.

41. At that meeting Clinton reportedly assured Rugova, "We will not allow another Bosnia to happen in Kosovo" (Elaine Sciolino and Ethan Bronner, "Crisis in the Balkans: The Road to War—A Special Report. How a President, Distracted by Scandal, Entered Balkan War," *New York Times*, April 18, 1999).

42. Defense Secretary Richard Cohen was quoted as saying, "We will not be the air force for the KLA." Some analysts have charged that Milosevic interpreted this as a "green light" to increase the Serbian offensive.

43. Buckwalter, "Madeleine's War," 12.

44. UN Security Council Resolution 1199, September 23, 1998.

45. Statement by Secretary of State Albright, New York, September 23, 1998, in Auerswald, *Kosovo Conflict*.

46. Statement by President William Jefferson Clinton, September 23, 1998, in Auerswald.

47. In what some might call a self-serving press conference on October 28, USAID declared that "a humanitarian disaster has been averted in Kosovo" (USAID/OFDA Kosovo DART Situation Report #9—October 29, 1998).

48. Raymond Apthorpe, "Was International Emergency Relief Aid in Kosovo 'Humanitarian'?" *Humanitarian Exchange* 20 (March 2002): 22.

49. WHO, First Mobile Health Clinic Monthly Morbidity Report for January 1999, based upon daily epidemiological data submitted by MSF, MDM, IMC, and IRC. Reported in USAID/OFDA DART Kosovo

Situation Report #81, March 4, 1999.

50. USAID/DART Situation reports and various case evaluations.

51. NGO personnel, interviews with author (January/February 2005).

52. USAID/DART Kosovo Situation Report #77, February 26, 1999.

53. USAID/OFDA Kosovo DART Situation Report #55, January 20, 1999.

54. CARE, CRS, DOW, and Mercy Corps were among the NGOs disseminating independent situation reports and humanitarian analysis of the crisis—a function highlighted in CARE's in-house evaluation: In late 1998, the CARE FRY team were sending out regular sitreps describing the changing situation within Kosovo as it affected humanitarian relief." From "Care International's Response to the Kosovo Crisis: Lessons Learned Review" (Internal Report), Nick Harvey, Hermen Ketel, Barney Mayhew, January 2000.

55. S/RES/1199 (1998), September 23, 1998.

56. In addition to the KVM monitoring missions, "Operation Eagle Eye" provided aerial surveillance for NATO starting in November.

57. USAID/OFDA DART Situation Reports.

58. US government internal report, "Interagency Review of U.S. Government Civilian Humanitarian and Transition Programs" ("The Halperin Report"), "Annex I: Kosovo" www.gwu.edu/~nsarchiv/NSAEBB.

59. Ibid.

60. Halperin Report, Annex I.

61. USAID/OFDA DART Situation Reports 83 (March 9), 84 (March 10), 85 (March 11), 87 (March 16).

62. Cable, "Kosovo—Possible Scenarios for USG Contingency Planning and Assistance," March 17, 1999.

63. Cable, March 22, 1999.

64. Ibid.

65. NGO personnel, interview with author.

66. NATO Press Statement (1999) 041, Statement by Secretary General Dr. Javier Solana, March 24, 1999.

67. Transcript: President Bill Clinton's news conference, March 18, 1999, CNN, allpolitics.com.

68. Astri Suhrke, Michael Barutciski, Peta Sandison, Rick Garlock, "The Kosovo Crisis: An Independent Evaluation of UNHCR's

Emergency Preparedness and Response," UNHCR, Evaluation and Policy Analysis Unit, Geneva, February 2000; and Larry Minear, Ten van Baarda, and Marc Sommers, "NATO and Humanitarian Action in the Kosovo Crisis," Occasional Paper #36, The Thomas J. Watson Jr. Institute for International Studies, Brown University, Providence, RI, 2000.

69. Bruce Nardulli, Walter L. Perry, Bruce R. Pirnie, John Gordon IV, and John G. McGinn, *Disjointed War: Military Operations in Kosovo, 1999*, Rand, Santa Monica, CA, 2002.

70. Joint Ops LL, Disjointed War, 112.

71. "CARE International's Response to the Kosovo Crisis: Lessons Learned Review," Internal Report prepared by Nick Harvey, Herman Ketel, and Barney Mayhew, January 2000. "CARE International's Response to the Kosovo Crisis: Lessons Learned Review," Internal Report prepared by Nick Harvey, Herman Ketel, and Barney Mayhew (January 2000). "On the eve of the air strikes, one major power told UNHCR that air strikes might provoke massive refugee outflows—perhaps 500,000 refugees. This message was not 'heard' by UNHCR senior management, partly because the message was sent by a low-level channel, and the message contradicted that same major power's public pronouncements. As far as the review team is aware, this was the only prediction of this scale of refugee outflow, and it was not made public."

72. Minear, Baarda & Sommers, "NATO and Humanitarian Action in the Kosovo Crisis," 15.

73. OSCE reports that all told, approximately 863,000 Kosovar refugees fled Kosovo for Albania, Macedonia, or Bosnia and Herzegovina (OSCE, "Kosovo/Kosova as Seen, as Told: The Human Rights Findings of the OSCE Kosovo Verification Mission," parts 1 and 2 [Vienna: OSCE Secretariat, 1999], chap. 14).

74. Buckwalter, "Madeleine's War."

75. Ibid.

76. Apthorpe, "Was International Emergency Relief Aid in Kosovo 'Humanitarian'?"

77. Joanna Macrae et al., "Uncertain Power: The Changing Role of Official Donors in Humanitarian Action," *HPG Report* 12, December 2002.

78. A military perspective on the Kosovo response suggests that part of this phenomenon may be due to a gender dynamic between the NGOs and military: "Finally, I was struck by the number of women

who work within the humanitarian agencies, often over 50% . . . Their numbers were in stark contrast to our male dominated Army, and they were too often dismissed by arrogant officers—many senior—who tended to either brush their opinions aside, condescendingly attempt to ingratiate themselves or were simply distracted!" From Tim Cross, Director General, Defence Logistic Support, DLO Andover, "Comfortable with Chaos: Working with UNHCR and the NGOs; Reflections from the 1999 Kosovo Refugee Crisis," *Journal of Humanitarian Assistance*, October 30, 2001, www.jha.ac/articles/u42.htm.

79. Harvey et al., "CARE International's Response to the Kosovo Crisis: Lessons Learned Review"; Minear et al., "NATO and Humanitarian Action in the Kosovo Crisis"; Rieff, *Slaughterhouse*.

80. Antonio Donini, "Kosovo Study Abstract," unpublished document from Humanitarianism and War Project, Tufts University, 1999.

CHAPTER SIX

SOME CONCLUSIONS
FROM THE THREE CASES

By reviewing the cases of Somalia (1991–92), Bosnia (1992–95), and Kosovo (1998–99), I set out to demonstrate the following information about complex political-humanitarian emergencies:

- Humanitarian NGOs provide the bulk of the information that shapes officials' understanding of the situation and upon which they base their decisions.

- This information feeds up the implementer-donor channel through regular reporting and informal communications.

- In some cases the compelling narrative of a thwarted humanitarian response can instigate a decisive policy response to the conflict (i.e., the humanitarian efforts precede and draw in the political response).

- Paradoxically, the information that centers on an operational humanitarian perspective can lead to suboptimal or undesirable policy responses from the humanitarian perspective.

- And typically, once the political/military response is under way, the humanitarian information is no longer valued or sought after the way it was prior to the response.

In Bosnia, international political actors seemed to proffer an exclusively humanitarian response when political and military responses were indicated. In Kosovo, these same actors moved aggressively to resolve the conflict politically and militarily, while cloaking it in a humanitarian mantle. The action taken in the name of "humanitarian intervention," however, induced an acute humanitarian crisis where one had not existed before. How much did NGO information and humanitarian framing contribute to this policy outcome? As mentioned at the beginning of that chapter, the United States and its NATO allies had a stronger sense that their collective national interests were at stake. The elements favoring an aggressive US-led international stance were in place early on after a decade of Balkan conflict had soured the international community against Milosevic and taught lessons about the human cost of delayed intervention. (US Senator Joe Biden, writing about why the United States decided to intervene in Kosovo, said the reason "could be summed up in two words: Slobodan Milosevic."[1]) Conflict in Kosovo was also genuinely feared as a potential trigger for a greater regional war in southern Europe. So even though the humanitarian warnings, and the 1998 winter scare in particular, had the effect of pushing the policy agenda forward faster and intensifying the diplomatic activity, it could be argued that the course toward intervention had been set and would have eventually been completed regardless of the humanitarian presence on the ground. Nevertheless, there are lessons to be drawn from Kosovo about the potency of humanitarian information from the field and its impact on policy.

One such lesson is that the greater part of the information stream emanating from crisis settings (the hard data, the guesstimates, the rumors, and the daily updates on events) sprang from the operations of the humanitarian providers—the NGOs—on the ground. Policymakers in governments, certainly those in the US government via the cables from the field, were tuned to this humanitarian frequency as they were formulating their policy responses. This basic fact is often overlooked by the humanitarians themselves. The Tufts study quoted some NGO representatives, who, arguing against engaging with policymakers, make statements that clearly underestimated their role in building the information base: "Governments have their own intelligence sources, they pointed out, and aid groups were well-advised to focus on their own bread-and-butter activities rather than taking on intelligence-sharing functions." In truth, what Kosovo and the other cases have shown is that other intelligence sources are in extremely short supply, and aid groups, whether they intended to or not, have served this role. The internal US government review of its humanitarian action notes that in Kosovo,

> the USG was significantly constrained by intelligence deficiencies, especially as regards Milosevic's war strategy and the numbers and calculations of internally displaced Kosovars. This became far worse with the withdrawal of external monitors and relief workers just prior to the onset of the NATO bombing campaign. . . . There had been no preplanning for NATO involvement in humanitarian operations in neighboring states. . . .[2]

Policy analyses of the Kosovo conflict (and other political/humanitarian emergencies) that take as their point of departure the doings in the foreign offices in Western capitals, yet do not look carefully at the operational and informational structures in the field, miss an important piece of the decision-making equation. The actual information sources on the ground, and the channels by which the information flows to policy makers, is alluded to in the vaguest of terms. One such Kosovo narrative speaks of the time when "Western journalists and human rights groups descended on the region,"[3] when in fact their numbers remained quite low relative to the aid worker presence, and they relied heavily on the humanitarian infrastructure to acclimate them and help them move about. The OSCE monitoring mission ultimately reached a few hundred personnel (from an envisaged two thousand) before it was withdrawn in late March, but only seventy-five of these staff members were actually engaged in the monitoring and investigation of human rights abuses.[4]

Like all so-called complex emergencies, Kosovo began as a political conflict—in this case, an insurgency and a counterinsurgency campaign that entailed egregious human rights abuses. There were people at various times in need of food and shelter assistance, surely, but the *humanitarian* crisis in pre-war Kosovo was overstated; the overriding needs were for *protection*, which the relief operation was not in any way equipped to provide. Once they could no longer run the convoys, the international aid community was out of options for helping displaced people. Raymond Apthorpe noted this deficiency in one of his articles on Kosovo: "The emphasis on emergency assistance meant that no framework was in place in which even the ICRC could carry out its protection activities from March to June 1999. No provision for protection was available for civilians, either on the ground or from the air."[5] A more "traditional" humanitarian emergency, of course, began after and as the indirect result of the air war.

A second lesson, therefore, and one that could also be extracted from the Somalia experience, is that information from the humanitarian community can provoke a policy response, but once it is set in motion, the form of that response is typically devoid of humanitarians' input and often contrary to their interests, as in the example alluded to earlier regarding the US military's controversial airdrops of food parcels into Afghanistan during the 2001 offensive against al-Qaeda and the Taliban. For many years prior to the war, no US government personnel had been on the ground inside, save for two short visits by OFDA staff. When in November concerns surfaced about the nutritional situation, the solitary piece of documented information came from a survey undertaken by Save the Children with CDC,[6] which identified serious nutritional deficiencies in the northwest Faryab province. This information, according to USAID officials, factored very heavily into OFDA planning, and was passed on to the military, who subsequently decided to initiate air-drops of food. The air-drops, however, were universally criticized by the humanitarian community as an American PR stunt at best, and dangerous to Afghan civilians at worst. (It didn't help that the early food packages had identical yellow coloring to the cluster bombs that were also being dropped at the time.)

Another point that the Kosovo case should drive home is that humanitarian information can at times be incomplete, misleading, or downright wrong. The Catch-22 of relief programming is that to be truly effective it must be based on a sound assessment of needs, but in the situations of greatest need relief workers are often too busy or too much at risk to achieve this standard. The reports from Kosovo demonstrate this problem in citing repeated instances of delayed or incomplete health/shelter/nutrition surveys and other assessment attempts, and the aid community's ongoing uncertainty about IDP numbers and needs. Reasoning that it is better to err on the side of caution might naturally lead humanitarian organizations to overstate rather than risk understating needs, and to issue hyperbolic warnings of "impending catastrophe," as were seen in the Kosovo winter scare. Apart from any damage this might cause to the organizations' future credibility, however, this approach risks provoking precipitous action that makes matters worse. NGOs also can and have served as unwitting channels of information (or misinformation) from political actors. For example, the DOW expatriate staffers who worked in Kosovo at the time now believe that one or more of their local staff members were in direct contact with the KLA before the group emerged from the shadows. At key points they recall being given hints that "things were going down" and that DOW aid packages should be stepped up.

No one could fairly accuse the NGOs working in Kosovo prior to the air strikes of either gross incompetence in reporting or deliberate manipulation of the information they conveyed. The worst that can be said is that the picture they helped paint was exaggerated in places, and too centered on their narrow sphere of operations so that it skewed the view of the situation. Humanitarians like Fred Cuny in the Bosnia case knew the power of humanitarian obstruction as a motivator for government involvement, and in Kosovo this theme was sounded anew. Ultimately, an emphasis on convoy operations and the need to clear the way for humanitarian deliveries must inevitably detract from the greater needs of civilians for protection from political violence and forced migration. Most agree that humanitarian NGOs cannot and should not try to provide direct physical protection or to recommend specific military or political strategy, but they should broaden their view enough to be clear about what the needs are, rather than focus on the Band-Aid solution of "getting the food through."

Notes

1. Senator Joseph R. Biden Jr., "Foreword," *The Kosovo Conflict: A Diplomatic History through Documents*, ed. Philip E. Auerswald and David P. Auerswald. Kluwer Law International, Cambridge/The Hague (August 2000).

2. US government internal report, "Interagency Review of U.S. Government Civilian Humanitarian and Transition Programs" ("Halperin Report"), 12. Copy of report, U. S. Dept. of State, January 2000. Released under FOIA, obtained from the National Security Archive, George Washington University.

3. Samantha Power, *A Problem from Hell: America and the Age of Genocide*. New York: Basic Books, 2002.

4. OSCE, Annual Report 1999.

5. Raymond Apthorpe, "Was International Emergency Relief Aid in Kosovo 'Humanitarian'?" *Humanitarian Exchange* 20 (March 2002): 22.

6. Fisum Aseefa et al., "Malnutrition and Mortality in Kohistan District, Afghanistan, April 2001," *JAMA* 286, no. 21 (December 5, 2001), 563–571.

CHAPTER SEVEN

THE HUMANITARIAN ALERT IN "FORGOTTEN EMERGENCIES"

The previous chapters have sought to demonstrate how the information relayed from humanitarian NGOs in the field has impacted upon US government decisions to take action in response to complex emergencies. Decisive action need not be defined strictly as military intervention, but can also encompass assertive diplomacy on the part of political actors to manage, resolve, or significantly influence the conflict. In this chapter we look at emergency cases that are considered among the "forgotten" or "neglected" emergencies, where Western powers have not devoted forceful and sustained efforts toward a decisive resolution, but in effect have allowed conditions of conflict and state failure to continue while civilians suffer violence, displacement, and deprivation. Over the years, Angola, Sudan, and the Democratic Republic of Congo (DRC) have all merited places on this list, according to humanitarian organizations that try to call attention to neglected crises.[1] This chapter examines this phenomenon from the standpoint of the operational humanitarian presence and the information function of humanitarian organizations. If the humanitarian information and framing proved catalytic in Somalia, Bosnia, and Kosovo, why has it not had the same effect on policy around these forgotten emergencies?

Chronic Emergencies and International (In)Action

The cases of Sudan, Angola, DRC, and other countries on the list of the world's neglected emergencies share a few key common features. The first is a situation of protracted low-level conflict amid the absence or failure of governance that in its durability seems inexorable. Recent research on war economies points to the economic incentives of belligerents to perpetuate the violence and anarchy to gain control over natural resources and exploit the opportunities of regional and global black and gray markets for drugs, arms, oil, and diamonds.[2] Such states of affairs, arrived at after years or decades of underdevelopment and ineffective or corrupt governance, come to be accepted by outside observers as simple grim reality, and conditions that on a humanitarian level constitute an emergency have instead become the norm. Even some aid organizations have taken to the term "complex development scenarios" to describe such environments.[3]

In the case of South Sudan, some have suggested that the civil strife and the coordinated humanitarian response within Operation Lifeline Sudan became routinized and normalized in a way that, for over a decade, kept Sudan on the back burner of Western government foreign offices. As a US government internal review concluded, "The 'business as usual' approach to Sudan belies the extreme nature of the crisis."[4] Although OLS has been the subject of some critical reviews over its long life span,[5] on the whole it has been justly praised as a remarkable achievement by the humanitarian community—both in terms of obtaining agreement by the warring parties to allow aid to get through to civilians, and in its effectiveness in reaching many in desperate need. Since its inception, OLS has served as the primary and essential conduit for international aid to South Sudan.[6] It therefore becomes uncomfortable for humanitarians to consider that its very success may have helped to prolong the conflict or lessen the incentives for the international policy community to address it. The issue has its parallel in the Bosnia case, where at times the convoy operation appeared *too* effective, in that it created complacency among politicians already reluctant to intervene. Even when faced with belligerents' violations of the "Ground Rules," that is, the humanitarian principles that underpin the OLS operation, some of its participants at times seemed more concerned with preserving the OLS structure than addressing the broader humanitarian issues, and the problems of OLS were played down in deference to safeguarding its continued existence. The centrality of OLS in discussions of the crisis in South Sudan arguably stunted innovative thinking and new approaches or initiatives.

A report by the Humanitarian Policy Group on "The Changing Role of Aid Policy in Protracted Crises" traces the evolution of thinking about assistance in chronic emergencies.[7] Through most of the 1990s, the international aid community promoted the concept that emergency relief and development exist as points on a continuum along which countries progress after a disaster or conflict. Using this conceptual framework, appropriate aid strategies would complement and reinforce each other: relief aid would provide the basis for and a smooth transition to ongoing development, and development aid would render a country less vulnerable to crisis due to natural disaster and even less prone to conflict. The first-generation thinking "stagnated," according to the HPG report, in part because the donor structures keep pace with the thinking and remain divided between relief and development structures. The current "second-generation" framework, as the report terms it, does not proceed from the concept of crisis as an inevitably temporary aberration or setback on the road to development, but acknowledges the existence rather of failed states and protracted conflicts and draws the link between them and the security policies of the donor governments.[8] Although it may be early yet, there is nothing to demonstrate that this framework either has made a practical policy impact vis-à-vis the approach to neglected emergencies, despite evidence of this new-generation thinking in some governments' donor agency documents.[9] And the US government, for one, retains the long-standing divisions of its donor bureaucracy and funding mechanisms between emergency relief on the one hand and development assistance on the other.

The fact of the matter remains that the idea of a short-term aberration has continuing salience among Western policymakers that generates a sense of urgency and directs new energy to the crisis, which is seen as a problem that can and should be fixed. A paper by Craig Calhoun identifies this concept in what he terms the "emergency imaginary": "'Emergency' is a way of grasping problematic events, a way of imagining them that emphasizes their apparent unpredictability, abnormality and brevity, and that carries the corollary that response—intervention—is necessary."[10] The idea of the humanitarian emergency, Calhoun writes, "naturalizes" the problem and provides the international community with a way of taking hold of these multifaceted crises. As the cases of Somalia, Bosnia, and Kosovo demonstrated, humanitarian action has provided the entry point to political actors into what were in fact complex political problems. Similarly, in the long-running conflict and state failure scenarios, rapid declines in humanitarian conditions or eruptions of violence and displacements in certain areas can create an acute emergency within a protracted emergency. The recent violence and IDP crisis in Darfur provides a perfect example of the acute emergency within the chronic emergency, the fresh horrors inciting new international public attention and policy movement around long-suffering Sudan.

Aid money flows faster and more copiously to sudden emergencies, even though the needs in the long-running crises may be greater. The funding generated for tsunami disaster in Southeast Asia reveals how a rapid onset, and a natural as opposed to conflict-related disaster (all are innocent victims in natural disasters), can unleash the world's generosity. The inhabitants of Banda Aceh in Sumatra, Indonesia, who have been beset by civil conflict and in need of humanitarian assistance for years, are now set to become the beneficiaries of an estimated $4 billion in international aid contributions.[11] The quickly unfolding refugee emergency in Kosovo in 1999 (aided, needless to say, by the fact that it was located in Western Europe's backyard) garnered $207 per victim in response to the UN appeal, as opposed to just $8 for continuing needs of victims in the DRC that same year.[12] In less extreme cases, while it is true that aid dollars concentrate on "high profile" disasters, one might ask how they came to possess the high profile. The conventional wisdom holds that the humanitarian population follows the money and media attention, but the money and media attention can also follow the initial humanitarian response. As the previous chapters have shown, OFDA and a few NGOs can beget a policy momentum within the US government that leads from humanitarian to political action. Moreover, as is well known, the joint UN-NGO appeals for funding in humanitarian emergencies are based *not on levels of need but rather on what the appealing organizations are prepared to do*. In difficult and dangerous settings like South Sudan, DRC, and Angola the capacity of organizations is limited, and so is the funding that comes in (typically short of the requested amount).[13] This fact, perhaps as much as political preferences, may explain why certain housing expenditures for international actors in Kosovo topped out at "more than the entire annual appeal for Angola."[14] The countless articles and reports that gauge the level of international interest and response to a crisis based on dollar contributions alone may be off the mark. Over the past ten years Bosnia and Kosovo did receive more aid money than Sudan, but nonetheless Sudan has consistently ranked among the top-ten annual recipients of bilateral humanitarian aid from Western governments, as has Angola.[15] The neglect is manifest not so much in money, but in the paucity and feebleness of political and diplomatic initiatives to address the underlying problem. In protracted and complex political crises, donor fatigue tends to be far less of a problem than political inertia.

Then again, even a crisis of unprecedented scale and rapidity may not be sufficient to provoke an international response, particularly if there is no "humanitarian entry point." In that regard, before proceeding to the other factors that inhibit international action in chronic emergencies, it is worth examining another of the greatest crises in the 1990s, which did involve rapid and massive loss of life, but in which the international community refused to intervene, and in fact intervention was actively discouraged by the United States. Neither media coverage nor calls for action from NGOs were sufficient to provoke a US response to the genocide in Rwanda. It is interesting to note, however, that the humanitarian presence and the type of information and appeals that emanated from the NGOs present were very different than in the other cases reviewed here.

The Rwanda Genocide

Among the most often cited explanations for why the United States not only refused to engage but actively thwarted an international response in Rwanda[16] is President Clinton's aversion stemming from the "Black Hawk Down" incident in Somalia. If the United States had been reluctant to enter the civil violence in the former Yugoslavia, a Rwanda intervention presented an even less "doable" prospect. As Samantha Power writes, "U.S. officials opposed to American involvement in Rwanda were firmly convinced that they were doing all they could—and, most important, all they should—in light of competing American interests and a highly circumscribed understanding of what was 'possible' for the United States to do."[17]

Only once Rwandan refugees flooded into Goma and humanitarian NGOs began their relief programs did the United States and the other Western powers kick into action with large infusions of assistance. In other words, until the crisis had shifted from one of pure violence to one of a standard "humanitarian emergency" involving Rwandan refugees in neighboring countries, there was no comfortable entry point for any sort of US response. Julia Taft, then president of the Washington-based NGO consortium Interaction, is quoted as saying that NGOs "got virtually no money whatsoever" during the massacres, but this changed dramatically when humanitarian NGOs streamed into the country to assist the refugees who were dying of cholera in large numbers.

Unlike Somalia, where a core group of operational NGOs hunkered down throughout the violence and continued to try to deliver humanitarian aid, all but a few NGOs evacuated Rwanda during the genocide. The Dunantist organizations that remained, ICRC and MSF, along with various human rights organizations, did not maintain the same kind of funding and communication relationship between ground-level implementer and donor as the other NGOs did in Somalia. Nor were the NGOs in Somalia in the habit of sharing information with the UN peacekeeping mission. The absence of a field-to-government information stream was key, because as in Somalia, there were no official information sources, and any political information and intelligence from ground-level Rwanda was a rare commodity. General Romeo Dallaire recounted in his book *Shake Hands with the Devil* that in the weeks leading up to the massacre he was enormously disappointed and frustrated over the lack of political information available to his mission or the SRSG's office. "The NGOs for the most part treated UNAMIR as if it were one of the belligerents, and handed their excellent information over to the news media, not us."[18]

An internal US government report describes this state of affairs as follows: "When U.S. officials locked the Embassy and evacuated from Rwanda on April 10th as ordered by Department of State officials, Washington policymakers lost both this ground-level view and the capacity to influence events in Rwanda."[19] In the absence of the implementing humanitarian organizations, the traditional advocacy tactics of the human rights organizations were received by government officials, noted the report, but "their impact on U.S. policy was limited."[20]

The US State Department cables note the only remaining directly operational organization ("the only organization in control of its distribution") was the ICRC, whose representatives were relaying very different messages to the US government about what was needed than the US NGOs had in Somalia. The ICRC's head of operations, Jean de Courten, met with State Department Undersecretary for Global Affairs Tim Wirth on May 17, expressing "serious concerns" over Rwanda and comparing the "mass killings" to "the genocide in Cambodia." According to a report of the meeting, he urged that "UN peacekeeping forces should be brought in, not to protect the voluntary organizations or relief convoys, *but to protect the civilian population who are being killed*," as "ICRC *has not been prevented from delivering relief supplies*"[21] (emphasis added). MSF also made it very clear in their public statements that the crisis was the lack of protection of civilians, not the lack of humanitarian aid: "Genocide cannot be stopped with doctors!" read one of several MSF press releases made in April–June 1994 calling for military intervention.[22]

Unlike Somalia, the substance of the Rwanda cables, informed by accounts from peacekeepers, not NGOs, was military movements and details of the fighting, and requests for airlift support, more troops, and acceleration of the political decision-making process. Relief supplies played a decidedly secondary role. It was human rights groups applying the most pressure for action, and they were urging that aid be *denied* to Rwanda while its purported interim government presided over the massacres. Samantha Power has concluded that the United States failed Rwanda as a result of a lack of the requisite attention and "strong leadership" on the issues, without which the policymaking system tends toward the easiest and safest options. Human rights organizations and the ICRC rightly identified the principal need of Rwandans as protection against the government-sponsored militias conducting the killings. However, an intervention to provide protection for civilians was not considered as a reasonable option for the United States.[23]

Even more starkly than in Bosnia and Kosovo, protection of civilians was the principal need in Rwanda, not relief assistance, but this left policymakers with the sense that it was futile and risky to get involved in such a mission. Aid convoys are easier to protect than populations. It fits in with the "ancient hatreds" explanation of ethnonationalist conflict that places equal culpability on every party, and leaves the international community with no policy option beyond sending in aid—for it was not deemed worth the domestic political costs to put US forces in harm's way to interfere in seemingly intractable conflicts.

Access, Coverage, and Security:
Sparser Humanitarian Presence, Weaker Voice

Rwanda was anomalous in the scale and speed of its horrific violence. Countries undergoing the other sort of neglected emergency endure years of low-level violence and instability, stalled development, and deteriorating humanitarian conditions among civilian populations. Aside from the chronic nature of the crises, another common feature—and, I would contend, a major contributing factor to the international policy inertia—is the relative lack of a concentrated international humanitarian presence. The inordinate difficulty of humanitarian access in these cases owes both to the geography of the countries and the large area over which recipients are dispersed, and to reasons of security, which make it impossible for international organizations to move freely or to establish large mission presences.

Though it may seem a prosaic observation, Sudan and DRC are enormous countries. In terms of sheer geographical space, they rank as the tenth- and twelfth-largest countries in the world, respectively, and furthermore have the lowest density of road networks and other forms of transportation (see Table 2). Angola shows a similar size-to-transport capacity discrepancy. Unlike Somalia, where IDPs and the aid efforts clustered mainly in and around Mogadishu, and grouped in camp settings in other parts of the country, there have been no single mass concentrations of victims that would be amenable to the camp or convoy situations that the humanitarian community favors for its operations.

Table 7.1: Emergency Case Comparisons

Country	Area (sq km)	Total Pop. (mil.)	Paved/ total roads (km)	Km roads per 1000 sq km of land	Estimated affected population at peak of crisis	Humanitarian presence (UN agencies/IOs/ NGOs)
Angola	1,246,700	11.0	5,349/ 51,429	41	4 million (IDPs, 2001)	90
Bosnia & Herzegovina	51,129	4.0	10,422/ 21,846	427	3 million (IDPs, 1995)	>250
DRC	2,345,410	58.3	NA/ 157,000	69	2.3 million (IDPs, 2004)	100
Kosovo	10,686	2.1	1,543/ 3,800	356	.86 million (Refugees, 1999) (.2 m IDPs before air strikes)	>300 (60 just before air strikes)
Somalia	637,657	8.3	2,608/ 22,100	35	1.5 million (at imminent risk of starvation, 1992)	40 (just before intervention)
Sudan	2,505,810	39.1	4,320/ 11,900	5	4.4 million (IDPs, 2004)	62 (South Sudan) 78 (Darfur)

Source data from CIA Factbook, ReliefWeb, UN DESA, OCHA, IRIN, USAID/OFDA, and World Bank

Security risk for humanitarian personnel poses another serious obstacle to humanitarian access and coverage in these countries. In terms of incidents of violence directly affecting humanitarian workers (including landmines), Angola, DRC, and Sudan are all among the ten most dangerous places to work (Sudan ranks number three, just after Somalia and Afghanistan).[24] While the deliberate targeting and obstruction of humanitarian efforts has shown to be a catalyst for policy action in the past it seems that a significant operation must first be there (the port operations in Somalia, convoys in Bosnia and Kosovo) to obstruct. Unlike UN agencies, NGOs are essentially free to choose the countries they will run programs in and to which emergencies they will respond.[25] In Angola, Sudan, and DRC, the United Nations has found implementing humanitarian assistance extremely difficult, in large part because there are not enough NGO implementing partners on the ground to do the work.

An August 2004 report by the UN Office for the Coordination of Humanitarian Affairs described the access problems facing humanitarian action in the DRC:

> One of the major unmet humanitarian needs in the Democratic Republic of Congo remains the lack of operational capacity to assist an enormous vulnerable population living throughout a vast and difficult to access terrain. There are currently only 95 international NGOs and representatives from the Red Cross Movement implementing programs in a country with millions of affected populations spread throughout 2.3 million km (a region 213 times the size of Kosovo, 86 times the size of Burundi, and 24 times the size of Liberia). Due to this shortage of operational partners, when humanitarian assistance does arrive in favour of vulnerable groups, like newly displaced persons or returnees, it rarely meets international standards, such as those outlined in the Minimum Standards in Disaster Response (SPHERE Project).[26]

The small numbers of NGOs that maintain an operational presence have seen access and security conditions worsen rather than improve in many areas since the peace agreement. In July 2005, following the kidnapping of two staff members, MSF announced it was halting operations in northeastern Ituri, where an estimated one hundred thousand displaced persons required aid. The head of MSF in DRC expressed his frustration with the inability of international actors to address or even gauge the scope of the humanitarian emergency:

> [A]n organization like MSF cannot get a clear picture of what is happening. Why? Because accessibility is difficult. What we know is that when we had the possibility to work in different camps surrounding Bunia, we knew the situation was not good. Medically speaking, we had some mortality rates that were already two or three times higher than those that are acceptable as emergency situations. So, in many places we surpassed these emergency levels. Now that we have withdrawn, we can easily imagine that the situation is just getting worse, and what is worrying us the more is that not a single actor has accessed these areas to know what is taking place there.[27]

Of course it is not just humanitarian action but peacekeeping efforts as well that are wholly overwhelmed by the enormity of the need in DRC.

Despite being the largest UN peacekeeping operation in the world, MONUC has proven seriously deficient in providing any sort of lasting stability or protection in the remote reaches of DRC, and in fact the civilian staff is often occupied with humanitarian efforts that humanitarian organizations are in too short supply to cover. The humanitarian presence in such situations will likewise be dispersed, ground-level information more scarce, and the humanitarian voice diluted. As the OCHA report on the DRC details:

> In a context where information is often lacking due to the absence or limited presence of humanitarian partners, clearly defining all unmet humanitarian needs in a country like DRC is a daunting task. There are even some regions, like Bas-Uele and Haut-Uele Districts, Orientale Province (together 2 times the size of Liberia), where vulnerable populations have never benefited from humanitarian assistance because of the reduced presence of humanitarian partners. Another major problem inhibiting the identification of humanitarian needs and the implementation of assistance programs in war torn zones is the absence of a road infrastructure, particularly in the provinces of Maniema, South-Kivu, Orientale, the two Kasais and Equateur.[28]

Where NGO information sources are absent, information is short all around. According to US officials, even the official intelligence services have drawn upon NGO information for much of their source material, as noted in chapter 3. In Sudan, faulty intelligence from the CIA indicating a threat to the US diplomatic community prompted an evacuation in 1996, followed by the discrediting of over one hundred CIA reports from the country.[29] Throughout the years of civil war in South Sudan, the UN agencies and most NGOs have not maintained permanent presence on the ground in Sudan, but have programmed their aid through OLS—the interagency cross-border operation based in Kenya. Other organizations, including the ICRC, based their operations in Khartoum. The limited access into vulnerable areas in Sudan, due to risk and deliberate restriction by the government and the rebels, has not allowed the NGOs to forge the ground-level familiarity and contacts that in other settings have made them key sources of information.

> As the desk officer of an NGO working in Sudan explained, "Access is the key word in such situations. If there is no access to certain areas, the governments that do not want to get

involved can say that they don't know. Even if there are rumors, testimonies of atrocities . . . there is no proof." . . . For the areas they cannot access, humanitarian workers have to work with demographic data given by local authorities, with all the bias this implies. In accessible areas, the information gathered is often most selective, due to the lack of free interaction with the local population. The program is then applied almost blindly, and there is no mean to correct it a posteriori, for future programs: aid agencies cannot monitor the impact of the food deliveries. Khartoum and the SPLM forbid almost all nutritional surveys and other common tools for evaluating the efficiency of aid programs, under the threat of expelling the delinquents, as happened to the NGO Action Contre la Faim in 1997.[30]

The humanitarian footprint was even smaller in affected parts of Angola before the ceasefire. The former UN humanitarian coordinator in Angola attests to a "constant shortage of information" on IDP whereabouts, movements, and needs that only began to improve after the war when humanitarian access became easier.[31] A US National Intelligence Council Report stated, "Heavy fighting and the combatants' unwillingness to provide humanitarian access to noncombatants are putting many critical areas out of the reach of aid deliveries and increasing the risks for international relief workers and IDPs alike."[32]

Failed states and chaotic, violent conditions represent one cause for the absence of a significant international humanitarian presence. Conversely, humanitarian access can be impeded by the actions of a strong and intact government. If the estimates are correct, the worst humanitarian disaster in the world today is occurring in North Korea, where prolonged famine has claimed an estimated 2 million lives, and left over a third of the population, some 8 million, heavily dependent on international donations of food aid.[33] The World Food Programme's operation in North Korea is the organization's largest anywhere, delivering amounts to feed 6.5 million,[34] but the government of the DPRK has not allowed for international monitoring of the government-run aid distributions to ensure that the food is actually reaching the people who need it, or for any independent NGO programming or needs assessments at the ground level. Because of Pyongyang's intransigence and enforced silence on the humanitarian crisis, a group of the major NGOs working to aid North Korea—ACF, CARE, MDM, MSF, and Oxfam—withdrew their programs in 2002.

When it has served as the entry point for Western powers' intervention, humanitarian action first possessed the requisite level of space and the stability to launch a response and build up a policy momentum behind it. The provision of humanitarian relief to civilians represents something that can be grasped, both by the public imagination and by policymakers as an item in their toolbox, in a way that snipers on rooftops and machete-wielding mobs defy understanding and inhibit action.

The Hierarchy of National Interests and the Prospect of a Hobbled OFDA

During the post–Cold War, pre–September 11, 2001, decade of the 1990s, it has been observed, "a foreign policy vacuum" emerged that allowed humanitarian concerns to take center stage in the West's approach to conflicts in the developing world. The United States began to experience an "interest-threat mismatch," as Donald Snow coined it, where in those areas that held vital US interests there were no threats to peace, and vice versa.[35] With superpower security stakes no longer riding on political outcomes in many of these countries, a new doctrine of humanitarian intervention could be promoted whereby a nation's right to sovereignty was contingent upon its living up to its "responsibility to protect"[36] its citizenry. The "Clinton Doctrine," established after the NATO operation in Kosovo (and reflecting a strong sense of regret of failing to act in Rwanda), called for the United States to intervene anywhere in the world where crimes against humanity were occurring. In Al Gore's presidential campaign he too stressed the idea that humanitarian values were part and parcel of the country's interests.

In the minds of the US senior leadership, the attacks of September 11, 2001, undeniably ushered in a new "A-list" threat, to use Nye's term, against the national survival of the United States. As a result, "humanitarian values" as a concept, though they may be invoked, are unlikely to carry the same influence or disinterest as during that short-lived period.[37] What might this mean for neglected emergencies? For a select few it may spur direct international policy action, perhaps intervention, and accordant increased humanitarian assistance. Afghanistan, which for years languished as one of the worst humanitarian situations on the planet, found itself in the center of the new security calculus of the United States owing to the presence of bin Laden and training camps. As a result, Afghanistan has been the recipient of intense international engagement, a US-led regime change, and foreign aid at levels not seen since the Soviet occupation during the Cold War. (It follows that had the Sudanese government not expelled Osama bin Laden in 1996, Sudan might have found its position reversed with Afghanistan's.)

It remains to be seen whether Somalia, still essentially stateless after the ill-fated intervention in the 1990s, will rise to a top spot on the US foreign policy agenda. There are signs pointing toward this possibility. The 2004–2009 Strategic Plan of the US Department of State and USAID[38] (the first of its kind), prepared to be in alignment with the president's 2002 *National Security Strategy of the United States*, has singled out failed states as "the source of some of our nation's most significant security threats" in that they may become host to transnational terrorist groups and staging grounds for attacks against the United States and its allies. USAID has increased its institutional focus and attention on failed states and has devoted new institutional resources to the issues of democracy, good governance, and building stable states. Somalia has been singled out in particular as a potential "next Afghanistan" in terms of serving as a haven for Islamist terrorist organizations. To date, however, these initiatives exist more on paper than in practice.

The primacy of great power security interests will also continue to *prevent* international action for certain countries undergoing conflict. Colombia and Chechnya provide two examples. Both states are beset by violence and urgent humanitarian need, including, in the case of Colombia, mass internal displacement. Yet the US interests and military involvement in Colombia under the Andean Counterdrug Initiative, and Chechnya being a disputed territory of the Russian republic, effectively rules out any direct engagement or intervention by the broader international community, humanitarian-driven or otherwise.

Finally, there are signs that the NGO-OFDA dynamic that acted as the wedge to drive policy action during the 1990s may be blunted due to recent Bush administration actions. It was suggested that OFDA director Bear McConnell was forced to step down after he suggested that putting Iraq humanitarian assistance under US military control would put NGO and OFDA staff at risk for political reprisals. Andrew Natsios commissioned a report (reportedly presented in verbal, not written, form) which found that by all appearances "OFDA has forgotten it is part of the US government."[39] In addition to the change in leadership, a new mandate for OFDA was drawn up on the basis of that report, which makes OFDA's relationship to government objectives more clear.[40] While the mandate seeks to give it a more prominent role in strategic planning and a louder voice in the government field to contribute to joint USG objectives, the fear for some is that this will bring OFDA's sphere of action more firmly under the joint strategic plan objectives and will be less able to protect the apolitical humanitarian space it had quietly carved out for itself. The semi-immunity from politics OFDA has enjoyed in the past was made possible by the legislative architecture of USAID that allows OFDA to automatically trigger an aid response to an emergency, whether or not the country has no diplomatic relations or hostile relations with the United States, and can waive certain cumbersome regulations when they slow down the aid response.

Prospects for Darfur: Beginnings of a New Humanitarian Impetus?

The cases in the previous chapters examined the effect of the humanitarian advisory on policy toward conflict-related emergencies during the pre–9/11 period. The cases in no way suggest that humanitarian action ever took precedence over security matters, for quite the opposite is true (a lesson driven home by the way the humanitarian field was subordinated and marginalized once the military became involved). Rather, they demonstrated how policy can be activated by nongovernmental humanitarian interests in some instances where there are no compelling security interests a priori. Although the sphere of strategic interests for the United States has ostensibly broadened in the post–9/11 security environment, it has not encompassed the countries enduring protracted conflict and chronic humanitarian need.

Sudan, with its vast territory, high level of risk to humanitarian workers, poor access, and low coverage of humanitarian assistance efforts, might seem an unlikely candidate for the humanitarian-driven dynamic described in the previous chapters to instigate significant policy action, or to set in motion the next humanitarian intervention. Prospects have been complicated further by the international policy community's desire to focus on and safeguard the Naivasha peace process, which at the same time was edging toward a negotiated resolution to civil war in the South; and by framing of the conflict as Arab versus non-Arab Sudanese and its implications for international relations between the West and the Islamic world.[41] The US government, distracted and stretched by its military commitments in Iraq, has also faced conflicting domestic interests vis-à-vis Sudan within the United States—on the one hand, the oil and gum arabic lobbies that pushed for better relations and lifting of sanctions against Khartoum, and on the other, the Christian religious right, which has been a strong voice for US-led action to stop the violence and forced displacement in Darfur.[42] Despite these impediments, however, a closer look behind the scenes reveals some significant policy movement already, and if not the probability then at least the potential for more assertive international action, including the use of force. After what he called a late start, author Hugo Slim has also noted the "continuous and determined diplomacy by individual states, notably Chad, the United States, the Netherlands and the UK, and by Germany mobilizing political commitment within the European Union. . . ."[43]

Guerrilla offensives began in January 1993 and retribution by government-sponsored Janjaweed militias started in February. In late September the extent of the crisis became known when the government of Chad and NGOs raised the alarm about the refugees and made guesstimates about needs and the displaced inside Darfur. Chad began a diplomatic effort that culminated in international talks in N'djamena, where the United States, European Union, Britain, France, the Netherlands, and the African Union all participated. However, humanitarians were still systematically being denied access; humanitarian efforts could not get started until the second half of 2004, and they did not get going in any major way until the summer of 2004. (At the time of this writing there is still a great deal of concern that the international humanitarian capacity in Darfur is not up to the task.) Also during that summer Secretary of State Colin Powell made a highly publicized visit to the region and a few months later stated that, as far as the United States was concerned, what was happening in Darfur constituted genocide.[44] Powell's visit had followed another high-profile visit by UN Secretary-General Kofi Annan, both of which signaled a high level of international attention and concern, and set the stage for continuing diplomatic activity to resolve the Darfur crisis in Abuja and at the United Nations in New York.

In Washington during the summer of 2004, high-level meetings (NSC deputies) were taking place on an almost daily basis, and OFDA and USAID senior leadership confirmed that, although it had not been much noted in the press, the administration was particularly "seized of" and energized about the Darfur issue.[45] At the same time, there have also been familiar signs of a humanitarian operations focus that was seen to cause suboptimal outcomes in the previous cases. The USAID/OFDA information machine has naturally centered on the issue of roads and food delivery rather than the political conflict and forced displacement that caused this crisis, and the need to disarm the militants.

Therefore, while the international community has yet to achieve "concerted diplomatic lift-off,"[46] it cannot be said that Darfur—the acute emergency within the chronic emergency—was the victim of outright political neglect. Moreover, although it may appear plodding and dilatory in real time, the diplomatic movement around Darfur has so far not been shown to be any slower than in Somalia, where there was even more media attention and many more were dying.

Hugo Slim notes the prominence of the humanitarian issue in these negotiations as an important and useful development: "Urgent humanitarian discussions rightly have a priority of their own in such situations, but can also play an important vanguard role in engaging the parties around a process of talks which may then become wider and turn to matters of political substance. Equally, such talks can then revert to humanitarian matters when progress on politics stalls."[47]

Slim's first point echoes the spear-tip analogy of humanitarian action in policy responses to conflict, as this book has tried to demonstrate. Likewise, it is conceivable that the humanitarian action in Darfur, if and once it gets up to speed, may repeat the pattern seen in cases such as Somalia and Bosnia. (By way of a possible first step, an OFDA DART mission in Sudan was enlarged and established in four locations in response to the Darfur crisis in February 2005.)

Notes

1. An Oxfam report from 2000 highlighted neglected emergencies in Angola, DRC, Sierra Leone, and drought victims Ethiopia, India, and Pakistan (Oxfam, "An End to Forgotten Emergencies?" May 2000, http://www.oxfam.org.uk/what_we_do/issues/conflict_disasters/forgotten_emergs.htm). MSF's list of 2004's top-ten most underreported humanitarian stories includes Burundi, Chechnya, Colombia, DRC, Ethiopia, Liberia, North Korea, the disease tuberculosis, and the conflict in Northern Uganda (MSF, "Beyond the Headlines: 'Top 10' Most Underreported Humanitarian Stories from 2004," http://www.msf.org).

2. Mark Duffield, "Aid Policy and Post-Modern Conflict: A Critical Review," Occasional Paper 19, School of Public Policy, University of Birmingham, 1998. See also Matts Berdal and David Keen, "Violence and Economic Agendas in Civil Wars," *Millenium* 26, no. 3 (1997): 795–818.

3. Nancy Lindborg, Mercy Corps International, interview with author.

4. Halperin Report, Annex 3: "Sudan Case Study," from the National Security Archive, US government internal report, "Interagency Review of U.S. Government Civilian Humanitarian and Transition Programs" ("Halperin Report"), 12. Copy of report, U. S. Dept. of State, January 2000. Released under FOIA, obtained from the National Security Archive, George Washington University (http://www.gwu.edu/~nsarchiv/NSAEBB/NSAEBB30/index.html/#doc).

5. Critiques have focused primarily on operational issues within OLS, but have reaffirmed its value and concluded it should remain. See Barbara Hendrie, ed., "Operation Lifeline Sudan: A Review," July 1996, and Larry Minear et al., "A Critical Review of Operation Lifeline Sudan: A Report to the Aid Agencies," Humanitarianism and War Project, Tufts University, October 1990.

6. "Since the beginning of the international humanitarian operation, the US has been the major donor to OLS: Its overall contribution between 1989 and March 2001 amounted to $1.2 billion, and represented some 68% of OLS's $180 million annual budget between 1989 and 1998. On average, 75% of the funding is channeled through NGOs and 25% through UN agencies" (Severine Autessere, "United States 'Humanitarian Diplomacy' in South Sudan," *Journal of Humanitarian Assistance*, March 2002, http://www.jha.ac/articles/a085.htm).

7. Adele Harmer and Joanna Macrae, eds., *Beyond the Continuum: The Changing Role of Aid Policy in Protracted Crises*, HPG Research Report No. 18 (London: ODI, July 2004).

8. Ibid.

9. For instance, in 2004 the first-ever joint Strategic Plan of the US State Department and USAID proclaims that "USAID will increase its attention toward failed and failing states, which the President's National Security Strategy recognizes as a source of our nation's most significant security threat" (U.S. Department of State and U.S. Agency for International Development, *Security, Democracy, Prosperity: Strategic Plan Fiscal Years 2004–2009: Aligning Diplomacy and Development Assistance,* Washington, DC: US State Department/USAID, August 2003).

10. Craig Calhoun, "Fear, Intervention, and the Limits of Cosmopolitan Order," Background paper for conference series hosted by the Social Science Research Council, New York, 2004.

11. Jane Perlez, "Asia Letter: As Aceh Aid Pours In, How Will It Be Spent?" *International Herald Tribune,* January 27, 2005.

12. Oxfam, "An End to Forgotten Emergencies?" May 2000, http://www.oxfam.org.uk/what_we_do/issues/conflict_disasters/forgotten_emergs.htm.

13. At times funding may even exceed what is possible to accomplish. According to a case study, "There is a fluctuating relationship between levels of funds and access in the DRC—at times, funds for response have eclipsed agencies' ability to access beneficiaries, while at other points it has been the reverse." Nicola Reindorp and Peter Wiles, "Humanitarian

Coordination: Lessons from Recent Field Experience," a study commissioned by the Office for the Coordination of Humanitarian Affairs (New York: OCHA, June 2001), 64.

14. Toby Porter, "The Partiality of Humanitarian Assistance: Kosovo in Comparative Perspective," *Journal of Humanitarian Assistance*, June 2000, http://www.jha.ac/articles/a057.htm.

15. *Global Humanitarian Assistance 2003* (London: Development Initiatives, 2003), 32.

16. Samantha Power's and others' research on the Clinton administration's policymaking around Rwanda found that "staying out of Rwanda was an explicit U.S. policy objective" (Samantha Power, "Bystanders to Genocide," *Atlantic Monthly*, September 2001; see also Power, *"A Problem from Hell": America and the Age of Genocide* [New York: Basic Books, 2002]).

17. Power, "Bystanders to Genocide." The Atlantic Monthly Online: (http://www.theatlantic.com/doc/200109/power-genocide), 1

18. Romeo J. Dallaire, *Shake Hands with the Devil: The Failure of Humanity in Rwanda* (Toronto: Random House, 2003), 173.

19. US government unclassified cable, "Subj.: UNAMIR Commander Dallaire pleads for Immediate US Military Support in Meeting with AID Administrator Atwood," May 1994.

20. Ibid.

21. Cable "Subj.: Undersecretary for Global Affairs Wirth's Meeting with Director of Operations for ICRC, Jean de Courten, May 17, 1994," May 24, 1994.

22. Laurence Binet, *MSF Speaking Out: Genocide of Rwandan Tutsis 1994* (Brussels: MSF, 2003).

23. Power, "Bystanders to Genocide."

24. Preliminary data compiled by the CIC/HPG project "Humanitarian Action in the New Security Environment: Policy and Operational Implications." Sources: UN OCHA, UNHCR, US Department of State, ReliefWeb, and agency reports.

25. A field evaluation by ODI's Humanitarian Policy Group confirmed the well-known but not always acknowledged fact that in places such as "Sudan and Somalia, insecurity and the restrictions placed on access by the warring parties were found to be the main determinants of whether and how an agency responded to humanitarian needs" (James Darcy and Charles-Antoine Hoffman, "According to Need? Needs Assessment and Decision Making in the Humanitarian Sector," HPG

Report 15 [London: ODI, September 2003], 51). Of course, the needs tend to be greatest in areas that can't be accessed.

26. UN OCHA, "Situation Report: Democratic Republic of Congo Report for July 2004," August 13, 2004, http://www.cidi.org/humanitarian/hsr/04b/ ixl41.html.

27. IRIN, "Interview with MSF head of mission in DRC, Jerome Souquet," August 22, 2005.

28. Ibid.

29. Mansoor Ijaz and Timothy Carney, "Intelligence Failure? Let's Go Back to Sudan," *Washington Post,* July 30, 2002.

30. Autessere, "United States 'Humanitarian Diplomacy' in South Sudan."

31. Erick de Mul, former UN Humanitarian Coordinator for Angola, interview with author.

32. National Intelligence Council, "Global Humanitarian Emergencies: Trends and Projections, 1999–2000," August 1999.

33. Jean-Fabrice Pietri, "Manipulating Humanitarian Crisis in North Korea," *Humanitarian Exchange* 20 (March 2002); InterAction, "Member Activity Report: North Korea," September 2002.

34. "North Korea needs more food aid despite health gains, U.N. says," Deutsche Presse Agentur, March 7, 2005.

35. Donald M. Snow, *When America Fights: The Uses of U.S. Military Force* (Washington, DC: CQ Press, 2000).

36. The UN secretary-general invoked the concept of the right of intervention and the responsibility to protect in his Report to the 2000 General Assembly.

37. Abby Stoddard, "Trends in US Humanitarian Policy," in *The New Humanitarianisms: A Review of Trends in Global Humanitarian Action,* ed. Joanna Macrae (London: Overseas Development Institute, April 2002).

38. U.S. Department of State and U.S. Agency for International Development, *Security, Democracy, Prosperity: Strategic Plan Fiscal Years 2004–2009: Aligning Diplomacy and Development Assistance,* Washington, DC: US State Department/USAID (August 2003).

39. US NGO representative, interview with author.

40. "Administrator's Mandate: Office of U.S. Foreign Disaster Assistance (OFDA)," USAID, October 26, 2004.

41. Alex de Waal has observed that the West's insistence on defining the Darfur conflict as North ("Arab") vs. South ("African") has dangerously simplified the complex ethnic and cultural dynamics and led to an externally imposed construction and militarization of identities in the region.

42. Autessere, "United States 'Humanitarian Diplomacy' in South Sudan."

43. Hugo Slim, "Dithering over Darfur? A Preliminary Review of the International Response," *International Affairs* 80, no. 5 (August 2004): 811–833.

44. Glenn Kessler and Colum Lynch, "US Calls Killings in Sudan Genocide—Khartoum and Arab Militias Are Responsible, Powell Says," *Washington Post*, September 10, 2004.

45. William Garvelink, interview with author.

46. Slim, "Dithering over Darfur?" 813.

47. Ibid., 824.

CONCLUSION

The work of humanitarian NGOs has constituted an indispensable element of the international response to complex emergencies over the past twenty years. The presence and professionalism of a core group of organizations has helped to draw greater attention to human needs, and provoke stronger action to address those needs, in crises that would have undoubtedly seen much worse human tolls had NGOs not been there. Despite humanitarian aid's bad reputation as a fig leaf to disguise governments' inertia, conversely we have seen how the aid response once launched can create a momentum of its own within donor governments toward more full-blooded policy action. As we have also seen, those policy responses do not always play out in the best interests of the humanitarian victims. The dearth of ground-level information sources for international actors in many of these complex emergencies has made it so that the humanitarian information often becomes the sole empirical basis for decision making. In such cases, paradoxically, when the international humanitarian effort becomes the central narrative, the policy outcomes are frequently out of kilter with the primary needs of the beneficiaries.

Past experience has shown that the self-referential advisories from humanitarian actors can have negative consequences. It was of no small importance to get food to the starving people of Somalia, but to design the initial military operation as little more than heavily armed escorts for food convoys, rather than as a force to disarm and separate the militias, set the stage for the mission's failure. Likewise in Bosnia, the single-minded focus on food convoys, corridors, and safe areas for the delivery of aid created even worse protection problems for Bosnian Muslims, and helped to prolong the limbo period before settlement was finally reached. In Kosovo, erratic and hyperbolic humanitarian messages helped to precipitate an ill-advised bombing strategy that caused a genuine refugee catastrophe. Another example not included in the preceding chapters can be found in the case of the Rwandan refugees' return from Goma. The refugees had been languishing in the camps for two years after the genocide and RPF takeover. When the Rwandan government decided to call for camp closures and mass repatriation, many humanitarian agencies protested. The abrupt closings and forced march back to Rwanda would be inhumane, they said, and they appealed to the authorities in Zaire and Rwanda to let them set up transit camps along the way, and return people more slowly, in phases. The Rwandan government refused to hear of it, and as it happened there were some anecdotal accounts of sick people being forced to leave their cots and start walking, and other brutalities. Overall, however, the return was amazingly quick, orderly, and successful, and people were resettled in their home communes much sooner than the humanitarians' plan would have allowed. Even some of the humanitarian practitioners who initially protested were forced to admit that morbidity and mortality would have been far worse if the transit camp plan had been enacted.

While the NGOs' primary responsibility is to get on the ground and be of help, they must also be conscious that their operational presence and the information they communicate to political actors may carry much more weight than they realize. They therefore must be cognizant of both its impact and its import in terms of policy decisions. On the other hand, the NGOs' humanitarian advocacy has not proven effective in terms of changing state policy vis-à-vis humanitarian objectives, even though it may have value and meaning as a motivating force for many organizations. In fact, no studies have been undertaken to determine the effectiveness of particular advocacy strategies or of humanitarian advocacy overall, and such efforts seem at times to be undertaken more for the sake of the advocates than for their clients—efforts, as David Rieff observed, that have been principled but hollow. NGO advocacy campaigns can point to some successes in the development context, but in complex emergency settings the NGOs have found for the most part that the louder and more strident they make their voices, the less they are listened to.

The "back-to-basics" movement is an understandable, but ultimately futile and counterproductive, reaction to the negative effects of what has been called here the humanitarian alert. Some humanitarians, awakening to the realization that they have aided and abetted certain policy actions that in humanitarian terms have done more harm than good, have decided the safest solution is to withdraw to a more circumscribed, ever more rarified humanitarian sphere so as not to be a part of the problem. This response is futile in that the idealized "humanitarian space" is a fiction:

Militaries, corporations, amateur organizations, and private individuals can all lay equal claim to the humanitarian endeavor, and to argue otherwise, as Hugo Slim points out, is a kind of irrational elitism. But more importantly it is counterproductive in that it stands to weaken rather than strengthen the humanitarian voice.

When the question is put to them, it seems the majority of humanitarian NGO representatives would insist that the answer is "not to depoliticize humanitarianism, but to humanitarianize politics." Even the adherents of the back-to-basics approach have not abandoned the idea that humanitarian action must strive to encompass means of protection—the nexus between human rights and humanitarian action that is the greatest need of many of these populations but the hardest thing to accomplish in practice.[1] For humanitarians to relinquish protection as a goal would be tantamount to a return to the days of the "well-fed dead." Yet if protection remains the goal, it will only be reached by finding new ways of engaging with the political sphere, not by withdrawing from it. A senior UN official recently expressed his frustration with the NGOs on this score as follows, "We've reached a stage where humanitarian agencies don't know how to deal with political issues. They hide behind humanitarian principles and put forward proposals that are not addressing the broader context of conflict, but strictly focusing on need. They're not solutions."[2]

What Is the Problem?

What prevents the humanitarian NGOs from effectively engaging as a community to promote a humanitarian agenda? The problem lies not with the vast size and complex biodiversity of the NGO population, for in the reality of international emergency response it is quite clear who the principal NGO actors are, and they number less than two dozen (being generous). Neither is it as simple as economic competition over funding, for this same group has functioned fairly comfortably as a virtual oligopoly going on three decades. Rather, the main impediment, as I have tried to describe in these pages, stems from the philosophical difference between the two main segments of the NGO community regarding the appropriate positioning of humanitarians vis-à-vis governments, more precisely the governments of the powerful Northern/Western industrialized states. At the heart, the issue comes down to whether they are seen as cooperating with their state-patron in a Wilsonian project to bring aid to the world, or instead circumventing and providing a counterforce to states in the Dunantist tradition. The "coherence" debate, as some have called it, is complicated further by the fact that most of the large NGOs work also in development and postconflict transitions, where they are more likely to act as partners with local and international governments toward objectives that were set by a broad political (and Western) consensus.

The battle over coherence has undeniably intensified since the post–September 11, 2001, military campaigns led by the United States. The feelings of repugnance and helplessness that have spurred the back-to-basics movement have led Dunantist organizations like MSF to begin to sound more circumspect about what they may do and talk about than the ICRC—the erstwhile parent against which they rebelled. With such narrow parameters, however, NGOs run the risk of providing more fig leaves and Band-Aids—or as one practitioner put it, "giving cowardly politicians an escape clause." It is the type of critique historically associated with the pragmatic, "service delivery"–focused Wilsonian NGOs. In fact, in an almost surreal development, the coherence debate produced a series of articles in which the MSF representative argues that humanitarians must stick to their knitting and stay out of politics, and a representative of CARE counters with an appeal for a politically attuned human rights–based approach to aid.[3]

Why Does It Matter?

Why is it even important for the NGOs to bridge this divide and pursue a common humanitarian agenda? Certain NGOs have argued that it is not. The organizations are independent entities after all, pursuing their own individual mandates and comparative advantage. Attempting to bind them together would only work against the independence and flexibility that have lent them an important role in humanitarian response. On the other hand, when faced with the magnitude of human suffering exacted by some of the world's worst crises, not even the largest NGO amounts to more than a drop in the ocean in terms of their capacity to respond to the needs. Surely, it would be the worst sort of NGO hubris of all to value organizational independence over potentially better humanitarian responses that are able to reach more people in need through coordinated efforts. The strength in numbers that underpins enhanced humanitarian response operations also stands to raise the volume of the NGO voice in political chambers.

Despite the debates that continue to swirl around the coherence issue, the major operational NGOs are truly not all that far apart on matters of basic principle, and have in a number of ways grown closer over the past ten years, speaking a common language and sharing a sense of global priorities. It is conceivable that the NGOs could find middle ground and work effectively together in a role that combines the information and advocacy functions in a form of expert advisory grounded in firsthand field experience.

It would seem that if the humanitarian NGOs are to truly surmount the ethical-political obstacles that divide them, and to present a credible and legitimate face of principled expertise, the major US NGOs simply cannot get around the need to find and create new sources of funding to free them of their near total dependence on the US government donor. Saying no to government donor funding for reasons of neutrality and independence is a viable option for most of the major European NGOs, while for the vast majority of the Americans it remains an unimaginable luxury.

Better Quality Information, More Considered Advocacy: The Merging of Expert and Moral Authority for Better Humanitarian Outcomes

The inroads made by the NGO "Big Five" group at the UN Security Council, as described in chapter 2, may provide clues to a possible way forward. By combining field expertise and real time, ground-level information with astute diplomatic strategy, those NGO representatives have managed to serve as more than issue advocates or a hectoring pressure group. They have fashioned themselves into a cadre of experts who provide information and counsel that is valued and respected by the UNSC members. Some NGO representatives in Washington cite a similar dynamic that has emerged with members of Congress and their foreign policy staffs. NGOs work best with the legislature, said one, when they are seen not as "groups with an axe to grind" but as experts with the empirical evidence to back up their assertions.[4] It is well known to the cadre of people working at the forefront of humanitarian advocacy that in order to have any chance of impact with policymakers, their statements "must derive from field reality." The policymakers are hungry for information, and the NGOs' role in providing it is "their hook, their seduction."[5] Advocacy with no firsthand information behind it is not credible, and not sought after, while sometimes the act of providing information on a crisis is itself a form of advocacy, implying the necessity of a response. In this regard, some of the most promising pieces of work by NGO policy sections have been the publications of field studies, as well as analytical reports that follow in the vein of the 1998 "blood diamonds" report[6] by Global Witness, mentioned in chapter 2.[7] IRC made headlines in 2001 when it released the findings of its DRC mortality study that reported 3.3 million civilian deaths as a result of the war.[8] That report, released at the same time as a massacre of one thousand people near Bunia in Ituri province, seemed poised to help prod new policy action on the situation. However, diplomatic initiatives have heretofore been concentrated at a national and regional level; the international community seems to have developed a considerable tolerance for local-level violence in the country.[9] (It could also not have helped when MSF publicly criticized IRC's report, finding methodological flaws with the survey and lowering the death toll estimate to a figure closer to 1 million.)

As this book has put forward, NGO field-based information may have a greater policy impact than NGO advocacy efforts, but that impact is often inadvertent, haphazard, and ill-considered. NGO policy staffers acknowledge the need to make a stronger link between getting the information in the field and making the case in capitals. This will always be a challenge in emergency settings as the lead time is often so short. Nonetheless, the way NGO information is presently gathered, processed, delivered, and translated into programming is flawed—a fact that many in the NGO community are starting to understand and address. A study on the practice of humanitarian needs assessment by the Humanitarian Policy Group of the Overseas Development Institute recently brought to light many of the shortcomings of NGO field-based information. The report found that very often program decisions are only rarely driven by hard data on humanitarian "key indicators" such as mortality, morbidity, and malnutrition rates. (And when they do use more rigorous methods and a standardized set of indicators, they opt usually to get a snapshot of needs from one-off surveys, rather than a system of ongoing surveillance that would track changes over time and give a clearer picture of the community's well-being.) Rather, as has been commonly acknowledged in humanitarian work, the system operates on a supply-driven basis. In other words, when proposing projects to donors the NGO (or UN agency) will think at least equally about what they are prepared to do as what is needed on some objective measure. Medical NGOs will naturally highlight health needs, food-focused NGOs nutritional needs, etc.

The HPG report identifies the trap in needs assessment that echoes the humanitarian advisory problem—that is, that this loosely defined practice of "needs assessment" in fact amounts to "finding a common 'narrative' about the situation in question that fits the priorities of agency and donor alike, and allows the two to be reconciled . . . [P]roblems are 'constructed' and 'solved' in ways that may bear little relation to actual needs."[10]

MSF's Nicholas de Torrente writes about this phenomenon as well, noting that it often involves constructing definitions or images of the victims that simplify the underlying political dynamics of the crisis: "Aid workers, consciously or not, select information based on their own judgment of what constitutes need and on their organization's capacity to handle it. . . . Deeply rooted images put a premium on the innocence of victims, making children, who are by definition blameless, the ideal recipients of care."[11] (David Rieff's book deals with the innocent victim image also, and notes how Save the Children in this way has set itself as the morally easiest mandate.) Such caveats are important for NGOs to take on board as they work toward extracting better, more accurate, and more objective field data. As Haas points out, "While epistemic communities provide consensual knowledge, they do not necessarily generate truth."[12] Or, to put it more bluntly, as a participant in a recent humanitarian conference expressed misgivings about NGOs serving as expert-advocates, "What if we're wrong?"

In the heat of an acute crisis, the information relayed by NGO workers in the field is understandably colored by emotion, humanitarian agendas, and no small amount of confusion. Often aid agencies will be fed disinformation by local sources which they then pass on. For example, when the Hutus fled eastern Rwanda to Tanzania in 1994, the refugees told MSF workers who were setting up the camps that they were fleeing massacres by the RPF forces that were then sweeping across the country, when in actuality they had been moved out in an orderly way by Hutu commanders after killing their Tutsi neighbors.[13] This is not to say that the RPF did not kill Hutu civilians anywhere, or that those particular refugees were not under duress, but those accounts allowed NGOs to frame the refugee crisis as innocent civilians fleeing horrific violence, and the real perpetrators of genocide were recast as leaders of the refugees.

The dramatic, emotive language often used by NGOs and indiscriminate use of terms such as "famine" and "catastrophe" may help bring in funding, but can backfire by reflecting badly on their objectivity, credibility, and professionalism. NGOs should also be aware that the window of influence accorded to their information is relatively brief. As learned and relearned in every humanitarian crisis that begat a Western intervention, the humanitarian information that is such a prized commodity before the policy action is taken often becomes fish wrap shortly after.

Notes

1. Most often humanitarian protection has been limited to technical measures in relief operations such as the proper placement of latrines and lighting in camp setting to prevent rapes and other crime, or to wishful thinking in terms of the deterrent effect of a humanitarian presence or humanitarians' "promotion of international law." In general it has been talked about much more than implemented. Fiona Terry and others have written how humanitarian assistance can be in conflict with

protection goals—for instance, by luring people to unsafe areas to col-
lect their aid and providing a source of spoils for belligerents. Terry,
"The Limits and Risks of Regulation Mechanisms for Humanitarian
Action,"*Humanitarian Exchange,* October 2000, Overseas
Development Institute (www.odihpn.org).

2. Representative of the UN Office for the Coordination of
Humanitarian Assistance, interview with author (June 2003).

3. Nicholas de Torrente, "Humanitarian Action under Attack:
Reflections on the Iraq War," *Harvard Human Rights Journal* 17
(Spring 2004), 1–29; Paul O'Brien, "Politicized Humanitarianism: A
Response to Nicholas de Torrente," *Harvard Human Rights Journal* 17
(Spring 2004), 31–39.

4. Andrew Johnson, director of policy in emergencies, Save the
Children US, interview with author.

5. Ibid.

6. Global Witness, "A Rough Trade: The Role of Diamond
Companies and Governments in the Angolan Conflict," December
1998.

7. "In the cases of both Angola and Nigeria, NGO reports assessing
the private sector role in conflict have appeared two or three years earlier than academic journal articles addressing the same subject matter.
At the moment, NGO reports are the most analytical and informative
writing that has yet been published on the relationship between the oil
industry and the civil war in Sudan. . . . While NGO reports are by no
means perfect, they can offer academics current and timely information
from countries and conflicts where alternative sources of good information are often scarce." From Scott Peg and Alissa Wilson,
"Corporations, Conscience and Conflict: Assessing NGO Reports on
the Private Sector Role in African Resource Conflicts," Paper presented
to the forty-third annual meeting of the International Studies
Association, New Orleans, Louisiana, March 2002.

8. International Rescue Committee, "Mortality Study, Eastern
Democratic Republic of Congo," February–April 2001.

9. Severine Autessere, "United States 'Humanitarian Diplomacy' in
South Sudan," *Journal of Humanitarian Assistance,* March 2002,
http://www.jha.ac/articles/a085.htm.

10. James Darcy and Charles-Antoine Hoffman, "According to
Need? Needs Assessment and Decision-Making in the Humanitarian
Sector," Humanitarian Policy Group Report 15 (London: ODI,
September, 2003), 56.

11. Nicholas de Torrente, "Preface," in *Civilians Under Fire: Humanitarian Practices in the Congo Republic, 1998–2000,* ed. Marc Le Pape and Pierre Salignon (Paris: Médecins sans Frontières, 2003), viii.

12. Peter Haas, "Do Regimes Matter?" 23.

13. Jean-Hervé Bradol, "How Images of Adversity Affect the Quality of Aid," in *Civilians Under Fire: Humanitarian Practices in the Congo Republic, 1998–2000,* ed. Marc Le Pape and Pierre Salignon (Paris: Médecins sans Frontières, 2003), 6.

BIBLIOGRAPHY

Books, Articles, Reports, and Papers

Allison, Graham. *Essence of Decision: Explaining the Cuban Missile Crisis*. New York: Harper Collins, 1971.

"Americans and Foreign Aid: A Study of American Public Attitudes." Steven Kull, principal investigator. Program on International Policy Attitudes, University of Maryland, March 1, 1995.

Anderson, Mary B. *Do No Harm: How Aid Can Support Peace—Or War*. Boulder, CO: Lynne Rienner, 1999.

———. *Do No Harm: Supporting Local Capacities for Peace through Aid*. Collaborative for Development Action, Cambridge, MA, 1996.

Anheier, Helmut, Marlies Glasius, and Mary Kaldor, eds. *Global Civil Society 2001*. Oxford: Oxford University Press, 2001.

Annan, Kofi. *Facing the Humanitarian Challenge: Towards a Culture of Prevention*. New York: UNDPI, 1999.

Auerswald, David P., ed. *The Kosovo Conflict: A Diplomatic History through Documents*. Kluwer Law International, Cambridge/The Hague, August 2000.

Austin, James E. *The Collaboration Challenge: How Nonprofits and Businesses Succeed Through Strategic Alliances*. San Francisco: Jossey-Bass Publishers, 2000.

Barnett, Michael, and Raymond Duvall. "Power in International Politics." *International Organization* 59 (Winter 2005).

Barnett, Michael, and Martha Finnemore. *Rules for the World: International Organizations in Global Politics*. Ithaca, NY: Cornell University Press, 2004.

Benthall, Jonathan. "Humanitarianism and Islam after 11 September." In *Humanitarian Action and the "Global War on Terror": A Review of Trends and Issues*, edited by Joanna Macrae and Adele Harmer. London: Overseas Development Institute, July 2003.

Berkowitz, Bruce D. "Information Age Intelligence." In *The Domestic Sources of American Foreign Policy: Insights and Evidence*, edited by Eugene R. Wittkopf and James M. McCormick. Lanham, MD: Rowman & Littlefield, 1999.

Bossuyt, Jean, and Patrick Develtere. "Between Autonomy and Identity: The Financing Dilemma of NGOs." *The Courier* ACP-EU No. 152 (July–August 1995); www.oneworld.org/euforic/courier/152e_bos.htm.

Bradol, Jean-Hervé. "How Images of Adversity Affect the Quality of Aid." In *Civilians Under Fire: Humanitarian Practices in the Congo Republic, 1998–2000*, edited by Marc Le Pape and Pierre Salignon. Paris: Médecins sans Frontières, 2003.

———. "Introduction: The Sacrificial International Order and Humanitarian Action." In *In the Shadow of Just Wars: Violence, Politics, and Humanitarian Action*, edited by Fabrice Weissman. Ithaca, NY: Cornell University Press.

Brauman, Romy, and Joelle Tanguy. "The Medecins Sans Frontières Experience." MSF; http://www.doctorswithoutborders.org/reports/msfexperience.htm, 1998.

Bryans, Michael, Bruce D. Jones, and Janice Gross Stein. "Mean Times: Humanitarian Action in Complex Political Emergencies—Stark Choices and Cruel Dilemmas," Report of the NGOs in Complex Emergencies Project, Program on Conflict Management and Negotiation. Toronto: Centre for International Studies, University of Toronto, 1999.

Buckwalter, David T. "Madeleine's War: Operation Allied Force." In *Case Studies in Policy Making and Implementation*, edited by David A. Williams. 6th edition. Newport, RI: Naval War College, 2002.

Calhoun, Craig. "Fear, Intervention, and the Limits of Cosmopolitan Order." Background paper for conference series hosted by the Social Science Research Council, New York, 2004.

Calkins, Barkely. "Improving InterAction's PVO Standards through the Pursuit of Excellence." *Monday Developments*, October 23, 2000.

Center on International Cooperation with Lester Salamon and Associates. "The Preparedness Challenge in Humanitarian Assistance." New York: Center on International Cooperation, 1999.

Chartrand, Sebastien. "Politics of Swedish Humanitarian Organizations: Exporting the Welfare State?" Paper P02-301, Wissenschaftszentrum

Berlin for Sozial Forschung, January 2002.

Clarke, Walter, and Jeffrey Herbst. "Somalia and the Future of Humanitarian Intervention." *Foreign Affairs* 25 no. 2, March/April 1996.

Clinton, Bill. *My Life.* New York: Knopf, 2004.

Cobb, Roger W., and David A. Rochefort, eds. *The Politics of Problem Definition: Shaping the Policy Agenda.* Lawrence: University Press of Kansas, 1994.

Cross, Tim. "Comfortable with Chaos: Working with UNHCR and the NGOs; Reflections from the 1999 Kosovo Refugee Crisis." *Journal of Humanitarian Assistance*, October 30, 2001; www.jha.ac/articles/u042.htm.

Curtis, Devon. *Politics and Humanitarian Aid: Debates, Dilemmas and Dissension.* London: Overseas Development Institute, London, 2001.

DAC News, OECD Development Assistance Committee, June 7, 2000; www.devinit.org/dac.htm.

Dallaire, Romeo J. *Shake Hands with the Devil: The Failure of Humanity in Rwanda.* Toronto: Random House, 2003.

Darcy, James, and Charles-Antoine Hoffman. "According to Need? Needs Assessment and Decision-Making in the Humanitarian Sector." Humanitarian Policy Group Report 15. London: ODI, September 2003.

Davidson, Lisa Witzig, Margaret Daly Hayes, and James J. Landon. "Humanitarian and Peace Operations: The NGO/Interagency Interface." Report of the conference held at the National Defense University, April 1996. NDU Press Book, December 1996; http://www.dodccrp.org/ngoIndex.html.

De Torrente, Nicholas. "Humanitarian Action under Attack: Reflections on the Iraq War." *Harvard Human Rights Journal* 17 (Spring 2004).

———. "Preface." In *Civilians Under Fire: Humanitarian Practices in the Congo Republic, 1998–2000*, edited by Marc Le Pape and Pierre Salignon. Paris: Médecins sans Frontières, 2003.

Deutsch, C. "Unlikely Allies Join with the United Nations." *New York Times*, December 10, 1999.

Development Initiatives. "Summary." In "Global Humanitarian Assistance 2000." Independent report commissioned by the IASC; http://www.devinit.org/hum2.htm.

De Waal, Alex. *Famine Crimes: Politics and the Disaster Relief Industry in Africa.* Oxford: James Currey with Indiana University Press in association with the International African Institute, 1997.

Dichter, Thomas. "Globalization and Its Effects on NGOs: Efflorescence or a Blurring of Roles and Relevance?" *NonProfit and Voluntary Sector Quarterly* 28, no. 4 (1999). Supplemental Issue: "Globalization and Northern NGOs: The Challenge of Relief and Development in a Changing Context." ARNOVA, Sage Publications Inc.

Dobbins, James, John G. McGinn, Keith Crane, Seth G. Jones, Rollie Lal, Andrew Rathmell, Rachel Swanger, and Anga Timilsina. *America's Role in Nation-Building: From Germany to Iraq*. Rand, 2003; http://www.rand.org/pubs/monograph_reports/MR1753/.

Duffield, Mark. *Global Governance and the New Wars*. London: Zed Books, 2001.

———. "Governing the Borderlands: Decoding the Power of Aid." *Disasters* 25, no. 4 (December 2001); London: Overseas Development Institute, 2001.

———. "Relief in War Zones: Toward an Analysis of the New Aid Paradigm." *Third World Quarterly* 18, no. 3 (February 1997).

Edwards, Michael. "International Development NGOs: Agents of Foreign Aid or Vehicles for International Cooperation." *NonProfit and Voluntary Sector Quarterly* 28, no. 4 (1998).

Fawcett, John, and Victor Tanner. "The Political Repercussions of Emergency Programs: A Review of USAID's Office of Foreign Disaster Assistance in the Former Yugoslavia (1991–1996)." A report to USAID/BHR/OFDA. Washington, DC: Checchi Consulting and Co., 2002. From "Review of USAID's Office of Foreign Disaster Assistance in the Former Yugoslavia, 1991–1996," 2002.

Forman, Shepard. "Underwriting Humanitarian Assistance." In *A Framework for Survival*, edited by Kevin Cahill. London: Routledge, 1999.

Forman, Shepard, and Rita Parhad. *Paying for Essentials: Mobilizing Resources for Humanitarian Assistance*. New York: Center on International Cooperation, 1997.

Forman, Shepard, and Stewart Patrick, eds. *Good Intentions: Pledges of Aid for Post-Conflict Recovery*. Center on International Cooperation. Boulder: Lynne Rienner, 2000.

Forman, Shepard, and Abby Stoddard. "International Assistance." In *The State of America's Nonprofit Sector*, edited by Lester Salamon. Washington, DC: Brookings Institution Press, 2002.

Giving USA 2001. A publication of the AAFRC Trust for Philanthropy, the Center on Philanthropy at Indiana University; www.aafrc.org.

Gray, Bradford H. "World Blindness and the Medical Profession: Conflicting Medical Cultures and the Ethnical Dilemmas of Helping."

The Milbank Quarterly 70, no. 3 (1992).

Graybill, Lyn S. "CNN Made Me Do (Not Do) It." *Sarai Reader*, 2004; http://www.sarai.net/journal/04_pdf/22lyn.pdf.

Grunewald, Francois. "Questioning the Sphere." Urgence réhabilitation développement; http://www.urd.org/debaloby/sphere/question.htm.

Haas, Peter M. "Do Regimes Matter? Epistemic Communities and Mediterranean Pollution Control." In *International Organization: A Reader*, edited by Friedrich Kratochwil and Edward Mansfield. New York: Harper Collins, 1994.

————. "Introduction: Epistemic Communities and International Policy Coordination." *International Organization* 46, no. 1 (Winter 1992).

————. *Saving the Mediterranean: The Politics of International Environmental Cooperation*. New York: Columbia University Press, 1990.

Harmer, Adele and Joanna Macrae, eds., *Beyond the Continuum: The Changing Role of Aid Policy in Protracted Crises*, HPG Research Report No. 18. London: ODI, July 2004.

Hendrickson, Dylan. "Humanitarian Action in Protracted Crisis: An Overview of the Debates and Dilemmas." *Disasters* 22, no. 4 (December 1998); London: Overseas Development Institute, 1998.

Holbrooke, Richard. *To End a War*. New York: The Modern Library, 1998.

Humanitarian Charter and Minimum Standards in Disaster Response. The Sphere Project London: Oxfam Publishing, 2000.

Huntington, Samuel. "The Erosion of American National Interests." In *The Domestic Sources of American Foreign Policy: Insights and Evidence*, edited by Eugene R. Wittkopf and James M. McCormick. Lanham, MD: Rowman & Littlefield, 1999.

"The International Response to Conflict and Genocide: Lessons from the Rwanda Experience." Published by the Steering Committee of the Joint Evaluation of Emergency Assistance to Rwanda, March 1996; ReliefWeb: http://www.reliefweb.int/.

Johnston, Philip. *Somalia Diary*. Atlanta: Longstreet Press, 1994.

Jones, Bruce, and Abby Stoddard. *External Review of the Inter-Agency Standing Committee*. New York: UN Office for the Coordination of Humanitarian Affairs, December 2003.

Judge, Anthony. "NGOs and Civil Society: Some Realities and Distortions. The Challenge of 'Necessary-to-Governance Organizations' (NGOs)." Adaptation of a paper presented to a seminar on State and Society at the Russian Public Policy Center, Moscow,

December 6–8, 1994, under the auspices of the Council of Europe; Union of International Associations: http://www.uia.org/.

Keck, Margaret E., and Kathryn Sikkink. *Activists beyond Borders: Advocacy Networks in International Politics*. Ithaca, NY: Cornell University Press, 1998.

Keen, David, and K. Wilson. "Engaging with Violence: A Reassessment of Relief in Wartime." In *War and Hunger*, edited by Joanna Macrae and Anthony Zwy. London: Zed Books, 1994.

Kent, Gregory. "Humanitarian Agencies, Media, and the War against Bosnia: 'Neutrality' and Framing Moral Equalisation in a Genocidal War of Expansion." *Journal of Humanitarian Assistance* (August 2003); http://www.jha.ac/articles/a141.pdf.

Keohane, Robert O., and Joseph S. Nye. *Power and Interdependence*. Boston: Little, Brown and Company, 1997.

Kratochwil, Friedrich. "Constructing a New Orthodoxy? Wendt's 'Social Theory of International Politics' and the Constructivist Challenge." *Millennium: Journal of International Studies* 29, no. 1 (January 2000).

Kremmer, Janaki. "Australia Scrutinizes Influence of Nongovernmental Groups." *Christian Science Monitor*, September 5, 2003.

Leader, Nicholas, ed. *The Politics of Principle: The Principles of Humanitarian Action in Practice*. Humanitarian Policy Group Report. London: Overseas Development Institute, 2000.

Levy, Reynold. *Give and Take: A Candid Account of Corporate Philanthropy*. Boston: Harvard Business School Press, 1999.

Lindenberg, Marc. "Declining State Capacity, Voluntarism, and the Globalization of the Not-for-Profit Sector." *NonProfit and Voluntary Sector Quarterly* 28, no. 4 (1999).

Lindenberg, Marc, and Coralie Bryant. *Going Global: Transforming Relief and Development NGOs*. Bloomfield, CT: Kumarian, 2001.

Lindenberg, Marc, and J. Patrick Dobel. "The Challenges of Globalization for Northern International Relief and Development NGOs." *NonProfit and Voluntary Sector Quarterly* 28, no. 4 (1999).

Lindsay, James M. "End of an Era: Congress and Foreign Policy after the Cold War." In *The Domestic Sources of American Foreign Policy: Insights and Evidence*, edited by Eugene R. Wittkopf and James M. McCormick. Lanham, MD: Rowman & Littlefield, 1999.

Lofland, Valerie J. "Somalia: U.S. Intervention and Operation Restore Hope." In *Case Studies in Policy Making and Implementation*, edited by David A. Williams. 6th edition. Newport, RI: Naval War College. 2002.

Macrae, Joanna. *The New Humanitarianisms: A Review of Trends in Global Humanitarian Action.* London: Overseas Development Institute, April 2002.

Macrae, Joanna, and Nicholas Leader. *Shifting Sands: The Search for Coherence between Political and Humanitarian Action.* London: Overseas Development Institute, 2000.

Macrae, Joanna, and Nicholas Leader, eds. "Terms of Engagement: Conditions and Conditionality in Humanitarian Action." HPG Report 6. London: ODI, July 2000.

Macrae, Joanna, et al. "Uncertain Power: The Changing Role of Official Donors in Humanitarian Action." *HPG Report* 12. London: ODI, December 2002.

Martone, Gerald. "The Peculiar Compartmentalization of Humanitarian Action"; "Relentless Humanitarianism." Papers presented at International Expert Conference on Security and Humanitarian Action: Who Is Winning? A US-Europe Dialogue in the Wake of September 11. Columbia University, Arden House, May 24–25, 2002.

Minear, Larry. "Humanitarian Action in the Age of Terrorism." Background paper for International Expert Conference on Security and Humanitarian Action: Who Is Winning? A US-Europe Dialogue in the Wake of September 11. Columbia University, Arden House, May 24–25, 2002.

———. *The Humanitarian Enterprise: Dilemmas and Discoveries.* Bloomfield, CT: Kumarian Press, 2002.

Minear, Larry, Ted van Baarda, and Marc Sommers. "NATO and Humanitarian Action in the Kosovo Crisis." Occasional Paper Number 36. Providence, RI: The Thomas J. Watson Jr. Institute for International Studies, Brown University, 2000.

Morrow, James D. *Game Theory for Political Scientists.* Princeton, NJ: Princeton University Press, 1994.

"The Myth of Opposition to Foreign Assistance." USAID (accessed April 2001); www.info.usaid.gov/about/polls.html.

Nardulli, Bruce, Walter L. Perry, Bruce R. Pirnie, John Gordon, IV, John G. McGinn. *Disjointed War: Military Operations in Kosovo, 1999,* Santa Monica, CA: Rand, 2002.

Natsios, Andrew S. "Illusions of Influence: The CNN Effect in Complex Emergencies." In *From Massacres to Genocide: The Media, Public Policy, and Humanitarian Crises,* edited by Robert I. Rotberg and Thomas G. Weiss. Washington, DC: Brookings Institution, 1996.

————. "Remarks at the InterAction Forum, Closing Plenary Session." May 21, 2003; http://www.interaction.org/forum2003/panels.html.

————. *U.S. Foreign Policy and the Four Horsemen of the Apocalypse: Humanitarian Relief in Complex Emergencies.* Westport, CT: Praeger, 1997.

Newberg, Paula R. "Politics at the Heart: The Architecture of Humanitarian Assistance to Afghanistan." Working Papers, Carnegie Endowment for International Peace, Washington, DC, July 1999.

"New Global Affairs Undersecretary Wishes to Engage with NGOs." *Monday Developments* 19, June 25, 2001.

Nye, Joseph. "Redefining the National Interest." *Foreign Affairs* 78, no. 4 (July/August 1999).

Oakley, Robert B. "An Envoy's Perspective." *JFQ Forum* (Autumn 1993).

Ogata, Sadako. "Humanitarian Action in Conflict Situations." Introductory Remarks at the panel discussion organized by the Institute of Policy Studies, the Singapore Red Cross Society, and the Society of International Law, Singapore, January 9, 1998; http://www.unhcr.ch/refworld/unhcr/hcspeech/spe21.htm.

————. *The Turbulent Decade: Confronting the Refugee Crises of the 1990s.* New York: W. W. Norton & Co., 2005.

O'Brien, David. *Regional Burden Sharing for Humanitarian Action.* Discussion paper, New York: Center on International Cooperation, 1999; www.cic.nyu.edu.

O'Brien, Paul. "Politicized Humanitarianism: A Response to Nicholas de Torrente." *Harvard Human Rights Journal* 17 (Spring 2004).

OECD/Development Assistance Committee. "Aid Statistics." Updated 29 February 1999; http://www.oecd.org/dac/stats.

O'Malley, Steve, and Dennis Dijkzeul. "A Typology of International Humanitarian Organizations." Unpublished paper presented at International Expert Conference on Security and Humanitarian Action: Who Is Winning? A US-Europe Dialogue in the Wake of September 11. Columbia University, Arden House, May 24–25, 2002.

Mitchell, John, and Deborah Doane. "An Ombudsman for Humanitarian Assistance?" *Disasters,* June 1999, 23 (2), 115.

Organization for Security and Co-operation in Europe. "Annual Report 1999 on OSCE Activities (1 December 1998–31 October 1999)." Published by OSCE, 17 November 1999, Vienna.

————. "Kosovo/Kosova: As Seen as Told. The Human Rights Findings of the OSCE Kosovo Verification Mission." An Analysis of the

Human Rights Findings of the OSCE Kosovo Verification Mission, October 1998–June 1999. Published by OSCE Office for Democratic Institutions and Human Rights, Warsaw, 1999.

Patrick, Stewart. "Multilateralism and Its Discontents: The Causes and Consequences of U.S. Ambivalence." In *Multilateralism and US Foreign Policy: Ambivalent Engagement*, edited by Stewart Patrick and Shepard Forman. Boulder, CO: Lynne Rienner, 2001.

Paul, James. "NGOs and Global Policy-Making." Global Policy Forum, June 2000; http://www.globalpolicy.org/ngos/analysis/anal00.htm.

Porter, Toby. "The Partiality of Humanitarian Assistance: Kosovo in Comparative Perspective." *Journal of Humanitarian Assistance*, June 2000; http://www.jha.ac/articles/a057.htm.

Power, Samantha. *A Problem from Hell: America and the Age of Genocide*. New York: Basic Books, 2002.

"Press Coverage and the War on Terrorism, 'The CNN Effect': How 24-Hour News Coverage Affects Government Decisions and Public Opinion." Brookings Institution/Harvard Forum, January 23, 2002; http://www.brookings.edu/comm/transcripts/20020123.htm.

Price, Richard. "Reversing the Gun Sights: Transnational Civil Society Targets Land Mines." *International Organization* 52 (Summer 1998).

Pugh, Michael. "Military Intervention and Humanitarian Action: Trends and Issues." Overseas Development Institute. *Disasters* 22, no. 4 (December 1998); London: Overseas Development Institute, 1998.

Randel, Judith, and Tony German, eds. *Global Humanitarian Assistance 2003, Development Initiatives*. London: Earthscan Publications, 2003.

Randel, Judith, Tony German, and Deborah Ewing, eds. *The Reality of Aid 2000, Development Initiatives*. London: Earthscan Publications, 2000.

Rieff, David. *A Bed for the Night: Humanitarianism in Crisis*. New York: Simon & Schuster, 2002.

———. "Charity on the Rampage: The Business of Foreign Aid." *Foreign Affairs* (January/February 1997).

———. "Kosovo's Humanitarian Circus." *World Policy Journal* 17, no. 3 (Fall 2000).

———. *Slaughterhouse: Bosnia and the Failure of the West*. New York: Simon & Schuster, 1996.

Roberts, Adam. *Humanitarian Action in War*. Adelphi Paper 305. Oxford: IISS and Oxford University Press, 1996.

Rubin, Barnett R., Abby Stoddard, Humatun Hamidzada, and Adib Farhadi. *Building a New Afghanistan: The Value of Success, the Cost of Failure*. Center on International Cooperation, New York University, in cooperation with CARE International, March 2004.

Ruggie, John Gerard. "What Makes the World Hang Together? Neo-Utilitarianism and the Social Constructivist Challenge." *International Organization* 52, no. 4 (Autumn 1998).

Salm, Janet. "Coping with Globalization: A Profile of the Northern NGO Sector." *NonProfit and Voluntary Sector Quarterly* 28, no. 4 (1999).

Salomons, Dirk. *Building Regional and National Capacities for Leadership in Humanitarian Assistance*. New York: Center on International Cooperation, 1999.

Seiple, Chris. "The U.S. Military/NGO Relationship in Humanitarian Interventions, Peacekeeping Institute." Center for Strategic Leadership, U.S. Army War College, 1996.

Shawcross, William. *Deliver Us from Evil*. New York: Simon & Schuster, 2000.

SIPRI Yearbook 2000: Armaments, Disarmament and International Security. Stockholm International Peace Research Institute. London: Oxford University Press, 2000.

Slim, Hugo. "Dithering over Darfur? A Preliminary Review of the International Response," *International Affairs* 80, no. 5, August 2004.

Slim, Hugo. "By What Authority? The Legitimacy and Accountability of Non-governmental Organisations." Lecture at the International Council on Human Rights Policy International Meeting on Global Trends and Human Rights—Before and after September 11." Geneva, January 10–12, 2002; http://www.jha.ac/articles/a082.htm.

———. "The Continuing Metamorphosis of the Humanitarian Practitioner: Some New Colours for an Endangered Chameleon." *Disasters* 19, no. 2 (June 1995); London: Overseas Development Institute, 110–126.

———. "Doing the Right Thing: Relief Agencies, Moral Dilemmas and Moral Responsibility in War." *Disasters* 21, no. 3 (September 1997); London: Overseas Development Institute, 244–257.

———. "International Humanitarianism's Engagement with Civil War in the 1990s: A Glance at Evolving Practice and Theory." *Journal of Humanitarian Assistance* (March 1998); http://www.jha.ac/articles/a033.htm.

———. "Military Intervention to Protect Human Rights: The Humanitarian Agency Perspective." Background paper for the International Council on Human Rights' Meeting on Humanitarian Intervention: Responses and Dilemmas for Human Rights Organisations, Geneva, March 31–April 1, 2001.

———. *Relief Agencies and Moral Standing in War: Principles of Humanity, Neutrality, Impartiality and Solidarity, Development in Practice*. Oxford: Oxfam, November 1997.

Snow, Donald M. *Distant Thunder: Patterns of Conflict in the Developing World*. 2nd edition. Armonk, NY: M. E. Sharpe, 1997.

———. *When America Fights: The Uses of U.S. Military Force*. Washington, DC: CQ Press, 2000.

Stockton, Nicholas. "In Defence of Humanitarian Principles." *Disasters, The Journal of Disaster Studies, Policy and Management* 22, no. 4 (December 1998); London: Overseas Development Institute, 1998.

Stoddard, Abby. "Background Paper on Issues in Humanitarian Aid." New York: Center on International Cooperation, 1999.

———. "Trends in US Humanitarian Policy." In *The New Humanitarianisms: A Review of Trends in Global Humanitarian Action*, edited by Joanna Macrae. London: Overseas Development Institute, April 2002.

———. "The US and the 'Bilateralisation' of Humanitarian Response." HPG Background Paper. London: Overseas Development Institute, December 2002.

Strobel, Warren P. "The CNN Effect: Myth or Reality?" In *The Domestic Sources of American Foreign Policy: Insights and Evidence*, edited by Eugene R. Wittkopf and James M. McCormick. Lanham, MD: Rowman & Littlefield, 1999.

———. *Late-Breaking Foreign Policy: The News Media's Influence on Peace Operations*. Washington, DC: U.S. Institute of Peace, 1997.

Suhrke, Astri, Michael Barutciski, Peta Sandison, and Rick Garlock. *The Kosovo Refugee Crisis: An Independent Evaluation of UNHCR's Emergency Preparedness and Response*. Geneva: UNHCR, February 2000.

Talbott, Strobe. "Globalization and Diplomacy: The View from Foggy Bottom." In *The Domestic Sources of American Foreign Policy: Insights and Evidence*, edited by Eugene R. Wittkopf and James M. McCormick. Lanham, MD: Rowman & Littlefield, 1999.

Terry, Fiona. *Condemned to Repeat? The Paradox of Humanitarian Action*. Ithaca, NY: Cornell University Press, 2002.

Tharoor, Shashi. "The Future of Civil Conflict." *World Policy Journal* 16, no. 1 (Spring 1999).

UNHCR. *State of the World's Refugees 2000: Fifty Years of Humanitarian Action.* Geneva: United Nations High Commissioner for Refugees, 1999.

USAID. *2002 Voluntary Foreign Aid Programs: Report of Voluntary Agencies Engaged in Overseas Relief and Development (The VOLAG Report)*; www.info.usaid.gov/hum_response/pvc/pvcpubs.html.

US Department of State. "Ethnic Cleansing in Kosovo: An Accounting." US State Department Report. Washington, DC, December 1999; http://www.state.gov/www/global/human_rights/kosovoii/homepage. html.

US Department of State, Office of the Spokesman. "CARE's Work Saluted." Statement by Secretary of State Warren Christopher at CARE's 47th anniversary humanitarian awards luncheon. Washington, DC, May 14, 1993; http://dosfan.lib.uic.edu/ERC/ briefing/dossec/1993/9305/930514dossec.html.

U.S. Department of State and U.S. Agency for International Development. *Security, Democracy, Prosperity: Strategic Plan Fiscal Years 2004–2009: Aligning Diplomacy and Development Assistance.* Washington, DC: US State Department/USAID (August 2003).

US General Accounting Office. "USAID Relies Heavily on Nongovernmental Organizations, but Better Data Needed to Evaluate Approaches." GAO Report to the Chairman, Sub-Committee on National Security, Veterans Affairs, and International Relations, Committee on Government Reform, House of Representatives (GAO-02-471), 2002.

US House of Representatives, Subcommittee on National Security, Emerging Threats, and International Relations. "Testimony of James Kunder, Deputy Assistant Administrator for Asia and the Near East. Humanitarian Assistance Following Military Operations: Overcoming Barriers, Part II." Washington, DC, July 18, 2003; http://www.usaid.gov/press/speeches/2003/ty030718.html.

US UN Press. "Remarks by Secretary of State Colin Powell to the National Foreign Policy Conference for Leaders of NGOs in Washington D.C." October 26, 2001; www.USUNPRESS.state.gov.

Weiss, Thomas. "Principles, Politics, and Humanitarian Action." *Ethics and International Affairs* 13 (Winter 1999).

Wendt, Alexander. "Constructing International Politics." In *Theories of War and Peace: An International Security Reader*, edited by Michael

E. Brown, Owen R. Cote, Sean M. Lynn-Jones, and Steven E. Miller. Cambridge, MA: MIT Press, 1988.

Western, Jon. "Sources of Humanitarian Intervention: Beliefs, Information, and Advocacy in the U.S. Decisions on Somalia and Bosnia." *International Security* 27, no. 1 (July/August 1999).

Wittkopf, Eugene R., and James M. McCormick, eds. *The Domestic Sources of American Foreign Policy: Insights and Evidence.* Lanham, MD: Rowman & Littlefield, 1999.

Woodward, Bob. *Bush at War.* New York: Simon & Schuster, 2002.

Young, Kirsten. "UNHCR and ICRC in the Former Yugoslavia: Bosnia and Herzegovina." *International Review of the Red Cross* 843, 30 September 2001.

Unpublished Sources

Congressional records

Department of State embassy cables (containing situation reports, communiqués, and memoranda)

Minutes and reports of NGO-US and NGO-UN interagency meetings

Press accounts

UN Security Council resolutions

USAID/OFDA situation reports and OFDA/DART situation reports

USG internal documents, including the US Interagency Humanitarian Assessment (1993), the Interagency Review of Humanitarian and Transitional Assistance Programs (2000), unpublished papers by John Fawcett and Victor Tanner as part of the OFDA Former Yugoslavia Review (1991–1997) Washington, DC, 1999: "Birth of the Aid Juggernaut in Former Yugoslavia (1991–1992): Humanitarian Plot or Unintended Consequences? A Report to USAID's Office of Foreign Disaster Assistance"; "Breaking the Siege by Water: Fred Cuny in Sarajevo"; "Fighting Ethnic Cleansing with Humanitarian Action? A Report to USAID's Office of Foreign Disaster Assistance"

INDEX

About the Author

Abby Stoddard, Ph.D., is a senior associate at New York University's Center on International Cooperation, where she performs independent research and international consultations on issues in humanitarian assistance and postconflict reconstruction. She has a master's degree in International Affairs from Columbia University's School of International and Public Affairs and a Ph.D. in Politics from New York University. Before joining the Center on International Cooperation, she worked for ten years with relief and development organizations, first for CARE USA as desk officer for Russia and the CIS, and most recently as program director for Doctors of the World (Médecins du Monde–USA). She has authored several articles and book chapters on topics relating to humanitarian action, NGOs, and the US foreign aid architecture.

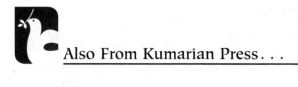

Also From Kumarian Press...

New and Forthcoming:

Non-State Actors in the Human Rights Universe
Edited by George Andreopoulos, Zehra F. Kabasakal Arat, and Peter Juviler

Development Brokers and Translators: The Ethnography of Aid and Agencies
Edited by David Lewis and David Mosse

Cinderella or Cyberella? Empowering Women in the Knowledge Society
Edited by Nancy Hafkin and Sophia Huyer

Development and the Private Sector
Edited by Deborah Eade and John Sayer

Of Related Interest:

Global Civil Society: Dimensions of the Nonprofit Sector, Volume Two
Lester M. Salamon, S. Wojciech Sokolowski, and Associates

Advocacy for Social Justice: A Global Action and Reflection Guide
David Cohen, Rosa de la Vega, and Gabrielle Watson

Worlds Apart: Civil Society and the Battle for Ethical Globalization
John Clark

Creating a Better World: Interpreting Global Civil Society
Edited by Rupert Taylor

Visit Kumarian Press at **www.kpbooks.com** or
call **toll-free 800.289.2664** for a complete catalog.

Kumarian Press, located in Bloomfield, Connecticut, is a forward-looking, scholarly press that promotes active international engagement and an awareness of global connectedness.